Love Sick

Frank Tallis is a writer and practicing clinical psychologist. He has held lecturing posts in clinical psychology and neuroscience at the Institute of Psychiatry and King's College London and is one of Britain's leading experts on obsessional states.

Frank Tallis is also the author of *Mortal Mischief*, the first in a trilogy of psychoanalytic detective thrillers published by Century.

He lives and works in London.

For further information visit: www.franktallis.com

Also by Frank Tallis

Non fiction
Changing Minds: The History of Psychotherapy
Hidden Minds: A History of the Unconscious

Fiction
Killing Time
Sensing Others
Mortal Mischief

Love Sick

Frank Tallis

arrow books

Published by Arrow Books in 2005

5 7 9 10 8 6 4

Copyright © Frank Tallis 2004

Frank Tallis has asserted his right under the Copyright,
Designs and Patents Act, 1988 to be identified
as the author of this work

First published in the United Kingdom in 2004 by Century

Arrow Books Limited
The Random House Group Limited
20 Vauxhall Bridge Road, London SW1V 2SA

www.randomhouse.co.uk

Addresses for companies within
The Random House Group Limited can be found at:
www.randomhouse.co.uk/offices.htm

The Random House Group Limited Reg. No. 954009

A CIP catalogue record for this book
is available from the British Library

ISBN 9780099445296

Penguin Random House is committed to a sustainable future for
our business, our readers and our planet. This book is made from
Forest Stewardship Council® certified paper.

Typeset by Palimpsest Book Production Limited,
Polmont, Stirlingshire

Printed and bound in Great Britain by Clays Ltd, St Ives plc

For Nicola
We must be mad

Contents

Preface

A Preliminary Observation

*H*arley Street, central London – a bright morning in April

Everything about the young man suggested depletion – a sapping of vital energies. He collapsed on the couch and allowed his body to slide from a seated to an almost horizontal position. Occasionally he would bang the heel of his shoe against the floor, like a petulant child who was being forced to keep still. The shadows beneath his eyes betrayed a week of sleepless nights – long hours, worrying in darkness.

I had asked him a few questions, but couldn't get him to engage. His responses were brief, uninformative and separated by long, uncomfortable pauses. They were unnerving, these pauses, like the lacunae in a Pinter play. I decided I would resist the urge to speak, just to see how long he would allow the silence to last. I sat back in my chair – and waited. Nothing happened. It was clear that his mind was wholly occupied. He stared straight through me. To my surprise, I noticed that his lips were moving – a barely discernable tremor of articulation. He was either remembering or rehearsing a conversation.

Only a few weeks earlier he had been a different person. He had burst through the door like a hurricane, shaking my hand vigorously and illuminating the room with a broad, fixed smile. He had required virtually no prompting. Indeed, he had spoken fluently, punctuating his conversation with extravagant hand gestures. His enthusiasm was feverish. He was boiling over with plans, schemes and ideas.

Yet, some fourteen days later, the hurricane had blown itself out. He was inert, cheerless, and exhausted. His face had dropped like melted wax and his eyes were made of glass.

What was wrong with him?

Was he clinically depressed? Had his preoccupations turned into obsessions? Had he been manic the last time I saw him?

None of these.

He was in love.

His partner had begun to express doubts about the quality of their relationship. I had invited her in for a joint session, but she had declined. In many respects, her position was understandable. They had never made each other truly happy.

Eventually, the session began to take shape. Monosyllabic answers gave way to sentences and, in due course, coherent speech.

'She can't leave me,' he said. 'You can't feel like I do – and it mean nothing.'

I gestured, indicating that he should continue.

'If you feel something this strongly,' he whispered, 'this deeply, things have got to work out. She's got to respond to this feeling – hasn't she? I don't believe in anything – I don't believe in God or anything like that – but I do believe in love.'

He stared into the pool of sunlight on the carpet between us.

'Last night,' he continued, 'I was lying in bed – awake – I haven't been sleeping. I was just lying there, thinking about

her. Willing her to want me. Willing her to love me.'

'And you think that might work?' I asked gently.

He looked up.

'It sounds stupid, I know, but yeah . . . I think it might work. That's what we're always told isn't it? That love will find a way?'

His eyes were suddenly hopeful.

I didn't want to encourage him – but at the same time I didn't want to trample over the closest thing he had to a spiritual belief.

'Yes,' I said neutrally. 'That's what we're told.'

Suddenly, his dead eyes flared with anger.

'And you don't believe that?'

It felt like an accusation.

'Sometimes,' I said wearily, 'no matter how much you love someone, they just don't love you back.'

The light behind his eyes flickered and went out. It was as though his consciousness had imploded, having become too dense with misery. Outside, I could hear the sound of children, coming to visit the dental practice next door.

'I don't know what I'll do if she leaves me.' He said the words slowly. 'It's difficult to imagine life without her.'

'What will you do?'

He shook his head, saying nothing.

I leaned forward, into his line of vision.

'What is it about her that makes you love her so much?'

'She's beautiful,' he said, without hesitation, and then added, 'Really beautiful', just in case I was in danger of underestimating the power of her radiance.

'And what else?'

'What else? I don't think it's something I can analyse.'

'Why's that?'

'All right, it's something I don't want to analyse. Love isn't something you should dismantle or pull apart.'

She was on a pedestal, held there by the sublime and incomprehensible forces of romanticism: forces that it would be sacrilegious to question.

'A few sessions back,' I said tentatively, 'you told me that she'd said some pretty hurtful things.'

'Yes. We've been arguing a lot lately.'

'How do you feel about her when she says things that hurt?'

'The same. I love her.'

'Even when what she says is unjustified – or insensitive?'

'Look, love isn't about liking. If you love someone, you love someone – and that's it. Whatever.'

'Wouldn't it be better if you did like her more?'

'Sure – but you can't choose who you're going to fall in love with.'

Again there was a long silence.

He closed his eyes tightly and clenched his fists. A tear trickled down the length of his cheek leaving a trail of silver.

'I'm sorry,' he said quietly.

'Yes,' I replied. 'So am I.'

He took out a handkerchief and blew his nose. When our eyes met, there was a hint of something different in his expression. Something lighter.

'Can I ask you a question?'

'Sure,' I said.

He exhaled forcefully, so forcefully his breath lifted the first page of my notepad.

'What . . .' *he paused for a moment before adding:* 'is love?'

I shook my head, unwilling to tackle such a momentous question. His expression coagulated with disappointment. He really wanted me to give him an answer.

'It's . . .' *I began, but stopped.*

Looking at him then – and being reminded of so many

other patients I had seen before in clinics and hospitals – I was tempted to reply: 'Love is a mental illness.' However, I suppressed the impulse.

'Well,' I began my sentence again, 'psychologists define love as a strong emotional attachment . . .' It was an unimpressive response. The words sounded sterile and empty. Hollow science.

He wasn't convinced – and to tell the truth, neither was I.

My first, unspoken answer was still resonating in my head. Love is a mental illness.

It seemed more accurate and more genuine than the respectable, sanitised definition that I had chosen to offer him. It seemed ripe with subtle truths.

I wondered about the relationship between love and madness.

A fat honey bee tapped at the window.

We both looked up.

It was spring again. Beyond the consulting-room walls, Regent's Park would be filling with young people. Couples – holding hands – would be making lazy progress around the lake and the air would be a haze of cherry blossom. Someone, somewhere, would be turning on a radio – and the sound of love songs would be carried across the water . . .

1

Latent Fire

Universals that stretch across cultures are rare and tell-tale.
The Ascent of Man, J. Bronowski

Love can exist in many forms; however, there is one manifestation of love that seems to have fascinated humanity since the dawn of recorded history. This is the love that two people share when they 'fall in love' – the love that is now more frequently described as passionate or romantic love. In this sense, love has a special place in human affairs. It has always been (and continues to be) a universal preoccupation.

Among the many states of being that characterise human existence, the state of being 'in love' seems to be the most mysterious. It is a unique and sometimes puzzling experience. For millennia, very different cultures have attempted to understand love – most notably in poetry and song – and in these forms of artistic expression we repeatedly encounter questions such as 'Why do I feel this way?' 'What is happening to me?' and, more precisely, 'What is love?' Thus, our preoccupation with love also represents an enquiry into its nature; the Muses preside over a vast reservoir of introspective and observational data that may not be scientific evidence, but nevertheless qualifies as evidence of a kind.

As soon as human beings were able to record their thoughts by writing, they began to compile a reference library of 'folk' psychology much of which concerns the causes, experience and consequences of love.

Even a superficial examination of artistic works on the theme of love will reveal a striking duality. Love is rarely described as a wholly pleasant experience. It is an amalgam of seemingly incompatible and ungovernable mood states. When in love, individuals describe odd combinations of pleasure and pain, rapture and grief, ecstasy and disappointment. Love seems to provide a shuttle service that operates between only two destinations: heaven and hell.

The effect of this emotional turmoil is often quite profound. Love changes people – the way they think and the way they behave. Moreover, these alterations are often associated with a general impression of mental instability. People feel less 'in control' and more volatile – less capable of making rational judgements.

Love is also strongly associated with a wide range of physical 'symptoms'. Lovers are often described as fevered, or pale and depleted – unable to sleep or eat. Thus, for as long as people have been writing about love, they have also been describing it as an illness. Indeed, the illness or sickness metaphor is one of the most consistent features of love poetry and love songs throughout the ages. There are many answers to the question 'What is love?', but 'A kind of illness' is one that appears (and reappears) with remarkable frequency.

Such an answer might be viewed in varying degrees as cynical, amusing, or absurd. It is certainly one that most would not take very seriously. Yet, it is an answer that the medical profession was willing to accept for over a thousand years, and one that – if given proper consideration within the context of modern scientific theories – may prove to be surprisingly apposite. Indeed, this answer – that love is a kind of illness – may contain within it a number of extremely revealing clues as to why we love, and why we experience love in the way that we do.

As we shall see, the illness metaphor is remarkably illuminating. If we are guided by its subtle logic, we will be able to answer questions such as: Why do men fall in love more than women? Why do women tend to become more addicted to love than men? Why do all lovers see their partners – at least for a time – as beautiful (irrespective of how they really look)? Why do people (when they fall in love) want to write love poetry (even if they've never written poetry before)? Why is heartbreak so painful? And why does wild, passionate love rarely last?

In addition, the illness metaphor reveals something very important about how we construe love. For millennia, it has been employed to emphasise the similarities that exist between love and madness. The metaphor has been so successful in this respect, that we now find it difficult to separate the two concepts. Thus, in the well-worn contemporary phrase – truly, madly, deeply – madness is supposed to be as significant an indicator of love's authenticity as honesty and depth. We do not want love to be rational. We want it to be audacious, overwhelming, improvident, and unpredictable.

But what are the consequences of this legacy? How has it affected the way we form intimate relationships? And how has it affected the quality of those relationships?

Sages as diverse as the philosopher Bertrand Russell and the present Dalai Lama have identified happiness as a rational goal. Moreover, they suggest that happiness is best achieved by pursuing a rational course of action. We might choose to do a particular job because it pays well, or develop a rewarding friendship because of shared interests. The preference can be justified. In matters of the heart, however, we proudly relinquish logic altogether. Perversely, we consider the formation of a meaningful, intimate relationship essential to happiness, but, at the same time, repudiate rationality because it is 'unromantic'. Thus, cold-hearted women and handsome scoundrels have become the staple of romantic literature, demonstrating that Cupid is a poor matchmaker, landing his arrows with unparalleled carelessness.

It may be that love's madness is part of the human condition. Something that is inescapable; however, acknowledging its power, understanding its processes, and being aware of its effect on the mind, may provide us with at least some protection against the torment (and misery) commonly celebrated by diehard romantics.

If love is construed as a kind of illness, then perhaps it has a cure? Or perhaps there are more satisfying, durable, and less troubled ways of loving? Although we are inclined to love madly, perhaps we should also consider the possibility of loving sanely.

What would loving sanely entail? How might love sickness be turned into love fitness? These, too, are questions to which we will look for answers.

To appreciate fully the degree to which the illness metaphor has shaped our beliefs about love, it is useful first to examine how it was employed in the early writings of the ancient and classical world. Love was swiftly identified with illness largely because of its physical manifestations; however, in due course, the emphasis shifted from the physical to the psychological. Thus, as classical civilisation progressed, the illness metaphor was used with greater specificity. Poets recognised that love didn't resemble just any illness, but, rather, a particular kind: mental illness. Even on the frayed papyrus and pottery pieces of the earliest civilisations, love was being linked with madness.

* * *

The oldest love poetry in existence was composed in eighteenth-dynasty Egypt. Tomb paintings depict banquets at which musicians, usually women, play on string and wind instruments while others sing and dance, and many scholars believe that these ancient verses were intended for performance with music as love songs. It is curious how these songs – written over three and a half thousand years ago – contain sentiments and phrases that are still found in many contemporary love songs: 'Never leave me, I beg', 'Your love ensnares me, I can't let go', 'She captures my heart.' The despair of young lovers has remained constant, even though the 'eternal' pyramids have crumbled.

Although these poems describe moments of great happiness, the experience of love is consistently associated with at least some level of distress. These anonymous poets describe feeling distracted, confused, and fretful. Their pulse is no longer steady: 'My heart quickly flits away when I remember your love.' One woman addresses her heart directly: 'Why do you behave so crazily? Be still.' There are other physical effects: 'If for a moment I am apart from her,' writes one young poet, 'my stomach is aflutter.' There are also references to sadness, and the sense of entrapment that accompanies obsessional love: 'With her hair she ensnares me, With her eyes she fetters me.'

In the most remarkable of these early poems, love is unambiguously described as an illness. The poet experiences a terrible longing, having been separated from his lover for a week. As a consequence of her absence, he experiences a 'sickness'. His body becomes 'heavy' and he neglects to take care of himself; however, he knows that his illness will not respond to medical attention or spiritual counsel: 'Should physicians come their drugs could not cure my heart, nor could the priests diagnose my disease.' Indeed, none of the remedies contained in a medical text which he calls 'The

Compendium' will alleviate his symptoms. The only effective treatment will be reunion with his beloved – consideration of which makes him feel no better because she is not expected back for a further seven days. The sense of each hour dragging on is quite palpable.

We know nothing of these early Egyptian poets. They are an anonymous cabal – an elite circle of ghosts who guard the wellhead of the 'romantic' literary tradition. However, examples of love poetry written nearly a thousand years later can be identified as the work of Sappho – a woman who is rightly fêted as the first great love poet. Her name has become synonymous with homosexuality, but she wrote love poems addressed to both men and women.

Sappho was born on the island of Lesbos. She married, had at least one child, and was the leading personality among a circle of women who were also her audience. Apart from one complete poem (an address to Aphrodite in which the goddess is asked to deliver her from the pangs of unrequited love for a girl), Sappho's work only survives in fragments. In one of these – known as 'The Ode to Anactoria' (or alternatively, 'To a Woman') – Sappho experiences love like an affliction. Her heart flutters in her bosom, she is struck dumb: 'and straightaway a subtle fire has run under my skin, with my eyes I have no sight, my ears ring, sweat pours down, and a trembling seizes all my body'. Her condition is deeply distressing, and she concludes: 'I am paler than grass, and seem in my madness little better than one dead.'

Sappho is acutely aware of love's dark side. She describes love as a 'fatal creature, bitter-sweet', and we easily recognise obsession and morbid jealousy in even the smallest vestige of what might once have been a fully developed poem: 'What country girl bewitches thy heart, who knows not how to draw her dress about her ankles.'

In many respects, Sappho's poetry is curiously haunting

because of its incompleteness. These intimate fragments come down to us through time, like pieces of a tantalising, fragile tapestry. Even so, her thoughts and impressions, however extenuated, allow us to enter a world that resonates with sensual pleasure – or at least its expectation: 'Mnasidica is more shapely than the tender Gyrinno', 'Much whiter than an egg', 'And down I set the cushion.' Sappho's vestiges, scraps, and scintillas are suspended in a shadowy vacuum that imagination rushes to fill. The scene is set: pillows on a marble floor, the scent of an exotic burning oil, trembling, aching Sappho, mad with love, lowers her head to kiss a pale body.

Legend has it that Sappho died for love, throwing herself off a cliff after being rejected. Thus, in myth (if not reality), love and mental instability are linked together in her person. As a culture, we have deemed it appropriate – even necessary perhaps – that our first great love poet should meet a violent and desperate end.

Love features significantly in many of the myths and legends of ancient Greece. The exact origin of these stories is unknown, but it is likely that they represent the distillation of a pre-existing and very lengthy oral tradition. Story telling has always been as much about instruction as entertainment, and this is particularly true of Greek literature. Human folly is amplified in the social commerce of kings, heroes, spirits, and gods. We are urged to beware of pride – but also of love. Both will lead to failures of judgement, but, with respect to love, the faculty of reason is so compromised, it is deemed to be a form of madness – *theia mania* – or madness from the gods. The term evokes a powerful image: love striking with the ferocity and suddenness of lightning.

The entire Trojan War arose because of Paris's precipitate love for Helen. By abducting the wife of another man, he set in motion a series of events that led to appalling carnage and the slaughter of thousands. When Orpheus descended into the underworld to rescue Eurydice, he was permitted to leave on one condition – that he didn't look back. Yet, when Orpheus saw the first light of the living world, he could not resist turning around to share his joy and, in doing so, lost Eurydice for ever. Western mythology is populated by beings who irrationally transgress for love. Edicts are broken. Infatuations compel forbidden unions, and mortal men refuse to heed terrifying prophecies.

In ancient Greece, epic poetry was complemented by elegiac poetry. If the former was executed on a large canvas, then the latter was the equivalent of a detailed miniature. Its purpose was to reflect the inner world – the world of thoughts, sentiments, and private mental events. It was, as such, more personal. In the sixth century BC, the elegiac form was frequently used to commemorate the dead – an association which has persisted to the present day. However, the elegy was also a very popular vehicle for exploring feelings about relationships. The first love poems in the elegiac form were said to have been written by Mimnermus, a poet who lived in Colophon in the second half of the seventh century BC. Although his principal subject was the pleasures of love, his poems were also said to be tempered with a certain melancholy.

The Latin poets followed Mimnermus's example, and wrote elegies not for the dead, but for the living – namely their lovers. In the custody of the Romans, the elegiac form became a short sequence of poems exploring the poet's relationship with his mistress. In some cases, the woman in question was real, while in others she was an imaginary figure employed to represent all women – a kind of female archetype.

The most celebrated Roman elegist was Catullus, who

was the first known poet to chart the course of a single relationship in verse. His lover, Lesbia, was married and occupied an elevated social position. Their affair ended, however, when Lesbia deserted Catullus, not for the sake of her husband, but for a young protégé of Cicero. Subsequently, Catullus's poems record an emotional journey from idyllic beginnings to disillusionment and anger.

Catullus was painfully aware of the emotional polarities of love. The joy, the despair, the desire and bitterness tore him apart: 'I hate, and yet I love thee too; how can that be? I know not how.' He appeared to be bewildered and confused by the simultaneous eruption of contradictory feelings. He described being 'love-crazed' and recognised that he must – in modern colloquial language – pull himself together: 'Miserable Catullus, put an end to this folly.'

Propertius is less well known than Catullus, but he was equally gifted when it came to self-analysis. From the very first poem of his four surviving books, it is clear that Propertius's experience of love was somewhat troubled. The opening is based on another work written a century earlier by the Greek poet Meleager. Propertius abandoned Meleager's stock image of being wounded in the heart by love's arrow, and exchanged it for a disease metaphor: love as an infection or contagion. Moreover, it is a disease that affected Propertius's mind. He was made to 'live by unreason' and complains: '. . . for a whole year now this madness does not leave me.' Consequently, he begged his friends to search out 'cures' for his 'insanity'. These opening images set the tone for much of the poetry contained in the subsequent volumes, which describe an individual who is afflicted, rather than affected, by love.

Outside the literary tradition, the first person to attempt a systematic analysis of the psychological consequences of love was the philosopher Plato. He recognised that falling in love, and being lovesick, are almost always experienced together, and subsequently sought to explain both by recourse to the metaphysics of his time.

In *Phaedrus*, Plato suggested that when a man sees his lover, the soul is reminded of the state of perfection it enjoyed before birth. This stimulates regeneration of the soul, which is described as the regrowth of its wings. The soul 'throbs' and is plagued by sensations of 'pricking', 'irritation' and 'pain', as the wings develop; however, the soul simultaneously experiences pleasure, because the pain is associated with the primal memory of perfection. These events on the spiritual plane have physical and mental consequences. The individual is afflicted with an illness – love sickness:

> In this state of mingled pleasure and pain the sufferer is perplexed by the strangeness of his experience and struggles helplessly; in his frenzy he cannot sleep at night or remain still by day, but his longing drives him wherever he thinks he may see the possessor of beauty.

Via the person of Socrates, Plato also remarked of a lover that 'the conventions of civilised behaviour, on whose observance he used to pride himself, he now scorns'. Lovers, like those tormented by madness, have little time for social niceties.

The fact that love and illness have always been linked, inevitably implies that doctors might be well placed to provide some help and advice. As we have discovered, even in the earliest love poetry of ancient Egypt, the physician is recruited as a kind of stooge: a social type who can be employed to strengthen and extend the illness metaphor. The lovesick poet doesn't really expect to be attended by a physician, because he already knows that his illness will not respond to medical intervention. The only thing that will cure him is the return of his beloved. Thus, we see the beginning of a long poetic tradition, in which languishing lovers implore doctors to heal them, while at the same time knowing that the doctor will be entirely impotent. This literary device serves several functions, the most important of which is to emphasise love's divinity: love is beyond the remit of science. The languishing lover also expects the doctor to recognise that the question, 'Can you not heal me?' is rhetorical. He does not expect the doctor to take it too seriously. But this is exactly what happened in second-century Rome: when the lovesick called for medical attention, doctors started coming.

Among these was the most important doctor in the history of Western medicine – Galen. Although his name is associated with Rome, he was of Greek origin, and his home town of Pergamum was the site of a famous shrine to Asclepius, the god of healing. At the age of sixteen Galen decided to become a doctor, and eventually studied at Alexandria, which was then the most important centre of medical learning in the world. He became the personal physician of the Emperor, Marcus Aurelius, and produced a body of work that exerted an influence on the practice of medicine well into the nineteenth century.

Galen's understanding of the human body was rooted in a collection of medical texts brought together around 250 BC and attributed to Hippocrates of Cos. The Hippocratic system recognises four body fluids or humours: blood, phlegm, yellow bile and black bile. In a healthy individual, the four humours are balanced; however, any imbalances will result in illness. This model probably originated by observation of sick patients, most of whom seemed spontaneously to evacuate an excess of one body fluid or another. For example, phlegm appears during colds, and yellow and black bile can be seen in vomit. Even blood, the humour most strongly associated with life, seemed to obey the same principle, being expelled from the body during nose-bleeds and menstruation (a phenomenon which eventually became the theoretical basis of blood-letting). Each of the humours was thought to be composed from the four elements, and each was associated with two of four qualities: hot, cold, wet, and dry.

The Hippocratic system has psychological implications, insofar as the relative predominance of a particular humour was supposed to influence temperament or personality. Thus, the four humours correspond with four personality types: sanguine (warm, pleasant), phlegmatic (slow-moving, apathetic), choleric (quick to react, hot-tempered), and melancholic (depressed, sad).

In spite of the 'psychological' possibilities of the humoral model, Galen did not write extensively on the subject of mental illness. In his major work, *On Prognosis,* he describes many case histories, but only three involve psychological disturbance. One is about a rich man's slave steward, who was depressed because of an audit. In another, Boethus's son was anxious on account of stealing some food. However a third, about Iustrus's wife, is altogether more interesting. Hers may be the first recorded case of love sickness to be diagnosed as such by a physician.

Iustrus's wife was suffering from insomnia and showing signs of considerable agitation. When Galen attended her, she refused to answer his questions, and brought their first consultation to an abrupt end by disappearing under the bedclothes. Undeterred, Galen continued to make house calls, until a chance observation allowed him to make a diagnostic breakthrough. He noted that his patient's expression and complexion changed when somebody happened to mention the dancer, Plyades. Galen swiftly applied his hand to her wrist, and noticed that the woman's pulse had become extremely irregular. On subsequent visits, he encouraged one of his followers to mention other dancers, but observed no change in her pulse. Then:

> On the fourth evening I kept very careful watch when it was announced that Plyades was dancing, and I noticed that the pulse was very much disturbed. Thus I found out that the woman was in love with Plyades, and by very careful watch on the succeeding days my discovery was confirmed.

By Galen's time, Hippocratic writings had already challenged the view that mental disturbances had a supernatural origin. For example, epilepsy, once described as 'the sacred disease' and regarded as an affliction sent from the gods, was now assumed to be nothing more than a brain abnormality. Galen was happy to follow the Hippocratic tradition and demote love in exactly the same way. The symptoms of love were nothing to do with divine intervention. He proposed that the lovesick individual, under the influence of a strong passion, experiences a humoral (or chemical) imbalance, which in turn promotes the occurrence of physical symptoms.

After Galen, love became the joint property of both poets and doctors.

A common misconception is that after the fall of Rome, very little was written about love until the twelfth century. It is assumed that the dark ages were a kind of cultural famine, which could not be brought to an end until the civil-ising influence of Christianity had spread across Europe, and that the poets of the world were struck dumb until the arrival of the troubadours. Then, this itinerant band of French minstrels burst into song, injecting the idea of romantic love into the Western literary canon.

In fact, ideas about courtly love and romance have a

literary provenance that predates the troubadours by centuries. During the dark ages, many love poems were composed in the Arab world, and a tradition of courtly poetry was established in the Middle East by the eighth and ninth centuries.

As the Arabic literary tradition developed, so too did Islamic science. In the ninth century, Caliph al-Mamum established a number of translators' colleges, where a cornucopia of Greek, Syriac, Persian and Sanskrit writings were made available in Arabic. He ordered the construction of a great Hall of Science in Baghdad, which housed an extensive library and was equipped with an astronomical observatory. While the West was still trying to recover from the collapse of classical civilisation, Islamic scientists had worked out how far the moon is from the earth, and one of their group – the eighth-century chemist Jabir ibn Hayyan – had already suggested that if it were possible to split an atom, enough energy might be released to obliterate a city. Islamic scholars were also responsible for tremendous advances in mathematics: we still employ an Arabic number system and frequently make use of al-jabr (algebra).

Among the sciences, however, medicine was particularly advanced – possibly because in the Qur'ān, medicine is praised as a discipline particularly favoured by Allah. Arab doctors possessed a thorough knowledge of human anatomy, and the circulation of the blood was understood centuries before Harvey. Although anaesthesia is generally considered a nineteenth-century innovation (ether was introduced in 1842), early Arab doctors frequently induced sleep with sponges soaked with hashish, opium, darnel and belladonna.

Arab doctors and scholars were not only interested in the body, they were also interested in the mind. Thus, by the tenth century, numerous works had been written on the subject of melancholia, and among the mental afflictions most readily recognised by doctors was 'ishq – love sickness, or, more accurately, love madness.

The term 'ishq does not appear in the Qur'ān, and appears to be a term originally employed to describe excessive religious fervour; however, many scholars resisted using the term in theological works, on account of it possessing a carnal or sexual connotation. This confusion of sacred and profane exemplifies how Arab culture was sensitive to the similarities that exist between the earthly desire for union with a loved one, and spiritual desire for union with God. By the ninth century, however, 'ishq had lost its spiritual connotation, and was being used specifically to describe excessive or obsessional love for another person.

It is of considerable interest that many of the Arabic words for love have disturbing overtones: they suggest unhappiness, or an implication of inevitable pain. The term 'ishq emerges from a linguistic seed-bed in which connections between love and emotional instability had already been firmly established.

The ninth-century lexicographer al-Asmai travelled extensively among the Bedouin Arabs, collecting information about the origins and definitions of word meanings, and among his writings, the following can be found:

> I asked a Bedouin Arab about 'ishq and he said, 'It is too sublime to be seen and it is hidden from the eyes of mortals, for it is concealed in the breast like the latent fire in a flint, which when struck produces fire, this fire remaining hidden as long as it is left alone.' Some of the Arabs say, "Ishq is a kind of madness. Madness has its varieties and 'ishq is one of them.'

In trying to understand the causes of excessive love, Islamic doctors turned to the recently translated works of the classical world – most notably, those of Galen. His system appealed to them, because it offered 'scientific' explanations for mysterious mental phenomena. Thus, medieval Islamic psychiatry was firmly rooted in the humoral tradition. The works of the physician al-Masuji are a particularly good example. He wrote an early medical textbook which eventually came to the West in Latin translation: first as the *Liber Pategni*, and later as the *Liber Regis*. It contains a theoretical discussion on the causes and signs of several 'psychiatric' conditions, including melancholia, lycanthropy, and love sickness. According to al-Masuji, passionate love is obsessional in nature, and linked with a number of physical symptoms: in particular, sunken eyes, rapid eye movements, emaciation, and changes in pulse.

The likes of al-Masuji, however, were all consigned to obscurity with the arrival in the tenth century of Abu 'Ali al-Husayn Ibn 'abd Allah ibn Sina: an Iranian physician who was destined to become the most influential philosopher-scientist of Islam, and immortalised by medieval scholars in the West as Avicenna. His two outstanding works are *The Book of Healing* (a vast philosophical and scientific encyclopaedia) and *The Canon of Medicine* – arguably one of the most celebrated books in the history of medicine and one which contains an extended section on the diagnosis and treatment of 'ishq. Ibn Sina's description of 'ishq is relatively detailed, and proved extremely influential in both East and West. With respect to the latter, his account of love sickness was completely absorbed into mainstream Renaissance scholarship and belles-lettres.

Ibn Sina is in no doubt that love sickness is a medical condition. Like Galen, he assumes that the physical symptoms of love sickness are the result of a chemical imbalance brought about by psychological factors: principally, obsessing about the loved one. This is a surprisingly modern view, insofar as it recognises continuities between mind and body.

For example, contemporary research has demonstrated that individuals who are confrontational, competitive, and driven are more likely to suffer from heart disease than those who are more easy-going. Mental states affect the chemical environment of the body, which in turn can lead to the development of organ disease (including the brain).

According to Ibn Sina, once love sickness is established, the power of reason is completely compromised; thinking becomes delusional and mood disturbance is apparent in the form of melancholia.

By the eleventh century, the medical treatise had shouldered its way on to shelves formerly reserved only for poetry, song and romantic epic. However, Islamic writers accepted that love was worthy of examination from yet another perspective, a perspective that offered a pleasing mixture of medical disinterest and passionate engagement – adab. The term is difficult to translate, but it is used to describe a work written as a form of intellectual entertainment. The objectives of adab are not dissimilar to those of contemporary scholars who seek to write commercially successful books for the 'educated layman'.

Among those who were influenced by this form was Abu Muhammad 'Ali ibn Muhammad ibn Sa'id ibn Hazm – known more commonly and concisely as Ibn Hazm. His treatise on love, *The Ring of the Dove*, is a thorough and agile investigation into the nature of human emotional life.

Ibn Hazm was born in Cordova on 7 November 994. Islam had been established in Andalusia for nearly three hundred years, and his family had converted from Christianity several generations earlier. Ibn Hazm was famous in his time for his prolific output, breadth of learning and mastery of Arabic. He published approximately four hundred works, exploring subjects such as logic, history, law, ethics, comparative religion and theology.

Ibn Hazm recognised that there are many different forms of love – spiritual, familial, amicable – but only one that is associated with extreme and intense emotional disturbance:

> In none of the other sorts of love does anything like this happen: the mental preoccupation, that derangement of the reason, that melancholia, that transformation of the settled temperaments, and alteration of natural dispositions, that moodiness, that sighing, and all the other symptoms of profound agitation which accompany passionate love.

Yet, in spite of the distress associated with being in love, he recognised that many aspire to the condition. It is thus, paradoxically, 'a baffling ailment', 'a delightful malady', and 'a desirable sickness'.

Ibn Hazm acknowledged the influence of medicine by noting the 'signs' or 'symptoms' of love. Although these include 'happiness' in the presence of the lover, the vast majority of the symptoms he described are troubling: 'a brooding gaze', 'extreme taciturnity', 'a fondness for solitude', 'emaciation' and 'weeping'. In addition, he noted swift changes of mood, poor concentration, uninhibited behaviour (such as excessive generosity), lassitude, and sleep disturbance:

> Sleeplessness too is a common affliction of lovers; the poets have described the condition frequently, relating how they watch the stars, and giving an account of the night's interminable length.

Although these symptoms can be very severe, Ibn Hazm chose to make a distinction between love sickness and mental illness. Love sickness may produce changes in behaviour that resemble mental illness, but being in love and being mentally ill are not the same thing. In his conversational and engaging style, Ibn Hazm describes sitting with his friends in the shop of Isma'il Yunus, a 'Hebrew physician' and 'clever physiognomist'. Together, they observe the slightly odd behaviour of one Abu 'L-Baqa, prompting a man called Mujahid to test Yunus's diagnostic skill.

> 'What do you say about this man?' He [Yunus] looked at him for a brief moment, and then said, 'He is passionately in love.' Mujahid exclaimed, 'You are right; what made you say this?' Isma'il answered, 'Because of an extreme confusion apparent in his face. Simply that; otherwise all the rest of his movements are unremarkable. I knew from this that he is in love, and not suffering from any mental disorder.'

However, passionate love is such a close relative of madness that the former often provokes the latter: 'Sometimes the condition progresses to such a point that the victim is no longer in possession of his senses; he is deprived of all reason, and becomes prey to insane fancies.' To illustrate this point, Ibn Hazm gave examples of two respectable and eminent gentlemen, who were separated from the slave girls with whom they had fallen in love. Both men 'lost their reasons and became deranged, so that they found themselves in chains and fetters'.

After elaborating on this theme, Ibn Hazm suggested that the intellectual and emotional disturbance produced by love can be so extreme, recovery is no longer possible:

> When the infatuated lover comes to this pass, all hope is cut off, and all expectation of a recovery must be abandoned; there is no remedy for him any more, neither in union with the beloved nor any other way. The corruption is firmly established in his brain; his consciousness is completely destroyed; the mischief has got the upper hand for him.

As the West began to recover from the fall of classical civilisation, it became more receptive to cultural influences from the East. The Arab courtly tradition was absorbed by Western literature in the form of *romans* – or romances – and love sickness became one the principal concerns of medieval medicine. Love sickness would continue to be regarded as an important medical topic for at least another five hundred years. Indeed, love, and its relationship to mental illness, was still the subject of learned dissertations well into the seventeenth century. However, it is doubtful whether the concept of love sickness would have enjoyed such a smooth transition from century to century without the lubricant of another medical condition with which it became strongly associated. This was melancholy or melancholia.

The European preoccupation with sadness was eerily presaged by one of Albrecht Dürer's most extraordinary copperplate engravings: his *Melencolia* of 1514. It is a bizarre and disconcertingly modern image. A winged female figure – looking like a sulky adolescent angel – is slumped down in a landscape of discarded objects and instruments. Her companion is a cherub who, rapt in thought, stares blankly at the ground. An hourglass – the lower chamber of which is full of sand – suggests that time is running out and, in the distance, the sun is setting. The total effect is one of abandonment. The two figures seem to have been washed up in this strange, desolate place: a world in which conversation is impossible – only stultifying, ruminative self-absorption. Although the work can be interpreted as a critical commentary on the affectations of self-obsessed scholars, its significance goes far beyond social satire.

Cultural historians suggest that the notion of self-awareness was not a feature of European art until the middle ages – and not properly exploited until the Italian Renaissance. Self-portraits began to appear in the late fifteenth century, and steadily increased in numbers until the seventeenth. Again, one of the earliest and most compelling examples of self-portraiture was produced by Dürer, in 1500. It is a face-on painting, in which the artist – depicted as a magus – stares directly into the viewer's eyes.

Dürer's self-awareness drew him inwards and, like many men of his age, he appears to have become increasingly interested in mental states. This, presumably, is why he chose 'Melencolia' as his subject. Melancholy was not a new phenomenon in the early sixteenth century – it had already been carefully described by both classical and Islamic physicians; however, sixteenth-century self-awareness seemed to increase the significance of melancholy as a feature of human mental life. Indeed, one senses the operation of a vicious circle, in which self-absorption encouraged melancholy, which in turn encouraged greater self-absorption.

Such a mechanism was almost certainly at work in the mind of Michel de Montaigne, whose famous *Essays* were published in 1580, and written largely under the influence of a severe bout of melancholy. Indeed, the *Essays* began as a kind of therapy, in which Montaigne sought to heal his mind by writing down his thoughts, but in doing this, he achieved something far greater. His writings are not so much essays, but assays. Montaigne was sampling his own consciousness – his own memories, values, attitudes and feelings. The end result – *The Complete Essays* – is the first modern example of self-analysis: a textual mirror in which the personality of Montaigne is faithfully reflected. Needless to say, melancholy is often the subject of his meditations.

References to melancholy are relatively rare in the literature of the early English Renaissance. Indeed, there are no protagonists or secondary figures who might be described as 'a melancholy type'. However, from the 1580s onwards, melancholy individuals begin to appear with much greater frequency, and among these are many who suffer from what came to be known as 'love melancholy'.

It is probably no accident that the increasing number of melancholy figures appearing in English prose writing and drama also coincided with the publication of an influential medical text: Timothie Bright's 1586 treatise on melancholia. This was the first English book of its kind, and made medical theories about melancholia much more accessible to the general reader. The Elizabethan historian Lawrence Babb has pointed out that this general readership must have included numerous writers (including Shakespeare), as Elizabethan playwrights seem extremely well informed about melancholia and its supposed medical origins. Such specialist knowledge would not have featured in a typical Elizabethan education based on religious instruction, literacy, numeracy skills, and limited exposure to selected classical texts.

The arrival of melancholy characters in English literature was also influenced by a curious trend. In Italy, many scholars subscribed to the Aristotelian notion that melancholy was the affliction of great minds. Thus, English gentlemen – once introduced to this doctrine on their European travels – often returned to their native country affecting a melancholy disposition to advertise their intellectual superiority.

By the end of the sixteenth century, a well-defined melancholy character type had been established in English literature. This was the malcontent – a man frequently described by others as 'discontent' or 'discontented'. He was usually distinguished by his penchant for black clothing, which was often worn in a slovenly fashion. Moreover, he possessed a fairly consistent cluster of psychological traits. The malcontent was unsociable, asperous, morose, ruminative, of economic speech, and prone to ranting when provoked. Apart from his taste in clothes – a piece of poetic licence –

all the other characteristics of the malcontent were taken from medical textbooks on melancholy. Essentially, he was a medical stigmatic whose psychological wounds were constantly on public display.

The malcontent was eventually developed into several character types, all sharing the core features of their medical condition. These were the melancholy man who resents others (because his superior abilities are not recognised), the melancholy villain, the melancholy cynic, the melancholy scholar and the melancholy lover.

Contemporary medical textbooks posited that amorous feelings were excited by an increased volume of blood. Because the liver was thought to be the organ which produced blood, the Elizabethans associated the liver, and not the heart, with romance. Thus, in *The Merry Wives of Windsor*, Falstaff describes Pistol as 'With liver burning hot', and in *As You Like It*, Rosalind suggests that Orlando might 'wash' his liver. These examples serve to underscore how closely Elizabethan writers understood emotions within the context of medical scholarship, thus strengthening the links between love and psychopathology.

In the sixteenth century, the ancient humoral account of mental and physical illness was still the dominant theoretical framework and so love melancholy was explained according to the peculiarities of this system. One of the inevitable consequences of the humoral model is that love melancholy is an illness that progresses through two distinct phases. Although this was rarely made explicit in medical textbooks, it is something of a logical necessity. First, the afflicted individual enters a sanguine stage, when the body is swollen with blood, and he becomes hot and moist. Then, the individual enters a melancholy stage – mediated by an excess of black bile – when he becomes cold and dry. This latter stage is associated with physical weakness, and the psychological symptoms of love sickness. If love becomes too intense, or lovers are separated from each other, there is a much greater danger of the sanguine stage progressing to the melancholy stage. This is because prolonged and intense heat was thought to putrefy or corrupt the humours. Melancholy – and particularly love melancholy – was attributable to an excess of not only black bile, but burnt black bile. In its burnt form, the humour was sometimes referred to as 'melancholy adust'.

This is an important point, because it implies that love is constantly on the brink of a terrible transformation. It is constantly threatening to become a mental illness. Indeed, the experience of love sickness may well be unavoidable. Love is booby-trapped – ready to explode as soon as the tripwires of desire and longing begin to tremble.

The underlying and inexorable physiology of love sickness is reflected in a wonderfully powerful speech, delivered by a young woman in Ben Jonson's *The New Inn*.

> My fires, and feares, are met: I burne, and freeze,
> My liver's one great coale, my heart shrunk up
> With all the [fibres], and the masse of blood
> Within me, is a standing lake of fire,
> Curl'd with the cold wind of my gelid sighs.

It was in the sixteenth century that the English also started 'falling in love'. The first use of the term – employed in the modern sense – is attributed to the scholar Palsgrave, who incorporated it into the sentence: 'I shall fall in love with her.' The phrase 'to fall in love' has since become the standard acceptation; probably because its innocent cadence conceals a number of alarming truths about love which the unconscious mind readily acknowledges (and which the conscious mind ignores at its peril).

We fall in love like we fall over, seemingly by accident –

not by design. Our emotional centre of gravity is displaced and we topple into the hands of fate. When we 'fall in love' we are again occupying the landscape of ancient Greece, where *theia mania* can strike us down at the whim of a minor god. Finally, there are sympathetic resonances shared between 'falling in love' and 'falling ill'.

The cultural conditions at the end of the sixteenth century in England could not have been more favourable for the consolidation of the concept of love melancholy. Ideas about courtly love were still an important inspiration to writers, medical explanations of love sickness were no longer in the possession of a few scholars, and the English had embraced melancholy as an emblem of sophistication. Perhaps more importantly, all of this was happening at a time when the English language had suddenly become self-empowered. The result was a golden age of artistic expression that would exert a massive influence on all future representations of love.

Sir Thomas Wyatt, in an exquisite, questioning poem, conveys the utter confusing desperation of love sickness: 'What meaneth this? When I lie alone, I toss, I turn, I sigh, I groan'; 'The clothes that on my bed do lie, Always methinks they lie awry: What meaneth this?' The same sentiments can also be found in a later poem by Sir John Suckling, whose questioning, however, is more rhetorical in nature:

> Why so pale and wan, fond lover?
> Prithee, why so pale?
> Will, when looking well can't move her,
> Looking ill prevail?

In 'Twicknam Garden', John Donne was 'Blasted with sighs, and surrounded with teares', and Katherine Philips observed that: 'Lovers like men in Fevers burn and rave.'

When we encounter Romeo for the first time – then still

besotted with Rosalind – he describes himself as a 'sick man', afflicted with a 'madness most discreet', and in *A Midsummer Night's Dream*, Theseus tells us that 'lovers and madmen have such seething brains'. And in the sonnets, liberated from dramatic demands and conventions, Shakespeare speaks more directly – and revealingly – for all of us. 'My love is a fever,' he says.

> Past cure I am, now Reason is past care,
> And frantic-mad with evermore unrest;
> My thoughts and my discourse as madmen's are,
> At random from the truth vainly express'd.

After the English Renaissance, the rose of romance would always be powdered with melancholy adust. Undoubtedly, to fall in love was to flirt with madness.

In the sixteenth century, medicine was beginning to mature as a scientific discipline, and the most reliable sign of this was the advent of anatomical studies. Prior to the sixteenth century, doctors were content to rely on classical authorities, but with the Renaissance came a new spirit of enquiry. The first modern master of anatomy was Andreas Vesalius, who popularised the discipline with dramatic public demonstrations. He was also the author of the first comprehensive textbook of anatomy, *On the Fabric of the Human Body*, published in 1543.

By the seventeenth century, the notion of anatomy had become extremely influential, particularly with respect to psychology. The mind, like the body, might best be understood as a community of parts. Moreover, the intellect itself might be employed as the principal tool of investigation. Self-anatomy, or the observation of the mind through introspection, became an increasingly important concept – a development reflected in the English lexicon. At about this time, we also see the first use of related terms such as 'self-examination', 'self-interest', and 'self-consciousness'.

The most significant anatomy of the self to appear in the early seventeenth century was Robert Burton's *The Anatomy of Melancholy*. It is an exhaustive survey of medical, philosophical and poetic writings on melancholia. Much of the lengthy 'third partition' is concerned with the causes and cure of love melancholy, which demonstrates how widely accepted the concept had become.

Robert Burton was not a doctor, but an Oxford fellow and clergyman. Even so, he felt sufficiently qualified to write about his topic for two reasons. Firstly, his knowledge of melancholy was encyclopaedic (he seems to have made an assiduous study of virtually every extant work on the subject); and secondly, Burton himself suffered from it. Burton led an uneventful, retiring life, dedicating himself almost entirely to the completion and revision of his *Anatomy*. He died on 25 January 1640, very near the time he had predicted on the basis of his astrological studies. This prompted a modest scandal among Oxford students, who suspected that Burton had committed suicide in order to validate his prediction. The fact that he had already written his own epitaph certainly gives some legitimacy to their morbid speculations. Given the nature of Burton's illness, however, it seems more likely that if he did take his own life, he did so because of depression, rather than scholarly pride.

The Anatomy of Melancholy first appeared in 1621, and was enjoyed by a large readership because Burton was writing for a sympathetic public: a melancholy generation who had been raised on a diet of Elizabethan dolour. It was revised and expanded through five subsequent editions, the last of which was published in 1651.

Unlike most scholarly works, *The Anatomy of Melancholy*

is extremely eccentric. It is something of a literary folly – the philosophical equivalent of Laurence Sterne's digressive *Tristram Shandy*. The reader enters a complex labyrinth of classical allusions, autobiographical vignettes, and is introduced to the most obscure pieces of information. Where else, for example, can one discover that it took Thebet Benchorat forty years or more to discover the motion of the eighth sphere? Yet, *The Anatomy of Melancholy* has a special place in the history of medicine. It represents the culmination of the humoral tradition; it is the last, triumphal statement of Hippocratic learning, articulated in an age when Galenic principles were still largely unchallenged.

In terms of subject matter, Burton's *Anatomy* can be divided into four broad sections. In the first of these, he attempts to define melancholy, while the second is devoted to cure. The third section is an extended treatise on all aspects of love melancholy (to which is appended a smaller and supplementary anatomy of jealousy), and the final section is concerned with religious melancholy.

What then, does Burton have to say about love melancholy?

Like many before him, Burton sets about understanding his subject by enumerating symptoms. These include the standard core features of love sickness – such as paleness, disturbed pulse, insomnia, and loss of appetite. However, Burton's obsessional temperament compels him to seek out more and more examples, until, overwhelmed by the task in hand, he is forced to concede that: 'the symptoms of the mind in lovers are almost infinite, and so diverse that no art can comprehend them'. Burton acknowledges that lovers can be 'rapt beyond themselves for joy', but concludes that in the final reckoning, love is perhaps better described as 'a plague, a torture, and hell, a bitter-sweet passion'.

Burton explains the symptoms of love melancholy with

recourse to the humoral model. In the same way that heat causes water to evaporate, so it is that passion dries up the 'radical moisture' – leaving a damaged and depleted body. In support of this position, he cites evidence from an autopsy conducted in ancient Greece on a man reputed to have died for love. The event was attended by the philosopher Empedocles, who, on inspecting the man's internal organs, discovered that 'his heart was combust, his liver smoky, his lungs dried up'. Empedocles asserted that the unfortunate's soul had been 'roasted through the vehemency of love's fire'.

For those who survive love's initial conflagration, the risk of mental illness is substantial. Those who have experienced an intense passion are likely to develop a condition which Burton calls *amor insanus*. They become 'no better than beasts, irrational, stupid, headstrong'. The prognosis, Burton points out, is poor: 'they will either run mad, or die'. Quoting an authority, he asserts that passion: 'makes the blood hot, thick, and black; and if the inflammation get into the brain . . . it so dries it up that madness follows, or else they make away themselves'. Yet, lovers are so deranged, they often view the prospect of death with equanimity. Of the typical lover Burton says: 'it would not grieve him to be hanged, if he might be strangled' using his beloved's 'garters'.

It is interesting that the last great work on love melancholy should be penned by an English cleric. The English are not renowned for their passionate and demonstrative natures – yet, for almost a hundred years, the psychological consequences of love became a major theme in English writing. Perhaps the clue to this interest lies in the English character itself. From a Hippocratic perspective, the celebrated cool exterior of the traditional Englishman suggests an interior environment of blasted livers and smoking hearts – the drained vessels and dehydrated brain of a lover whose soul has been consumed with passion.

The experience of 'falling in love', although complex, has been described through the ages and across cultures with remarkable consistency. Moreover, the repeated, indeed relentless, poetic linkage of love and madness merits more than just a knowing smile and a moment of embarrassed self-reflection. It is surely of some significance that the same metaphor has been employed so enthusiastically from the time of the earliest love songs to those of the present day. In addition, it must also be significant that doctors took love sickness very seriously for over a thousand years. Perhaps all this means something? Perhaps – if we suspend disbelief and provisionally define love as a mental illness – this definition will edge us towards some unexpected insights. Indeed, it may even be the key to a true understanding of what love is, and how it works.

2

Diagnosing Love

Love is a sickness full of woes,
All remedies refusing.
            Hymen's Triumph, Samuel Daniel

From the time of Galen to the seventeenth century, doctors considered love sickness a legitimate and useful diagnosis. It appears in many guises, from the exotic 'ishq, to the more familiar love melancholy. In many cases, doctors were happy to diagnose love alone, as it was assumed that love and its sickness were virtually inseparable. In terms of durability, love sickness has proved itself to be one of the most successful of all diagnoses. Most diagnostic terms used by contemporary psychiatrists are less than a hundred years old. Compared to love sickness, their clinical utility has hardly begun to be tested.

Love sickness as a diagnosis became less popular among doctors from the eighteenth century and lost currency completely in the nineteenth. By the twentieth century, it had more or less disappeared from the medical vocabulary. What had once been considered a significant and potentially fatal illness was now an inconsequential side-effect of falling in love – a disconcerting but harmless state of mind associated primarily with adolescent infatuations.

The demise of love sickness as a medical diagnosis is almost entirely due to the decline and eventual rejection of Hippocratic principles. Until the seventeenth century, Hippocratic medicine had provided doctors with a secure theoretical basis. However, after William Harvey's demonstration of blood circulation, many doctors realised that the practice of medicine would have to be guided by an entirely new set of principles. As medicine began to evolve into a modern science (based on experiment and observation) the humoral system looked increasingly suspect, and with it so did love sickness.

In 1664, the London physician Thomas Willis published an *Anatomy of the Brain*. Three years later, he followed this with a companion volume on diseases of the brain and the nervous system. Willis argued that many psychological problems previously attributed to either supernatural or humoral causes were, in fact, the result of neurological abnormalities. Approximately one hundred years later, this view had become widely accepted. In 1773, the Scottish physician, George Cheyne, published an influential treatise on melancholia: *The English Malady*. He attributed melancholy to a weakness in the nervous system, particularly among the elite of society.

The collapse of the humoral model deprived physicians of a ready explanation for the close relationship between love and mental illness. Desire was no longer incendiary. The brain could no longer be parched, nor bile burnt. The symptoms of love sickness still existed, but they required a new explanation. Thus, doctors chose to understand love sickness as an emotional reaction typical of individuals of a certain character – men and women of 'sensibility'.

The term sensibility was originally used by doctors to describe the degree to which a person might respond to various forms of stimulation (for example, flinching in response to a pin prick). By the mid-eighteenth century, the term was being employed by novelists to describe those who were not physically sensitive, but emotionally sensitive. Early examples of this character type can be found in Samuel Richardson's 'novels of sentiment', *Pamela* and *Clarissa*. It is interesting to note that Richardson's personal physician was one George Cheyne – suggesting, perhaps, a degree of mutual influence.

Towards the end of the eighteenth century, heightened sensibility was viewed as a significant risk factor with regard to the development of mental health problems. Symptoms that were previously associated with the diagnosis of love sickness were now understood to be a straightforward manifestation of 'too much sensibility'. Marianne – one of the two heroines of Jane Austen's *Sense and Sensibility* – falls into a perilous decline when she is rejected by Willoughby, a stranger with whom she has become romantically involved. She becomes tearful, 'deathly pale', loses her appetite and cannot sleep. These symptoms are readily attributed to 'general nervous faintness' or 'a nervous complaint'. In spite of their poetic advantages, there are no longer any references to burning livers, dried-up hearts, or melancholy adust. Literature had turned its back on the humoral model.

As medicine became fascinated by the nervous system, the symptoms of love sickness were absorbed into broad syndromes presumed to arise from constitutional vulnerabilities. Patients so afflicted appeared to be exquisitely sensitive – perhaps even hypochondriacal. The end point of this kind of thinking was the designation of disorders such as neurasthenia – a kind of mental breakdown due to the depletion of 'nerve force'.

These developments alone would have been sufficient to bury the diagnosis of love sickness, but there was more to come.

In the nineteenth century, doctors became less and less interested in love, and more and more interested in sex. Indeed, by the 1860s, the Viennese physician Moritz Benedikt had proposed that many psychological problems were the result of traumatic sexual experiences, and the German neurologist Richard von Krafft-Ebing had published his infamous and exhaustive study of sexual deviancy, *Psychopathia Sexualis*. Interest in sex and sexuality continued to grow, culminating in the psychoanalytic works of Sigmund Freud, who insisted that all psychological problems were the result of repressed sexual memories or fantasies. Psychoanalysis became extremely influential, not only as a method of treatment but also as a way of thinking about the mind and how it works. As a consequence, for much of the twentieth century, medicine and psychiatry were largely preoccupied with sex and sexuality.

Love – its origins, complications, and relationship to mental illness – had become completely irrelevant to the modern doctor. Or so it seemed.

In the *The Art of Loving*, Freud's erstwhile disciple Erich Fromm wrote: 'For Freud, love was basically a sexual phenomenon.' The tone of Fromm's statement is critical, but it is also correct. Freud believed that romantic love was generated by the suppression, repression or frustration of sexual desire. His ideas about the sexual foundations of love are dramatically illustrated in one of his most famous case studies, that of the Wolf Man (so called because of the patient's description of a dream of wolves which he reported during psychoanalysis). It was published in 1918 as 'From the History of an Infantile Neurosis'.

The Wolf Man was a young Russian aristocrat who had first consulted Freud in 1910. He had already been in the care of other doctors and had also spent time in several

German sanatoria. When Freud examined him, the young man exhibited a host of symptoms, many of which had begun in early childhood. These were of an obsessional nature and included problems such as unwanted distressing thoughts and compulsive rituals. Although Freud believed that the Wolf Man was suffering from a conventional 'obsessional neurosis', there was one feature of his obsessionality which was anything but conventional: the Wolf Man kept on falling in love. Even Freud was somewhat perplexed by this: 'The most striking phenomenon of his erotic life after maturity was his liability to compulsive attacks of falling physically in love which came and disappeared again in the most puzzling succession.'

It quickly became apparent, however, that the Wolf Man's affections were only aroused when he encountered women in a particular (and rather undignified) position – on their knees and viewed from behind.

> He [the Wolf Man] was walking through the village . . . when he saw a peasant girl kneeling by the pond and employed in washing clothes in it. He fell in love with the girl instantly and with irresistible violence, although he had not yet been able to get even a glimpse of her face.

After many sessions of psychoanalysis, Freud concluded that the ultimate cause of the Wolf Man's propensity for falling in love was a repressed infantile (and sexually arousing) memory of his parents copulating – with his mother on her knees. It was this sort of explanation for falling in love that Erich Fromm found unsatisfying. Even the Wolf Man himself (when traced and interviewed by a journalist in the 1970s) found Freud's theories 'terribly far-fetched'.

Freud gave sex a fundamental role, not only in the psychopathology of his patients, but also in his general account of human motivation. One of the postulates of psychoanalytic theory is the basic instinct (or drive) called Eros. It is supposed to correspond with what in lay terms would be described as the 'life instinct' – lending itself to the realisation of evolutionary goals such as survival and reproduction. However, in Freud's writings, the term Eros is almost always used with respect to the latter – it is the drive that makes human beings seek sexual gratification.

In 1925, Hollywood's legendary producer, Sam Goldwyn, offered Freud $100,000 to write a film script, because he considered him 'the greatest love specialist in the world'. This is not an assessment that has stood the test of time. It is now widely accepted that Freud had little to say about love, largely because of his preoccupation with sex. In Freud's scheme, love tends to be viewed as a secondary (almost unimportant) by-product of frustrated libidinous urges. Consequently, his analysis of love is described by many contemporary commentators as superficial or cursory. Yet, in one sense – a sense that is often overlooked – Freud offers another account of love, an account that is implied rather than stated. This more subtle reading of Freud is intriguing, because it recapitulates the ancient notion that love is a form of madness.

Although we have only one word for love, Western society acknowledges a distinction between mature, healthy love and immature, unhealthy love. This distinction is certainly upheld within institutions such as the law and medicine. There is an implicit divide between normal and abnormal forms of loving. It is normal to want the company of a loved one – but abnormal to achieve this by stalking. Similarly, it is normal for periods of separation to be associated with sadness – but not total despair. A boundary (however difficult to define) is assumed to separate those who love from those whose love is symptomatic of an underlying mental illness. The ancient humoral model was never so clear-cut:

the boundary that separated love from mental illness was always blurring. In many respects, Freud's understanding of love shares much in common with the humoral model. He, too, has doubts about the degree to which love can ever be regarded as rational or sane. This is because, for Freud, love can only ever be a form of self-delusion. In the same way that the dynamics of humoral theory make it difficult to love without becoming lovesick, so it is that psychoanalytic principles make it difficult to love without becoming divorced (at least to some extent) from reality. There are two reasons why this should be the case.

Firstly, falling in love is greatly influenced by prior learning and experience. For example, in the formative years of childhood, a classroom crush for a girl or boy with black hair might establish a hair-colour preference that becomes apparent in later life. However, memories of such events are not always accessible. They might be hidden away in the mind's basement – the unconscious. Therefore, we often have very little insight into our own behaviour. Like the Wolf Man, our most significant memories may have been repressed. It is only by entering psychoanalysis that such memories can be recovered. Without being able to identify the real causes of love, we will attempt to generate a series of post-hoc justifications – which may have no bearing on reality whatsoever. They will be nothing more than a set of convenient (and probably romantic) fictions: 'It was our destiny to be together', or 'It was love at first sight.'

Secondly, ideas about romance and romantic love allow us to disguise the true and troubling nature of our attachments. Just below the thin lacquer of civilisation, primitive sexual desires are a potent and unwelcome reminder of our animal ancestry. Thus, love is a cosmetic, clumsily applied to protect us from discomfiting self-knowledge. It operates within the psychic economy like a defence mechanism, warping reality along contours that cause the least offence – thus reducing anxiety.

If love always involves self-deception and delusion, then love must – by its very nature – be a close relative of mental illness. Indeed, in Freud's system, the basic principles that explain falling in love are also used to explain why people become mentally ill. Unconscious memories and defence mechanisms feature significantly in both. Here then, we have an intellectual framework that booby-traps love in much the same way as the humoral model. Love can only ever be close to madness.

Summarising Freud's position, Erich Fromm concluded:

> Falling in love always verges on the abnormal, is always accompanied by blindness to reality, compulsiveness, and is a transference from love objects of childhood. Love as a rational phenomenon, as the crowning achievement of maturity, was, to Freud, no subject matter for investigation, since it had no real existence.

It is ironic that Freud's emphasis on sex and sexuality has damaged his reputation as the world's greatest 'love specialist'. Because in actuality, Freud's ideas about love are much richer. Moreover, they show an unexpected degree of continuity with ancient wisdom.

As psychiatry became increasingly interested in sex and mental illness, the subject of love and mental illness was largely neglected – an extraordinary turn of events, given that the psychoanalytic framework which guided the practice of psychiatry for much of the twentieth century strongly implied that love is a delusional state.

Unlike medicine – which embraces the early practice of psychiatry – psychology is a relative newcomer. Although the human mind has been the subject of discussion and speculation since classical times, it was only in the twentieth century that psychology matured as an academic discipline.

In the nineteenth century, what we would now call psychology was largely in the hands of philosophers and physiologists, and the subject matter of psychology was poorly defined. However, as psychology developed, it began to identify itself as a science. Psychological research tended to take place in laboratories and the experiment was endorsed as the discipline's main investigative tool. Consequently, the scope of academic psychology was restricted to mental phenomena and processes that could be meaningfully studied and measured. Thus, a great deal of early psychology was concerned with the basic elements of cognition, such as memory and perception.

Although psychology eventually achieved scientific respectability, it did so by following a very limited agenda. Indeed, for most of the twentieth century, psychology failed to show any interest in those features of human mental life that are the most complex and distinctive. For example, in the first half of the century, only a fragmented literature existed on the whole area of human emotions. Virtually nothing was written about love.

In his 1958 presidential address to the American Psychological Association, Harry Harlow declared: 'So far as love or affection is concerned, psychologists have failed in their mission. The little we know about love does not transcend simple observation, and the little we write about it has been written better by poets and novelists.'

Since the 1950s, psychologists have become more interested in love. Yet, given its cultural significance, the literature on love is still relatively small: only a handful of theorists have attempted to explain love in the context of a general theory, and only a few of these theories have generated interesting research programmes. Be that as it may, a modern research literature does exist and its findings are of considerable interest – for this reason: every contemporary typology of love, theory of love, and description of love acknowledges at least one feature or mechanism that is associated with mental illness.

In seeking to answer the question 'What is love?', humanity has been unable to discover a single answer. This lack of success is not because love is a mysterious phenomenon, forever beyond the reach of rational analysis; it is because of the way we use language. There may not be a common factor underlying all the things we call 'love'. Indeed, two people said to be 'in love' might think, feel and behave very differently. As a general principle, scientific investigation cannot proceed effectively in the absence of definition – albeit a provisional or working definition.

A possible remedy to this problem is the creation of a classification system: a typology of love, in which precise terms are employed to describe different forms of love. This strategy is part of a tradition that goes back to ancient Greece. For example, in *The Symposium*, Plato makes a distinction between common and heavenly love. The former is base and fuelled by sensual desire alone, while the latter is nobler and more mature – a kind of deep, lasting attachment (but which might still be experienced as part of a sexual relationship). The first modern and extended typology of love was devised, not by a psychologist, but by the writer C.S. Lewis. In *The Four Loves*, which was published in 1960, Lewis distinguished four forms of love: Agape (altruism), Affection (attachment), Philias (friendship) and Eros (romantic love). Although Lewis's work was influential, his system did not take the study of love as shared between lovers very much further than Plato. Indeed, in this respect, one could even argue it represents a step backwards. Lewis does not attempt to define the types of love that might exist under the single heading of Eros.

The task of deconstructing the love shared between lovers was undertaken by John Lee, a Canadian sociologist whose research has since been claimed by psychology. Lee began by examining descriptions of love in various fictional and non-fictional works since classical times. These initial investigations were then supplemented by data collected after conducting carefully structured interviews. After collating and analysing his results, Lee was able to differentiate six forms of love (some of which owe a modest debt to Lewis's quartet). They are Eros (romantic), Storge (friendly), Ludus (playful, uncommitted), Agape (selfless), Pragma (logical or practical) and, finally, Mania (manic). Although individuals tend to have a dominant 'love-style', this is by no means fixed. Indeed, the type of love one experiences may change as a relationship progresses, and different types of love might be experienced with different partners.

In this new anatomy of love, a residue of melancholy adust seems to have blown across the centuries and collected in Lee's mania: an unhappy form of loving with obvious psychopathological resonances.

> The manic lover is obsessively preoccupied with the beloved, intensely jealous and possessive, and in need of repeated assurances of being loved. At the same time, the manic lover often holds back, fearful of loving too much before there is a guarantee of being equally loved in return. In many cases, the lover doesn't even *like* the beloved and would not choose him or her as a lasting friend.

This description of the manic lover evokes Catullus, who so powerfully described the self-contradictory nature of love – both loving and hating at the same time.

Lee suggests that manic lovers often appear to have 'lost

their senses'. They will go to bizarre extremes to 'prove' their love and are apt to dramatise feelings of jealousy with extreme 'displays'. Yet, interestingly, Lee does not view mania as psychopathological. His classification system was based on literary and contemporary descriptions of love as experienced by non-psychiatric individuals. It is certainly true that during the course of normal sexual development, most people's first experience of love tends to be imbued with manic qualities. Indeed, intensity, insecurity and ambivalence are typical of adolescent romance. Terms such as 'puppy love' – evoking comfortable images of innocent, loyal attachment – fail almost entirely to capture the confused, anxious and frankly miserable state that the majority of adolescents pass through on their journey to adulthood. Unfortunately – as a feature of normal human development – mania is not only associated with adolescence. It is also associated with the middle years and tends to reappear when an affair disturbs the equilibrium of a complacent marriage. The offending party (typically the male) assumes that the illicit relationship can be conducted in a businesslike fashion, but is suddenly overwhelmed by powerful and uncontrollable feelings, recapitulating the tormented world of juvenile obsession.

At roughly the same time as Lee was developing his typology of love, psychologist Dorothy Tennov began a research programme that eventually resulted in the identification of a form of love similar to Lee's mania. Tennov called it limerence – to distinguish it from other concepts of love – and it corresponds with mental states conventionally described as 'being in love' or 'falling in love'. The principal features of limerence are obsession, irrational idealisation, emotional dependency and a deep longing for reciprocation. Typically, limerent individuals pursue inappropriate partners, fail at relationships, and seem unable to learn from their experience. Moreover, like manic lovers, they are often compulsively attracted to partners who are objectively unsuitable. Given that the limerent individual does not learn from experience, he or she is likely to become trapped in a repeating cycle of unhappy relationships. Consequently, limerence is characterised by significant emotional distress and a sense of futility.

Again, it should be noted that, like Lee's mania, limerence is not supposed to be viewed as an abnormal state. It is merely a more precise description of what many people experience when they 'fall in love'. However, Tennov has suggested that limerence may be a state with which women – rather than men – are more familiar. Indeed, many of the non-psychiatric participants in Shere Hite's 1987 survey, *Women and Love*, describe relationships that are clearly limerent. For example:

> I care for a lover that I should hate. He's treated me bad and has little respect or understanding of who I've become, yet I want him. Why? I don't know and it takes all my strength to stay out of his life. I've got to let him go. It's destructive to me, to my self-worth and self-esteem.

Although the work of Lee and Tennov has inspired some academic interest, their ideas have not been widely accepted. This may be – in part – because their research is considered too close in flavour to 'pop psychology'. An approach to taxonomy that seems to have achieved a greater degree of academic respectability is that proposed by Yale psychologist Robert Sternberg. Unlike Lee's, Sternberg's taxonomy is closely linked to an underlying theory of love. Therefore, rather than just cataloguing different types of love, Sternberg is able to explain why and how they arise.

Sternberg's theory is known as the triangular theory, because it supposes that love is ordinarily a compound of three psychological elements: intimacy (or closeness), passion (which is mostly sexual in nature) and commitment. For the purpose of elucidating the principles that generate his taxonomy, Sternberg suggests that these three elements can be envisaged as forming the vertices of a triangle (Figure 1).

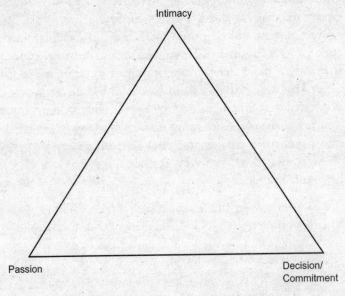

Figure 1: Love's three psychological elements

By combining these three elements in various ways, it is possible to derive seven types of love. Thus, Sternberg's theory produces a typology similar to that of Lee, but with much greater transparency (Figure 2). Put plainly, we can see how he gets them.

Consummate or complete love arises when all three of the basic components are present. It is the kind of love that most couples strive to achieve, and its accomplishment is associated with stability and satisfaction. However, when only one or two of the components of love are present, other forms of love are produced. For example, when a relationship is based

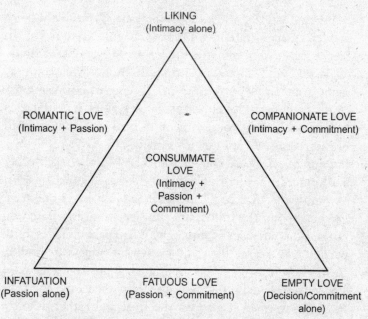

Figure 2: Sternberg's seven types of love

on intimacy alone, it is perhaps more accurately described as 'liking'. When commitment is added, the outcome is companionate love, which has the character of a deep, long-term friendship. When passion is added to intimacy, the outcome is romantic love. This term is used in a special sense here, to describe the kind of love that might be experienced during a holiday romance. Both parties may be drawn to each other physically and emotionally, but recognise that a lasting commitment will be neither likely nor possible.

Along the base of Sternberg's triangle, we find three forms of love which are associated with painful, distressing or deeply unsatisfying relationships. These are infatuation, fatuous love and empty love. The first two seem to correspond quite closely with the sanguine (or hot) stage of love sickness, Lee's mania, and Tennov's limerence.

Infatuation arises from passion alone. Typically, it has a sudden onset – but it will evaporate just as quickly. In Sternberg's taxonomy, it is the form of love most strongly associated with obsession and idealisation. When commitment is added to passion (in the absence of intimacy), the result is fatuous love. Sternberg describes it as fatuous because a lasting commitment is made on the basis of passion alone. A fatuous love affair can easily result in a fatuous marriage. A couple who hardly know each other and, indeed, may not even really like each other, make a commitment that has little chance of being honoured. Predictably, in the fullness of time, relationships based on fatuous love are usually unhappy. When passion fades, both parties may regret their 'moment of madness' – finding themselves in a marriage predicated almost entirely on a sterile contractual obligation. In effect, their love will then have transformed itself into the final and rather desolate love that Sternberg describes: empty love. This is the kind of love that is based entirely on commitment and nothing else. Many ill-conceived arranged marriages would fall into this category, being maintained only by a sense of religious or social duty.

By defining love in terms of three elements, and examining their different combinations, Sternberg's theory generates a complete taxonomy. It is self-contained and governed by a pleasing internal logic. There are no loose ends. However, its neatness has also invited a certain amount of scepticism. Many members of the academic community have questioned whether it is necessary to make quite so many fine distinctions, and others have questioned their legitimacy. For example, do relationships based on intimacy alone, or commitment alone, qualify as 'loving' relationships at all? Although there are undoubtedly relationships that can be sustained by closeness alone, or commitment alone, do they represent examples of what most people would recognise as love?

Lee's taxonomy is vulnerable to exactly the same criticism. For example, his ludus is a type of love that is playful, superficial, and non-committed. The ludic lover wants to have fun, does not experience the pain of 'falling in love', and will avoid partners who are possessive. Given these parameters, perhaps ludic lovers are merely people who flirt and enjoy uncomplicated sex? Similarly, agape – which Lee describes as 'selfless, giving, altruistic love' – is so saintly that it has more in common with spiritual than earthly love.

Clearly, to suggest that love is a unitary concept is inadequate. Love – even when considered only in the context of intimate relationships – seems to possess more facets than a single word can capture. Yet, extended taxonomies seem to generate more terms than are necessary, thus producing examples of love that appear hollow or unconvincing. As a consequence, modern research into love seems to have settled on a compromise.

It is now generally accepted that much of the evidence gathered since the 1950s suggests the existence of just two forms of love: passionate love and companionate love. These two forms are sometimes called by different names – for example, romantic love in the case of passionate love, and conjugal love in the case of companionate love – but the key characteristics are almost always the same. The terms passionate and companionate are intentionally broad headings, and both subsume many of the more precise varieties of love that can be found in the taxonomies of Lee and Sternberg.

Passionate love is generally described as a state of intense longing for the beloved. When reciprocated, passionate love is associated with joy, euphoria and ecstasy. However, these feelings are almost invariably shadowed by darker emotions such as anxiety, jealousy, and sadness. Therefore, it is difficult to experience passionate love in the absence of at least some psychological pain. When unrequited (or frustrated), passionate love will reliably engender a sense of emptiness and even despair. Passionate love is all-consuming, tending to dominate an individual's life to the exclusion of everything else; however, its intensity is short-lived. It seems either to burn itself out – in which case the affected individual falls out of love – or to reduce in intensity until it transmutes into companionate love.

Companionate love may be less intense than passionate love, but it is more stable. It is generally associated with commitment and feelings of profound closeness. This level of intimacy can only be achieved in a relationship that evolves over an extended period of time. The companionate couple enjoy a symbiotic partnership, sustained by common goals and shared experiences. Although companionate love may never recover the heady heights of passionate love, neither does it plumb its depths. Moreover, what companionate love lacks in excitement is amply recompensed by more subtle rewards: tenderness, understanding, sympathy, affection, support and care.

Passionate love – as described above – captures many of the features of Lee's mania, Tennov's limerence and Sternberg's infatuation. Moreover, companionate love seems to be an amalgam of several other (and similar) kinds of love described by the same theorists. Indeed, Sternberg actually uses the term companionate love.

In attempting to answer the question 'What is love?' psychology has chosen to begin with taxonomy. Although complex taxonomies seem to include forms of love that are either redundant, or unconvincing, a general consensus has emerged that a valid distinction can be made between passionate and companionate forms. This distinction is supported by a considerable amount of scientific research, but, more importantly, the distinction 'makes sense' to most people if they reflect on their own experiences of love. Anyone who has fallen in love will immediately be able to identify with descriptions of passionate love: the intensity, pleasure and pain. If they are in a long-term relationship, they will also recognise that their experience of love has gradually changed. Few couples are infatuated with each other several years into a relationship. Moreover, the special 'friendship' that characterises companionate love is very different from other forms of friendship. It has a unique emotional depth.

The striking feature of twentieth-century research into the nature of love is that it has rarely been able to refrain from employing the language of psychopathology. Passionate lovers are manic. They obsess and experience episodes of anxiety: they despair. Although psychologists have sought to describe ordinary, nonpathological love, they have been constantly forced to describe love using the language of ancient poets and scholars. We are constantly reminded of love sickness. The modern taxonomies of love share much in common with the psychological anatomies of the seventeenth century. When the body of love is opened, something that looks like disease is almost invariably identified.

After the collapse of the humoral model, doctors decided that love was no longer a mental illness. Yet, this decision had no impact on how people actually experienced love – indeed after the seventeenth century, romanticism swept Europe and people loved more madly and more deeply than ever – and the illness metaphor has continued to be exploited to the present day. The pop charts are saturated with young men and women who are crazy for love, mad for love, who are going out of their heads for love; they cry for love, sigh for love, and swear that they will die for love.

The illness metaphor has maintained a continuous presence in poetry and song for thousands of years and in cultures too numerous to mention. Moreover, contemporary psychological research has repeatedly identified features of love that imply psychopathology.

Does it really mean anything, then, that doctors have decided that love is no longer an illness? They have changed their minds – but the rest of the world doesn't seem to have taken much notice.

Of all the specialist sub-disciplines of medicine, psychiatry is the least secure – and arguably the least respected. This is largely because, unlike other areas of medicine, psychiatry has had enormous problems establishing a solid and coherent diagnostic system.

Diagnosis is not merely about the enumeration of symptoms. To give a diagnosis implies knowledge of causation and thus also provides a rationale for treatment. Consider, for example, the diagnosis of diabetes. The diagnosis of diabetes is given when there is insufficient or absent production of the hormone insulin by the pancreas. When this happens, a discrete set of symptoms will reliably appear. These include increased urination, excessive thirst, weight loss, hunger, and fatigue, and tests will show that blood glucose is abnormally high. However, the administration of insulin will correct blood glucose abnormalities and lead to the remission of symptoms. This outcome is more or less guaranteed.

Unfortunately, psychiatry does not operate within such a reassuring framework. Apart from a few exceptions, there has never been complete agreement with respect to what symptoms constitute a particular diagnosis; the causes of putative syndromes have never been fully identified; nor can a positive outcome be confidently predicted after a particular treatment has been administered. Even today, major diagnoses like schizophrenia are still the subject of heated debate. Although the term has been in use for over fifty years, there are still those who question the validity of current diagnostic criteria, and there are even some who doubt whether the term schizophrenia has any objective validity at all. For so-called radical psychiatrists, schizophrenia is merely a convenient and authoritative term used by the psychiatric establishment to disguise a very real poverty of knowledge. Although this position is somewhat extreme, it dramatises the importance of diagnosis in medical practice. It is a lynchpin, the removal of which can threaten the whole integrity of a profession.

In addition to these fundamental problems, psychiatric diagnoses have proved particularly vulnerable to the influence of cultural factors, giving the impression that they are groundless and unreliable. Diagnoses are introduced, modified, or rejected, in a manner that suggests the world of fashion rather than science. In the late nineteenth century, for example, the salons of Europe were full of swooning women who exhibited a bizarre collection of symptoms – all generally attributed to the very broad and accommodating diagnosis of hysteria. It was a condition that completely preoccupied the intellectual colossi of the time: Charcot, Janet, Freud and Breuer. After the First World War, the diagnosis of hysteria became increasingly rare and, by the end of the twentieth century, the diagnosis had all but disappeared. The symptoms of hysteria still exist, but the diagnosis is no longer popular, and its various manifestations have been absorbed into a range of other more precise diagnoses.

Today, the reputation of psychiatry is bolstered by two diagnostic Bibles: the International Classification of Diseases and Related Health Problems (ICD), (produced by the World Health Organisation), and the Diagnostic and Statistical Manual of Mental Disorders (DSM), (produced by the American Psychiatric Association).

Although a considerable amount of research and effort has gone into the development of these systems, they operate on a simple principle – the counting-up of symptoms (where symptoms are defined according to guidelines agreed by specialists). Thus, when a patient exhibits a certain number of symptoms that appear under specific headings (for example, Panic Disorder or Social Phobia), they are said to meet diagnostic criteria and consequently receive a diagnosis. It is possible to receive several psychiatric diagnoses at the same time – in the same way that it is possible to suffer simultaneously from two or more medical conditions (for example, eczema, migraine and a cold).

A problem with these diagnostic systems is that much depends on the attitude and opinion of the clinician making the diagnosis. For example, DSM contains diagnostic criteria such as 'The disturbance causes clinically significant distress or impairment in social, occupational, or other important areas of functioning.' The level of disturbance a problem must cause to be classified as 'clinically significant' varies from psychiatrist to psychiatrist (some being more liberal than others).

ICD and DSM are not meant to be definitive statements, but are work in progress. Although both systems broadly agree with each other, there are many differences with respect to detail. Moreover, both the ICD and DSM systems are frequently reissued in revised editions in which diagnostic criteria are slightly modified. ICD is currently in its tenth edition (ICD-10) and DSM is in its fourth (DSM-IV). If one compares editions, it is possible to observe a gradual process of attrition and deposition, leading to dramatic changes in the diagnostic landscape: features appear, change their location, or vanish completely.

Of course, this lack of certainty may be generic to psychiatry. The brain is the most complex object in the known universe, and human beings are extremely sensitive to their social and cultural contexts. Thus, the subject matter of psychiatry does not lend itself to rigid diagnoses and the identification of straightforward pathological processes. The brain is infinitely more complicated than the pancreas, and the course of 'schizophrenia' – unlike diabetes – can be influenced by a multiplicity of subtle factors. Even the barely discernable nuances of parental criticism have been shown to exacerbate the illness. It may be the case that psychiatry is not a poor science but a difficult science. Unfortunately, the academic community is unforgiving, and for those who practise more trustworthy forms of medicine, the edifice of psychiatry appears to be built on shifting sands.

Love sickness is no longer recognised as a medical condition. It does not feature in either the ICD or DSM systems, but, given the controversy surrounding psychiatric diagnosis, its absence doesn't really mean very much. It still looks like, feels like, and behaves like a mental illness. The *symptoms* of love sickness can still be found in ICD-10 and DSM-IV, where they congregate – to a greater or lesser extent – under several diagnostic headings. Moreover, love sickness has very similar consequences to mental illness. Clearly, a 'clinically significant' amount of distress and general impairment are an almost inevitable consequence of falling in love. How many people, for example, after declaring that they are in love, can function well at work the following day? One imagines very few. When we fall in love, we immediately begin to stumble across the boundary lines that psychiatrists use to cordon off abnormality.

As Robert Burton pointed out, falling in love seems to be associated with an overwhelming and sometimes confusing number of symptoms. This sentiment was echoed several centuries later by the eminent Victorian Sir Henry Finck, who suggested that: 'Love is such a tissue of paradoxes, and exists in such a variety of forms and shades, that you may almost say anything about it that you please, and it is likely to be correct.' Described in this way, love seems too Protean – too ephemeral – to be confined within a rigid set of diagnostic criteria. However, this is somewhat misleading. Although there are an enormous number of secondary (and even tertiary) symptoms, the primary symptoms of being in love are easy to identify and appear together with remarkable frequency. The diagnosis of love sickness is probably more coherent and reliable than many of the diagnoses that appear in ICD and DSM. Indeed, the parameters of love sickness are so well defined, that people without any medical training are able to diagnose it accurately (in themselves and others) from a relatively early age.

It was suggested above that love sickness looks, feels and behaves like a mental illness, and that many of the symptoms of love sickness can be found distributed through the ICD and DSM classification systems. This underscores the fact that being in love produces a symptom profile that would ordinarily suggest significant psychiatric disturbance.

When people fall in love, they reliably describe four core symptoms: preoccupation (with the loved one), episodes of melancholy, episodes of rapture, and general instability of mood. Symptoms such as these correspond closely with the conventional diagnoses of obsessionality, depression, mania (or hypomania), and manic depression. These will be briefly considered in turn.

In the context of love sickness, obsessional thinking was given considerable importance by doctors working in the Galenic tradition. Indeed, Ibn Sina (and his followers) believed obsession to be the primary cause of 'ishq (or love madness). Modern research is, for the most part, consistent with these early observations. Data collected from numerous interview, survey, and questionnaire studies all demonstrate that obsessing is a key feature of falling in love.

For psychiatrists, the term obsession is usually employed to describe thoughts, impulses, or images, that are recurrent, persistent, and difficult to dismiss. These 'intrusions' are generally unwanted, and characteristically reflect themes that are distressing to the sufferer: for example, sex, violence or blasphemy.

Recurrent and persistent mental intrusions can be a feature of several psychiatric problems; however, in the current ICD and DSM systems, the term obsession is most strongly associated with Obsessive Compulsive Disorder (or OCD). This is a rather complex condition, in which obsessions trigger high levels of anxiety, which the affected individual then attempts to reduce (often unsuccessfully) by performing certain actions. These 'compulsions' are often superstitious or ritualistic, and can be enacted internally (for example, repeating a lucky number) or externally (arranging objects symmetrically). Some individuals diagnosed as having OCD are described as 'pure obsessionals' or 'ruminators'. Although these terms describe slightly different problems, there is a considerable degree of overlap – the majority experience intrusive thoughts and images, which initiate (or form part of) extended episodes of preoccupation.

Although patients who are diagnosed as suffering from OCD and individuals who fall in love obsess about very different things, the quality of obsessional thinking in both groups is very similar. Lovers, too, experience thoughts, impulses and images that are recurrent, persistent, and difficult to dismiss: fantasies, day-dreams, and irresistible urges to send text-messages or make telephone calls are all typical of new love. During periods of separation, the threat of infidelity can easily turn a soft-focus day-dream through several degrees of menace into nightmare. When this happens, the resonances between OCD and love sickness are highlighted with respect to both quality and content: unwanted and intrusive sexual images can trouble the OCD patient *and* the lover. Finally, a further and somewhat obvious link concerning clinical obsessions and love obsessions is the degree to which both are usually very focused and absorbing. A single idea, person, or image may occupy awareness to the exclusion of everything else.

We have already considered how melancholy – a disturbance primarily of mood and now more frequently described as depression – extended the longevity of love sickness as a medical diagnosis well into the seventeenth century. Indeed, for Elizabethan dramatists and scholars such as Robert Burton, love sickness was simply a variant of melancholy. It is certainly the case that depression and love seem to fashion figures of a common type: sighing, lachrymose and listless. As with obsession, the similarities between love sickness and psychopathology are amplified under conditions of forced separation. When lovers part, they exhibit a number of symptoms that are usually attributed to depression. Consider, for example, the following: depressed mood (most of the day), diminished interest or pleasure in activities, loss of appetite, insomnia, fatigue, and diminished ability to concentrate. Exhibiting only five of these six symptoms sustained for a mere two weeks is sufficient to merit a diagnosis of major depressive episode according to DSM-IV criteria.

Another sobering link between love sickness and depression is suicide. Rejected lovers and individuals with a diagnosis of depression are both at risk; however, those individuals who are already depressed and subsequently break up with their partners seem to be particularly vulnerable. Indeed, contemporary suicide statistics (particularly for young men and women) suggest that those ancient physicians who considered love sickness a potentially fatal illness were correct to do so.

Although love and melancholy are closely related, to construe love solely as a form of depression is clearly inaccurate. Separation and rejection might well provoke the symptoms of depression, but love is much more than yearning, pining and sadness. It is also joy, euphoria and ecstasy. When such positive emotions are felt very intensely, they too can cause problems: for example, overconfidence, boastfulness, recklessness, and a failure to recognise realistic limits.

In psychiatry, something very similar occurs in patients suffering from mania, which is associated with increased levels of physical energy and abnormally elevated mood. In the first euphoric weeks (or even months) of love the symptoms of mania are clearly evident. These include expansive mood, inflated self-esteem, decreased need for sleep, a pressure to talk, racing thoughts, distractibility, increased activity (particularly sexual), and a general disregard for the consequences of pleasure-seeking (for instance, spending large amounts of money on gifts or dining). Again, only four of the above (including expansive mood) experienced for one week will be sufficient to meet DSM-IV diagnostic criteria for a manic episode. Less than a week of these symptoms would be sufficient to merit the lesser diagnosis of hypomanic episode.

Clinically, mania tends to alternate with episodes of depression. Thus, when psychiatric patients meet criteria for both mania and depression, they are described as being manic-depressive. This general instability of mood is also one of the most characteristic features of passionate love. When in love, the mind oscillates between two emotional polarities. Indeed both poetry and ancient medicine have always favoured the language of dichotomy to describe love: hot-cold, heaven-hell, moist-dry, bliss-misery – and so on, exhausting all antonyms. In many respects, manic depression is perhaps the most accurate psychiatric analogue of love, embracing as it does both extremes of the emotional continuum.

In addition to the diagnoses of obsession, depression, mania, and manic depression, the symptoms of love overlap with a number of other psychiatric problems, although perhaps to a lesser degree. For instance, the excitement that precedes meeting a lover is often accompanied by physical symptoms that appear during panic attacks: pounding heart, trembling, shortness of breath and feeling lightheaded. Excessive worry about the future of a relationship resembles generalised anxiety disorder; disturbances of appetite and appearance sensitivity are reminiscent of anorexia nervosa; and feeling as though life has become 'a dream' suggests phenomena such as derealisation (experiencing the world as unreal) and depersonalisation (experiencing the self as unreal). It is extremely easy, in fact, to show correspondences between the symptoms of love sickness and numerous forms of psychiatric illness.

In a sense, the exercise of testing the diagnosis of love sickness against contemporary diagnoses seems to fall foul of Sir Henry Finck's caveat. One can say almost anything about love and find it to be true. Nevertheless, the ease with which it is possible to show similarities between the experience of falling in love, and several forms of mental illness recognised by contemporary psychiatrists, is striking. The tiniest flexing of diagnostic parameters would confer psychiatric status on the vast majority of people who describe themselves as being 'in love'.

Although falling in love can be a painful experience, it is generally treated as something to celebrate – a golden thread on which we are able to string together the most important events of our lives. For the majority of the human race, these events usually take the form of engagement, marriage, and the naming of children. Today, particularly in the liberal West, even homosexual relationships may progress in an identical fashion, addressing the hitherto problematic issue of children by surrogacy or adoption. In spite of escalating divorce rates, rancorous financial settlements and painful disputes over child custody, the human race seems tirelessly optimistic when it comes to love. The principal landmarks of autobiography are predicated on love, and saluted with the ordnance of party poppers and champagne corks.

Yet, love is unique among those mental states that we generally assume to be positive. Although we celebrate love, we also recognise that it can resemble an illness. Thus, the word love is complemented by love sickness. There is no equivalent construction that relates to any other 'positive' mental state. People never become 'joy sick', and there is no such thing as 'delight sickness'. Psychiatry recognises abnormally elevated mood in the form of mania, but this has no colloquial equivalent. Although it is possible for people to become deliriously happy, in this context, the term delirium has no clinical overtones. It merely describes a higher and headier register of happiness. Only love has its own sickness.

If love looks like, feels like and behaves like a mental illness, then we must ask 'Why?' The process of answering this seemingly suspect question will be astonishingly revealing. Not only will it deepen our understanding of love, but it will also explain every significant human achievement over the last thirty-five thousand years.

3

A Necessary Madness

Love is only the dirty trick played on us to achieve continuation of the species.

A Writer's Notebook, W. Somerset Maugham

Charles Darwin was never a bold, romantic figure. His school career was undistinguished and he didn't have the stomach to follow his father into medicine – he found surgical procedures too distressing to watch – so he was sent to Cambridge to study divinity; then, a common fate for the less impressive sons of prominent families. While at Cambridge, Darwin became a student and friend of the cleric and botanist John Stevens Henslow. His canine loyalty and unassuming character meant that he soon became known as 'the man who walks with Henslow' – a telling epithet, as it suggests the total eclipse of one man's identity by the mere presence of another.

When Darwin was still relatively young, he became sickly and somewhat apprehensive. His condition deteriorated, resulting eventually in problems such as painful flatulence, vomiting, insomnia and palpitations. Many believe that he suffered from some form of anxiety disorder. He was certainly excessively cautious, and delayed publishing the details of his theory of evolution for years, because he did not want to offend devout Christians. Indeed, if the young biologist Alfred Wallace had not come up with exactly the same idea – forcing Darwin to publish – he might have procrastinated indefinitely.

Darwin was an atheist, but he never attempted to promote atheism as an alternative to Christian orthodoxy. He had no desire to disturb the status quo. Those who set out to challenge traditional values frightened him. Even nature scared him a little: 'What a book a Devil's Chaplain might write on the clumsy, wasteful, blundering low & horridly cruel works of nature!'

Darwin did not possess a poetic sensibility. In his auto-biography, he wrote: 'I have tried lately to read Shakespeare, and found it so intolerably dull that it nauseated me.' Years of scientific observation, classification, and rational prob-lem-solving had taken their toll. His imagination was blunted.

Many accounts of Darwin's character suggest an affable but rather unimpressive individual. When his 'big idea' was finally unveiled, and its awesome implications recognised, evolution was not regarded as a 'clever' theory, the kind of theory that could only ever be conceived in the mind of a genius. Even Darwin's greatest admirers seemed to belittle him as they praised his achievement. T.H. Huxley is reputed to have exclaimed: 'How extremely stupid not to have thought of that!'

Friendly, timid, nervous and, at times, sufficiently unim-posing to suggest mediocrity, a plodder – this was Darwin: the complete antithesis, in temperament, appearance and behaviour, of a romantic hero. Yet, his life was not without romance – in two ways.

Firstly, a romantic mythology surrounds his early life. The young Darwin leaves England on HMS *Beagle* and embarks upon an epic voyage. He travels around the world and, liberated from the restrictive thinking and practices of Victorian society, sees the universe with new eyes. He encounters nature in the raw, and a mystery is revealed. On his return to England, he can no longer pursue a career in the Church, and must dedicate his life to science. The dramatic structure of the Darwinian romance follows the conventions of ancient Greek story telling: our hero goes on a journey, is changed by wonderful, strange experiences, and then returns clutching the key to a mystery in his hands. The myth of the *Beagle*'s voyage contains a nugget of truth, but it owes much more to the imposition of a pleasing narrative by biographers.

Secondly, Darwin's life was also touched by romance in the more conventional way. He fell in love. Darwin – not the most passionate of men – was an unexpected triumph for Cupid.

He approached the idea of marriage with a curious degree of intellectual detachment. He had reached his late twenties, and recognised that marriage was one of those things that a successful young bachelor should be considering – but, like most young men, even today, he was not sure whether he was ready to commit himself. The problem was also compounded by the fact that he was considering marriage entirely in the abstract, having no wife-to-be in mind.

In an attempt to resolve his uncertainty, Darwin did something very unromantic. He drew up two columns, one headed 'Marry', and the other headed 'Not Marry', and then set about evaluating the costs and benefits associated with each. His instinct, therefore, was not to find love, but to examine its balance sheet. He took his first faltering steps towards the altar not as love's victim, but as love's auditor.

The costs that Darwin associated with marriage are very revealing: he would have less time for himself in general, less time to spend in gentlemen's clubs, and less time for reading. Worse still, he would have to waste time seeing his wife's relatives (who would no doubt expect him to be accommodating with respect to every trifling request). Clearly, for Darwin, time was a precious commodity.

He was also concerned that the financial austerities of marriage would limit his expenditure on books – not only would he have less time to read, but fewer books to read as well.

On the reverse side of his balance sheet he wrote:

> Then how should I manage all my business if I were obliged to go every day walking with my wife. – Eheu!! I never should know French, – or see the continent, – or go to America, or go up in a Balloon, or take a solitary trip in Wales – poor slave . . .

Darwin was a man who was accustomed to total freedom. He had spent five years on the *Beagle*, doing more or less whatever he wanted. His journal entries show that, at times, the wonders that he saw gave him an almost spiritual sense of satisfaction: 'To a person fond of natural history, such a day as this brings with it a deeper pleasure than he can ever hope to experience again.' Then, on his return to England, Darwin continued to enjoy the comfortable, privileged existence of a gentleman scientist; an existence entirely compatible with his temperament and intellectual needs. He liked books, clubs and clever conversation. Why on earth should he swap these for boring relatives and screaming children, expenses and worries? Life was difficult enough without all these additional burdens. Darwin even contemplated the possibility – with palpable discomfort – that, after marriage, he might have to do some form of work! Labour! Toil. Could anything be worse for a man who enjoyed full possession of his time and the leisurely pursuit of learning?

But what of the benefits of marriage? To what extent

would the connubial life recompense Darwin for his losses? In the 'Marry' column of his balance sheet, he attempted to enumerate the benefits of female company – a task which he found profoundly difficult. The best he could do at one point was to observe that a wife would be 'better than a dog'. Darwin found it so difficult to focus on the advantages of marriage that he ended up linking the few he could think of with what – as far as he was concerned – constituted its most significant disadvantage: 'Charms of music & female chit-chat – These things good for one's heath.– but terrible waste of time.'

Within a few months, however, everything had changed.

Darwin's balance sheet was written in July 1838. Shortly after, he fell in love with his cousin, Emma Wedgwood. In November of the same year, he proposed – and to his great surprise, she accepted. Thereafter, Darwin was a reformed character. The voice of the bullish bachelor was silenced by the besotted lover.

Darwin's correspondence shows how, every day, he anxiously waited for the post to arrive, in the hope that it would include a letter from his 'sweet Emma'. He was unable to sleep, because his nights were spent fantasising about the life he would enjoy with his future wife. He was eager – even desperate – to get married. He experienced moments of intense joy, followed by despondency. The rational, sensible, restrained gentleman scholar completely forgot self-interest, clubs and books. The immense and remarkable freedom that he had formerly enjoyed – to ride across the pampas with gauchos, experience the sublime in the great deserts of Patagonia, and climb the wooded mountains of Tierra del Fuego – was suddenly rendered irrelevant. As for solitary trips to Wales and ballooning – nothing could have been further from his thoughts. Instead, Darwin craved domestic captivity. He was no longer dismissive of 'female chit-chat' and prostrated himself before his wife-to-be: 'My own dear Emma, I kiss the hands with all humbleness and gratitude which have so filled up for me the cup of happiness. It is my most earnest wish that I may make myself worthy of you.'

His mind filled with cosy images of married life: Charles and Emma – husband and wife – wasting hour after delightful hour by the fireside. Suddenly, time wasn't quite so important any more. Even his scholarly pursuits seemed less attractive – somewhat cold and sterile: 'I think you will humanize me, and soon teach me there is greater happiness than holding theories and accumulating facts in silence and solitude.'

This process of conversion, from self-engrossed bachelor to devoted husband, continued well beyond the wedding day. Darwin's concerns about the cost of raising a family seem to have evaporated completely. Charles and Emma had ten children, seven of whom lived to adulthood. Also, he lost all interest in the clever conversation of his gentlemen peers, preferring the company of his wife and family, which he found inexpressibly rewarding.

Darwin was aware that he was a changed man, and he understood perfectly well what had caused this transformation. A few weeks before his wedding day, he wrote in his notebook: 'What passes in a man's mind when he says he loves a person . . . it is blind feeling. Something like sexual feelings – love being an emotion does it regard – is it influenced by – other emotions?'

In the throes of love, Darwin was grappling with the age-old question – 'What is love?' It is a salient question for a man who had been altered more by love in five months than in the five years he had spent circumnavigating the globe.

Darwin's succinct and disjointed answers are remarkably

perceptive. Love is first and foremost an emotional state, but a complex emotional state – both influencing, and being influenced by, other more basic emotions. Love is also linked to sexual interest. This essential feature distinguishes romantic love from other forms of love, such as parental love or love between friends. Darwin's language also echoes the cautionary expression 'love is blind' – a phrase that pithily recognises love's irrationality.

If the old, bachelor Darwin had met the new, engaged-to-be-married Darwin, how might the former have addressed the latter? It seems likely that he would have begged the new Darwin to think things through properly, rationally. He might have resorted to a basic technique, handing the new Darwin a crumpled balance sheet on which the insubstantial benefits of marriage were weighed against its severe and punitive costs – but one thing is absolutely certain: however reasonable, logical, or sensible his objections, the new Darwin would not have been persuaded to alter his course. The new Darwin was in love – and, as we all know, lovers cannot be persuaded to change their minds about anything by means of rational argument.

Our imaginative fancy suggests an image of the old Darwin, raising himself from the worn leather chair of a gentlemen's club and looking long and hard at his new incarnation. After a while, he might shake his head, and intone gravely: 'Sir. You have taken leave of your senses. You have become quite mad.' And at the periphery of awareness, we might detect a sympathetic resonance, amplified in the vast body of poetry, literature and song that extends back to the earliest of civilisations.

Darwin wrote his notes on the nature of love at about the same time as he was formulating his theory of evolution. It is significant that he begins his note 'What passes in a man's mind . . .', as it demonstrates his keen interest in psychology. It was inevitable, therefore, that Darwin would eventually seek to understand mental life from an evolutionary perspective.

In the mid-nineteenth century, psychology – if it can be said to have existed at all – was a relatively incoherent discipline: a loose coalition of romantic poets, philosophers, physiologists, and doctors. Psychological knowledge was fragmented, and desperately in need of a unifying framework.

In the last few pages of *On the Origin of Species by Means of Natural Selection*, Darwin wrote:

> In the distant future I see open fields for far more important researches. Psychology will be based on a new foundation, that of the necessary acquirement of each mental power and capacity by gradation. Light will be thrown on the origin of man and his history.

Unfortunately, the burgeoning discipline of psychology chose to ignore this subtle signal – an oversight that is perhaps forgivable, given the brevity of the passage and its relatively minor position in such a major work. However, the connections between evolutionary theory and psychology could not have been made more explicit than in Darwin's later publication, *The Expression of the Emotions in Man and Animals*. In this work, Darwin suggested that emotions could be understood in terms of their function or purpose.

Darwin was too large a figure for psychology to ignore completely. Thus, the discipline assumed that his theory of evolution was true, and that subsequently all psychological phenomena must have evolved according to Darwinian principles. Memory, language, emotion and consciousness itself were all assumed to have a function, and to be the result of millions of years of natural selection. However, the discussion did not proceed any further. There was no debate or lively exchange of ideas, and so, apart from the most super-ficial acknowledgement of Darwin's importance to psych-ology, academic textbooks included virtually nothing on him for over a hundred years. For the remainder of the nineteenth century, and the greater part of the twentieth, psychology failed to realise the potential of Darwin's vision – that of a mental science based on a 'new foundation'.

Darwin's theory of evolution was not the only theory of its kind. Indeed, different evolutionary theories had been proposed before (the earliest dating back to ancient Greece and China); however, all of these contending theories were – to a greater or lesser extent – wrong. Darwin's theory, on the other hand, was right, because it included the critical ingredient of natural selection. This made it not only an accurate theory, but a theory possessed of awesome explan-atory power.

What, then, are the elements of Darwin's theory of evolu-tion by natural selection? The basic tenets are easily summarised and deceptively simple.

He suggested that characteristics and traits, some of which are advantageous with respect to survival, are passed from one generation to the next. Novel and beneficial char-acteristics arise from new arrangements of genetic material, which result from either sexual reproduction (when differ-ent genes from each parent are recombined) or accident (because of genetic mutation). The resources necessary for animals to survive and reproduce are limited, and so there is always a struggle for survival. In a competitive environ-ment, some animals will be better equipped to survive than others. Consequently, their offspring will be better repre-sented in the general population. The converse is also true. Disadvantaged animals will be less well equipped to survive, will produce fewer offspring, and feature less significantly in the general population. Beneficial traits will gradually appear with greater frequency, while useless or redundant traits will gradually appear with less frequency. Some lines thrive, others dwindle, and many may become extinct. No living creature is descended from an ancestor who failed to reproduce. In *The Origin of Species*, Darwin managed to describe natural selection in one short sentence: 'Multiply, vary, let the strongest live and the weakest die.'

This relentless process, repeated with each generation, ensures that organisms become increasingly well adapted to survive in their specific environment. They are better able to find food, avoid predators, compete with rivals from their own species, and find mates. Thus, when we see an animal, we are in fact looking at a solution – an answer to the question, 'What sort of creature is best equipped to survive in this sort of environment?' The insensible, and infinitely patient, process of natural selection eventually discovers the solution through trial and error.

The engine of evolution can be represented as a circle, linking the three major concepts of variation, differential survival and reproduction. It progresses through endless revolutions, refining organisms so that they are adapted to maximise their 'fitness' – an evolutionary term which means the capacity to survive and reproduce.

The links between the physical form an animal takes, and the evolutionary pressures that shaped it, are relatively easy to identify. Life is sufficiently plastic (or variable) to fill almost every conceivable ecological niche – the solution to occupying a bird's ecological niche involves having wings, while the solution to occupying a fish's involves having gills. Darwin immediately saw that the same principle could be applied to mental life, and *The Origin of Species* contains a section on animal instincts and habits. However, Darwin did not extend his line of argument to explain similar phenomena in human beings. When *The Origin of Species* was published, he was still trying to understate the role of natural selection in human evolution, so as not to offend the religious majority.

Evolutionary theory suggests that all mental phenomena can be understood as adaptations (features shaped by natural selection which enhance fitness). So, we can begin to understand emotion better by asking the simple question: 'What function does it serve?' For example, fear – a complex set of psychological and physiological changes – prepares the human animal for conflict with an aggressor or escape (the so-called fight-flight response). This approach suggests that even something as apparently mysterious as love should yield to an evolutionary analysis. All that we have to do is shift the emphasis of our question. Instead of asking 'What is love?' (which requires a merely descriptive answer), we might choose to ask instead 'What is love for?' or 'What does love do?' These are questions which invite an explanatory answer. As a general rule, explanations are far more satisfying than descriptions. They tell us how things work.

Love, like every other characteristic, trait or feature of the human animal, has been shaped by natural selection because it is adaptive. It is a psychological lubricant that keeps the Darwinian wheel of variation, differential survival and reproduction turning in our favour. Without it, our fitness would be compromised.

To understand how love achieves its evolutionary objectives, and why it takes the form that it does, it is essential that we consider love in the context of sexual reproduction.

We will discover two things. Firstly, that what we call romantic love has its ultimate origins in the ancestral environment, that in which humans evolved between three million and 35,000 years ago; and secondly, that love is necessarily irrational.

* * *

Although Darwin believed that his principle of natural selection could account for almost everything he saw in the natural world, he had to acknowledge that there were some things that it just couldn't explain. Darwin's contemporary (and acquaintance) John Ruskin once wrote: 'Remember that the most beautiful things in the world are the most useless, peacocks and lilies for instance.' For Darwin, this was a troubling observation.

Natural selection abhors waste, and any useless or improvident characteristic should eventually be sifted out of the gene pool. Yet, living creatures often possess features that seem decorative and frivolous. The most striking example of this is (as Ruskin astutely observed) the peacock's tail. It does not help the peacock fly faster or higher, nor can it be used as a weapon. Indeed, at times, it seems to be nothing more than a handicap – providing tigers with something to pull on when a peacock is perched in a tree. So why is it there?

Darwin recognised that, in addition to natural selection, another selection process must be at work – a selection process that, for whatever reason, favoured the useless extravagance of the peacock's tail.

It was in *The Descent of Man and Selection in Relation to Sex* that Darwin offered a solution to phenomena such as the peacock's tail. He suggested that the male or female of a species might acquire superfluous features, if they are perceived as attractive to the opposite sex. Such features become ornaments that confer an advantage over sexual rivals. He concluded, then, that evolution must be driven by two mechanisms: natural selection and sexual selection – there is competition not only *between* species, but *within* species.

The importance of finding a mate in a sexually reproducing species cannot be overestimated. Obviously, even the best-adapted survival machine will produce no progeny if he (or she) is unable to find a mate. Thus, sexual selection in not an addendum to natural selection – it is of equal importance. You can't reproduce if you're dead, but neither can you reproduce if you're single.

A fundamental question concerning the evolution of the peacock's tail is simply, 'Why the tail?' Why should longer tails be aesthetically more pleasing to peahens than, say, longer beaks or longer claws? The answer may be 'No particular reason at all.'

The peacock's tail might have acquired its aura of desirability for an entirely arbitrary reason, the whim of peahens, if it is possible to imagine such a thing. However, once established as desirable by a critical number of females, a self-perpetuating bias would have been established. Peacocks with larger and brighter tails would be chosen as sexual partners in preference to peacocks with shorter, duller tails. Thus, tails would have tended to become progressively larger and larger. A renegade peahen, who bucked the trend by mating with a short-tailed peacock, would very likely waste her genes. Her short-tailed son would not be perceived as attractive by other peahens, and the genetic line would end there. Moreover, the female genes that produced a peahen with a 'kinky' preference for short-tailed males would also be deleted from the gene pool.

It should be noted that, as a result of this process, the genes for sexual preference and the genes for the selected trait will occur in the same offspring. A peacock born of the union between a long-tailed father and a long-tail-fancying mother will carry genes that ensure any subsequent male offspring will have long-tails and any subsequent female offspring will be long-tail-fanciers. The result of this linkage is that such traits spread very swiftly through the population and morphological change occurs at an accelerated rate.

Another possibility is that the peacock's tail serves as a

fitness signal. Peacock tails are very 'expensive'. They require energy to grow, must be preened, and are relatively heavy. Only a very healthy bird could sustain one. Thus, the extravagance is also a factor which preserves the tail's authenticity as a fitness indicator. A large, bright tail is a significant handicap that an unhealthy or weak peacock could not sustain.

The peacock's tail is just one example of how males and females of the same species evolve differently. When males and females of a species are physically different, they are said to show sexual dimorphism. Human males and females do not differ with respect to any single feature as spectacular as the peacock's tail, but they are still significantly different. Again, such differences may have originally served as fitness indicators, or have been the result of arbitrary sexual preferences.

The physical dimorphism that distinguishes men and women is complemented by a kind of psychological dimorphism. The minds of men and women *look different* too. These psychological differences have arisen because of sexual politics.

From an evolutionary perspective, men and women have somewhat different agendas. The optimal strategy for reproductive success is not the same for men as it is for women, and so, at times, there is a conflict of interest.

The sex that invests most in the process of reproduction (by carrying the child, giving birth to the child, and feeding it) is also the sex less able to make extra reproductive capital by seeking other mates. However, the sex that invests least – enjoying the luxury of more 'free time' – will be in a better position to take advantage of further mating opportunities. A male can increase his reproductive success by merely copulating more. A woman's reproductive success, however, is severely limited by a number of biological factors. The discrepancy between sperm and egg production serves as a particularly compelling example. A young man is manufacturing sperm at approximately 3,000 per second; a young woman possesses a lifetime's supply of only four hundred ova. The potential reproductive capacity of males is vast, while that of females is relatively small.

As a consequence of these gender asymmetries, there are two trends that characterise reproductive psychology. Males invest less, so tend to look for more partners, whereas females invest more, so tend to look for superior partners. Female discrimination also produces something of a reproductive bottleneck, meaning that males have to work harder to impress females. Thus, a pattern has been established whereby men typically court, and women choose. A man can propose, but acceptance is the woman's prerogative. Remarkably, this general pattern of behaviour is not only typical of humans, but reflects the behaviour of almost all gendered species – suggesting the operation of a very basic principle.

The reproductive strategies associated with gender are colourfully dramatised in the courtship rituals of numerous human societies. A fine example is included in J.G. Frazer's venerable study of cultural anthropology, *The Golden Bough*. Frazer notes that many cultures observe a courtship ritual involving some kind of race for the bride – a 'love chase'. The Kirghiz (a pastoral people of central Asia), for example, have developed a ritual in which the bride – on horseback and armed with a 'formidable whip' – evades a mob of suitors. Although she is expected to marry the suitor who catches her, she is permitted to exploit her equine advantage, and use her whip with as much force as she wishes, to deter those suitors whom she dislikes. This ceremony seems to provide a test of male resolve, commitment and physical fitness, while at the same time allowing the bride to exercise a very high degree of personal choice. Thus, it represents a cultural formalisation of fundamental male and female behaviour patterns.

In human societies, mate selection is not usually followed immediately by marriage. Typically, there is a delay or period of 'engagement'. Again, this tradition of extended courtship may have evolutionary roots. It does not always follow that a man who possesses resources will also be willing to share them. A period of delay might provide further opportunities to assess whether crude signs of fitness (such as health, strength and wealth) are complemented by other important attributes such as warmth and, more importantly, generosity.

Comparisons are often made between patterns of human sexual behaviour and the sexual behaviour of our closest genetic relatives, chimpanzees. Perhaps, in the social organisation of chimpanzees, we can discern an atavistic remnant of early human society.

Chimpanzees live in polygamous social groupings, where a power hierarchy among males determines access to females. It has been suggested that a similar social organisation characterised early human society. Males might have competed for access to the most attractive females, where attractiveness was identified with signals of fitness. In the very early ancestral environment, polygamy might not have been such a bad option for females. Living under the protection of a healthy, strong, resource-rich male might have been the best way to ensure offspring reached sexual maturity. However, it is unlikely that a rigid social hierarchy and polygamy (at least in its extreme form) were characteristic of hunter-gatherer societies. This is because hunting – an activity typically involving males – requires a high level of cooperation. There would have been a definite group advantage if rivalries (including sexual rivalries) were held in check. Hunting also encourages altruism. Because meat decomposes, families with excess meat would not suffer greatly by sharing their bounty. Such generosity would invite reciprocal gestures when fortunes were reversed. Again, such a system would not work so smoothly where sexual rivalries complicated such transactions. A further important factor is that meat decomposition limits the amount of food any single individual can amass. No single male – however strong – would have been able to monopolise resources to support an extended harem. Adopting a hunter-gatherer lifestyle would have had many repercussions, favouring the replacement of polygamy with monogamy as the preferred mating system, although males would still feel – and still do feel – a deep, instinctual urge towards polygyny.

Fortunately, evolution may have equipped women with a number of strategies – in the form of both biological and psychological adaptations – to deal with this problem.

When a female chimpanzee is ovulating, her fertility is brilliantly advertised by a large red swelling that appears on her rump. Female humans do no such thing. Ovulation takes place in secret. At first sight, concealed ovulation seems a curious evolutionary development if reproductive success is the goal. Surely a clear physical signal that invites sexual interest during periods of fertility must be a good thing? When ovulation is concealed, however, a male must be a diligent and frequent lover to guarantee reproductive success. If a male is promiscuous, then his chances of reproducing successfully are greatly reduced. The only way to be certain of success is to select a single female and mate with her for a complete cycle. As long as a male is engaged in the task of fertilising one female, he cannot afford to spend time with another. Thus, by concealing ovulation, the human female secures the exclusive attention of a male – a by-product of which might be the formation of a stronger pair-bond. Concealed ovulation might be a tactic, devised by selection pressures to encourage fidelity and emotional commitment in males – a very useful consequence if vulnerable offspring are to be properly cared for.

The adaptations that facilitate pair-bonding may not be the same as those that maintain it. Although concealed ovulation might create ideal conditions for initial bonding, a more durable cement might be required if those bonds of affection are to last. A conspicuous adaptation that might extend the longevity of pair-bonds in humans is our enhanced capacity to enjoy sex. Human beings seem to derive a unique degree of pleasure from sexual coupling, and human females – unlike other evolved mammals – are sexually receptive all year. Although romance is traditionally associated with the spring, human beings do not have a breeding season. Thus, pair-bonding is reinforced by pleasurable and unrestricted sexual activity.

The zoologist, Desmond Morris, has argued that the importance of sex in pair-bonding is emphasised by the evolution of many other distinctive physical characteristics. These include naked skin, full sensitive lips and relatively large sexual organs (breasts in women and the penis in males). In addition to these physical characteristics, the unusual behavioural feature of face-to-face coupling adds further weight to the argument. Clearly, the expressive power of the human face will secure a far more significant claim on the heart than either a rump or a neutral scene (that is, the respective prospects offered to males and females by rear mounting).

The pair-bond between men and women is also strengthened by the mere prospect of female infidelity. No male would want to waste his precious resources raising offspring that will carry a rival's genes into the next generation. This, in itself, encourages the development of a close, attentive relationship. Indeed, sexual jealousy – which is particularly strong in men – has almost certainly evolved for this reason.

Although human males are inclined to be less faithful than females, it would be incorrect to suggest that they are 'low investors' in an absolute sense. The human race has evolved such that both males and females must expend a great deal of energy on their young if they are to survive. A pattern of promiscuous couplings and swift departures would not have translated into reproductive success for the ancestral human male. Genes resulting in such behaviour would have been strongly associated with infant mortality and subsequently lost from the gene pool.

Sexual politics and evolutionary pressures have shaped the nature of human relationships. We are a largely (though not exclusively) monogamous ape, whose reproductive success depends on the formation of a mutual – sometimes jealous – pair-bond. The purpose of this bond is to ensure that vulnerable offspring survive to sexual maturity.

Clearly, many of the behaviours described above contain the germ of what we would now call romantic love. Evolutionary pressures have created a behavioural template that underlies many romantic conventions. Men pursue women – not the opposite; women, offered initial sexual advances, demur and want to be courted; during courtship, a man is expected to impress, to 'see off' other suitors and to woo with gifts. Romantic love is exclusive – men and women both demand fidelity, and a romantic relationship is always jealously guarded. While our remote ancestors were still dragging their knuckles across the plains of Africa, sexual selection and sexual politics were turning them – generation by generation – into romantics.

Emotions prepare the mind and body for action, and organise behaviour. Fear makes us vigilant, promotes the secretion of adrenaline, and makes us run away from danger. Love organises romantic behaviour in much the same way. It prepares the mind and body for action, and organises behaviour to increase the likelihood of reproductive success.

Firstly, love engenders a mental state characterised by thoughts and day-dreams about the loved one. This 'obsessional' feature of love ensures that the loved one is not forgotten. Secondly, love seems to take command of the reward and punishment centres of the brain. When the lover is in the presence of the loved one, the experience is rewarded by love's rapture; however, on separation, the lover is punished with feelings of heartache and despair. This reward-and-punishment system is mediated by brain chemistry, and encourages sustained periods of contact. Thirdly, and perhaps most interestingly, love seems to overthrow reason. Reproduction is so important from an evolutionary point of view that it cannot be left to humans to decide whether or not they want to procreate.

This final point is highly significant with respect to how we experience love, because human beings – unlike any other animal – have the ability to self-reflect and rebel against the evolutionary diktat. This is exactly what Darwin was doing when he composed his balance sheet. He was able to sit down and calculate the enormous personal cost of marriage: the wasted time, the financial difficulties, the restricted freedom, the obligation to squander hours talking trivia with uninteresting and boring relatives. Yet, in the final reckoning, all Darwin's logic was overthrown because – and only because – he fell madly in love.

Evolution does not plan ahead. It is an insensible process of reproduction, variation and selection. Organisms evolve in a piecemeal fashion, retaining elements of redundant adaptations as new ones are added. A feature designed for one function might be adapted for another, and problems are corrected by the steady acquisition of checks and balances.

The advantages of an adaptation like intelligence are obvious. It is our single most distinctive feature, and has allowed us to occupy a wide range of ecological niches. So useful is this adaptation that intelligence has permitted us to achieve a pre-eminent position in the power hierarchy of the natural world. No animal, however large, however fast, can overcome the weakest human who is armed with a loaded gun.

It is still unclear how intelligence developed in the human animal, and there are many competing theories, but it is very likely that intelligence was the result of many evolutionary pressures, some being more important than others at different periods in our history.

It is interesting that the fossil record indicates an initial increase in brain size approximately two million years ago. This coincides with a fundamental change of diet. The vegetarian Australopithecines were superseded by their meat-eating successors. This transition would have presented our ancestors with special intellectual challenges, and promoted increased levels of socialisation. Hunting, for example, would have necessitated the formation of larger groups, better communication skills, and the use of more advanced implements in the form of weapons and, perhaps, cooking utensils. Dietary change would also have resulted in more basic, biological consequences. The increased levels of nourishment made available by meat consumption would have provided excellent conditions for further brain growth.

This expansion in brain size, although adaptive, produced a major practical problem. Human babies have very large heads, so large they can only just pass down the birth canal – and even then, with extreme difficulty. The birth canal cannot expand any further, because bipedalism requires a small pelvis. Human labour is a long, painful and dangerous process, because intelligence is such a precious commodity. The disinterested calculations of evolution have deemed the risks associated with human labour acceptable because of intelligence.

Remarkably, evolutionary pressures have determined that brain size should be optimised still further. Given that the pelvis cannot become any larger – if women are to remain bipedal – there is only one other option: human beings can retain their big brains only if the brain passes through the birth canal before it has finished growing. Thus, all human babies are born about twelve months too early. This fact has enormous implications for human relationships.

The human infant is extremely vulnerable because of its prematurity. Moreover, its big brain – which grows at an incredibly fast rate in the first two years of life – has a large metabolic requirement. The human infant must have a high quality of care, and this is best delivered by two parents working together for an extended period of time – in effect, two parents in a monogamous relationship, sharing a strong pair-bond, the kind of pair-bond that results when people fall in love.

Intelligence may have been favoured by evolutionary pressures, but it is unpredictable with respect to its consequences. Take, for example, the use of tools by chimpanzees. It is well known that chimpanzees often use sticks to catch insects, and pebbles to crack nuts. Clearly, using tools in this way is highly adaptive, resulting in greater availability of food. However, some chimpanzees use tools in ways which have precious little to do with achieving evolutionary objectives. Female chimpanzees sometimes insert sticks and pebbles into their vaginas to increase stimulation while masturbating – and one particularly ingenious female was observed constructing a primitive vibrator from a trembling leaf stem.

As suggested above, evolution is a blind process – it does not plan ahead. Consequently, evolution did not anticipate that intelligence would permit the human animal to override instinctual urges – and most notably the urge to reproduce. Clearly, this ability has the potential to undermine evolutionary progress completely. In the 1970s, Richard Dawkins famously explained that genes are 'selfish'. They are not concerned about anything, except being copied from one generation to the next. From the gene's point of view, a human being is merely a vehicle; the personal happiness of a human being is of no consequence to the genes he or she carries. Yet, intelligence allows human beings to consider their own personal happiness. An individual with a sense of self can weigh the costs and benefits of a particular action, and decide 'for' or 'against' it. Darwin's balance sheet, with its 'Marry' and 'Not Marry' headings, exemplifies this process.

In *The Selfish Gene*, Dawkins underscored the unique freedom that human beings enjoy among sexually reproducing animals:

> Not only are brains in charge of the day-to-day running of survival-machine [human] affairs, they have also acquired the ability to predict the future and act accordingly. They even have the power to rebel against the dictates of the genes, for instance in refusing to have as many children as they are able to.

Although most would-be parents are relatively sanguine about starting a family, new arrivals do tend to have a detrimental effect on the quality of the mother and father's relationship. Research shows that marital satisfaction plummets after the birth of a first child. Subsequent children reduce marital satisfaction even further. Sometimes, there is an enormous discrepancy between what our genes make us do, and what actually makes us happy.

It is ironic that Darwin, who almost succeeded in talking himself out of marriage when young, became increasingly aware in later life of the tensions that exist between intellect and evolutionary objectives. The most compelling and direct example of this is the use of contraception. In a letter to a correspondent, Darwin wrote in 1878: 'I have lately reflected a little on artificial checks but doubt greatly whether such would be advantageous to the world at large at present . . . No words can exaggerate the importance in my opinion of our colonization for the future history of the world.'

The conflict between intellect and evolutionary objectives does not arise in animals for obvious reasons: animals simply follow their instincts. When it comes to sexual reproduction, they are simply automata – and, to a very large extent, so are we. However, the very fact that we can self-reflect, and rebel, has perhaps necessitated the evolution of a safety mechanism – an emotional swamping of the mental apparatus to ensure that fundamental evolutionary objectives are met. We call this safety mechanism 'love'.

Love must be, by its very nature, the antithesis of reason. This is probably why it is so frequently described as a form of madness. Indeed, for many, the authenticity of love is determined according to the degree to which it is experienced as irrational – a position succinctly captured by Robert Mallet's witty aphorism: 'I have every reason to love you. What I lack is the unreason.'

Committing to a single human being is a momentous investment, particularly for men. The male of the species must resist his natural instinct to mate with more than one partner, and be willing to share his resources (at least initially) with his family. This would suggest that, from an evolutionary perspective, it is more important for men to fall in love than women. Consequently, evolutionary pressures should have made men more love-prone – which does seem to be the case.

Psychological research shows that men fall in love more often than women, experience it more intensely, and are much more likely to celebrate love by composing poetry or songs. This disposition is exemplified by research into the phenomenon of love at first sight. In a large-scale survey conducted in America by Earl Naumann (now a marketing consultant but previously a Professor of Marketing and International Business at five different universities) it was discovered that – of those individuals who profess to believe in love at first sight – some 62.3 per cent of men claim to have experienced it, compared to 55.7 per cent of women. Although these figures seem close, the difference is in fact statistically significant. Similarly, men are significantly more likely to experience love at first sight on more than one occasion. It is also worth remembering that men are much more likely to remarry than women (showing scant regard for Dr Johnson's sardonic observation that a second marriage demonstrates 'the triumph of hope over experience'). The force with which love assaults the intellect in men is also reflected in literary, philosophical and medical writings, which generally contain more references to love-sick men than lovesick women. Indeed, in many early medical texts it is almost assumed that the lovesick patient will be male.

Women, on the other hand, although capable of experiencing love, tend to be less passionate and more pragmatic – being more inclined, for example, to marry for increased status or money rather than love. In a major study of sex differences conducted by American evolutionary psychologist David Buss – examining 37 samples drawn from 33 countries on six continents – women were much more likely than men to select partners on the basis of their financial prospects.

Evolutionary theory also explains another puzzling feature of love – its relative brevity. Although, when in the throes of love, we think that it will last for ever, this is rarely the case. Love diminishes, dies or becomes – over time – something closer to friendship (companionate love).

Evolution is parsimonious. Love, on the other hand, is florid and wasteful. Like the peacock's tail, love is splendidly profligate. The evolutionary psychologist Geoffrey Miller notes: 'The wastefulness of courtship is what makes it romantic. The wasteful dancing, the wasteful gift-giving, the wasteful adventures.' Perhaps, because love is so wasteful, evolutionary pressures have ensured that we fall in love for as long as it is necessary to achieve evolutionary goals, but no longer.

To ensure reproductive success, the pair-bond that keeps men and women together does not need to last for ever. It only needs to last long enough for one or two children to be produced and raised. In the ancestral environment, the earliest cut-off point would probably have been linked with the termination of breast-feeding. Thus, intense, passionate love might only be sustainable for a few years. This seems to correspond closely with psychological research and popular folklore, which recognises an upper limit of seven years (coinciding with the anecdotal 'seven-year itch').

At first sight, it seems extraordinary that evolutionary forces might conspire to shape something that looks like a mental illness to ensure reproductive success. Yet, there are many reasons why love should have evolved to share with madness several features – the most notable of which is the loss of reason. Like the ancient humoral model of love sickness, evolutionary principles seem to have necessitated a blurring of the distinction between normal and abnormal states. Evolution expects us to love madly, lest we fail to love at all. That way lies Darwin's vision of an uncolonised future – a world without men, women and, more significantly, children.

4

Incurable Romantics

Love, love, love – all the wretched cant of it, masking egotism, lust, masochism, fantasy under a mythology of sentimental postures, a welter of self-induced miseries and joys, blinding and masking the essential personalities in the frozen gestures of courtship, in the kissing and the dating and the desire, the compliments and the quarrels which vivify its barrenness.

The Female Eunuch, Germaine Greer

Romantic love has been described by the Jungian psychoanalyst Robert Johnson as 'the single greatest energy system in the Western psyche'. Although this sounds like a wildly extravagant claim, it is almost certainly true. Love – and in particular romantic love – is our great preoccupation. Almost every aspect of our life is affected, in some way, by the concept of romantic love.

The word 'romantic' is troubled by a long history. It is like an overworked canvas, the composition and brushwork of which cannot conceal the suggestion of earlier drafts. English dictionaries distinguish 'romantic' with several definitions, but in reality, such tidy divisions are misleading. When we use the word, these different meanings bleed into each other. To be romantically involved is an admission that carries a host of implications: passion, folly, obsession, anguish, recklessness, intrigue, and adventure; archetypes rise from varying depths and jostle with each other for recognition and influence.

As with any native tongue, we first speak the language of romantic love without being able to explain its grammar. The assumptions on which romantic love is predicated are buried in the unconscious mind, where they exert a powerful influence on our beliefs, attitudes, and expectations. We never pause to question their legitimacy. When a romantic hero decides he will sacrifice everything for love, no one will ask 'Is she really worth it?' or 'Can't he find someone else?' Romantic love has its own obscure logic which we all tacitly accept.

The roots of romantic love run deep. Indeed, the fundamental conventions of romantic love were consolidated on the ancestral plains of Africa, where evolutionary pressures determined that men should court women, that women should be coy, that relationships should be exclusive, and that love should storm the mind like a form of madness. However, since the rise of civilisation, these features have been increasingly complicated by ideological factors. The roots of romantic love are profoundly deep, but, now, they are also hopelessly tangled.

To understand fully the concept of romantic love requires an examination of its cultural history (in addition to its evolutionary history). Yet, even a superficial study reveals an underlying raft of contradictions: burning desire is yoked to self-denial; the sacred and carnal are confused; misogyny and beatification coexist in an uneasy alliance; and life becomes inextricably linked with death. In the contrary universe of romantic love, it was inevitable that madness should become a virtue.

* * *

In Chapter 1 it was pointed out that the first 'romantic' songs were probably sung by the Arab Bedouin, rather than the wandering minstrels of Provence. The southern Arabs in particular enjoyed a form of poetry known as Udhri', which has clear thematic links with the troubadour tradition. Indeed, it is possible that the word troubadour itself is derived from the Arabic word *tarab*, meaning music. Typically, in Udhri' poetry, the beloved is idealised, but the desire for union is denied, engendering melancholy and even madness.

The poet al-Abbas wrote poetry that was set to music in the court of Haroun al-Rashid – the caliph immortalised in *The Thousand and One Nights*. In the eighth century, al-Rashid ruled the Islamic world when its empire had spread extensively, and Baghdad was a place of wealth, luxury, and scholarship. The caliph (who was all-powerful) frequently fell in love with slave girls, only to find that the experience made him miserable. That such a potentate could be made wretched by a slave girl suggested to al-Abbas that love was an irrational yearning. Love could make a slave girl seem unattainable – thus precluding its own satisfaction.

During the middle ages, many anthologies were published, containing poems that examined love from a particular position or view. A very influential collection of this kind was *The Masari al-'ushshaq*, by the tenth-century poet as-Sarraj, which greatly promoted the idea that the consequences of romantic love were tragic. The word masari comes from an etymological root which has the connotation of 'throwing to the ground'. It is interesting that as-Sarraj described lovers who frequently fainted, fell down or lost consciousness. This same link – between love and falling – was of course also made by Palsgrave in the sixteenth century, when the term 'to fall in love' was introduced into the English language.

By the eleventh century, Islamic authors were writing love

poetry on a much grander scale. In effect, they were composing 'poetical romances'. The most famous of these include
Varqueh o-Golsha by 'Eyyuqi, and *Vis o-Ramin* by Fakhr
od-Din Gorgani. These extended works contain many
narrative elements that appear later in Western medieval
romances, and are the precursors of one of the most influential love stories ever written – the story of *Layla and
Majnun* by the twelfth-century Persian poet Nizami.

Various permutations of this epic romance existed long
before a definitive version was reached – which was probably well before Nizami's time. The character of Majnun is
a familiar trope in Islamic literature, in much the same way
as the 'knight in shining armour' or the 'damsel in distress'
are an integral part of the Western narrative tradition.

The term majnun is derived from the word djinn, and is
thus linked with the notion of possession by a supernatural
agency; however, in this case, the demon is love itself, for
the majnun – 'the demented one' or 'romantic fool' – is
driven mad by love. In some of the earlier Arabic versions
of the story, the link between love sickness and the supernatural is made explicit. Majnun cries: 'O doctor of the djinn,
woe unto you, find me a cure, for the doctor of humans is
helpless against my ill.' Once again, we are on familiar
rhetorical ground, where the impotent medical man serves
only to underscore the divine or elemental provenance of
love sickness.

Originally, *Layla and Majnun* was not a continuous
narrative. It was a story told through a collection of independent (but related) tales. In composing his epic, Nizami
took the traditional episodes, and combined them together
with some new ones of his own. The final product was
lengthy, but held together by a simple narrative.

Kais, the son of Sayyid (ruler of a Bedouin tribe), sees
the beautiful Layla for the first time at school. The young

couple fall in love instantly, but cannot be together because of tribal custom. Kais is tormented by his desire for Layla, and separation drives him insane:

> Having lost his heart, he now lost his mind. All he could do was wander around in a trance, extolling Layla's beauty and praising her virtues to everyone he met. The more people saw him and heard what he had to say, the more insane he appeared and the more bizarre became his behaviour. And everywhere the stares and pointing fingers, the laughter and the derision, the cries of 'Here comes the madman, the majnun.'

Kais (thereafter referred to in the text as Majnun) cannot be cured. He spurns Bedouin society (preferring instead the company of animals) and wanders in the desert, where he becomes a kind of hermit or mystic. Although he seems incapable of listening to reason, he can spontaneously recite and sing love poetry of astonishing beauty.

Layla is forced to marry another young nobleman, Ibn Salaam, but she refuses to consummate the marriage, and, in time, Ibn Salaam dies of a broken heart. This is of little consequence to Layla, who is fated 'by the icy touch of life's most trying tribulations' to die.

On hearing of his beloved's death, Majnun rushes to her grave:

> Majnun closed his eyes and lay down on Layla's grave, pressing his body against the earth with all that remained of his strength. His parched lips moved in silent prayer; then, with the words, 'Layla, my love . . .', his soul broke free and he was no more.

The tale ends with members of Layla's tribe and Majnun's tribe weeping by the grave, where the two lovers have finally been united in death.

The story of Layla and Majnun contains almost all of the elements that were later claimed as the hallmarks of romantic or courtly literature: love at first sight, a love triangle, forbidden love, idealisation, restless wandering, lack of consummation, and a tragic end in which the lovers die. Moreover, scenes from *Layla and Majnun* have surfaced in almost all of the great love stories written by Western authors. For example, the tribal gathering with which the tale ends anticipates the Montagues and Capulets renouncing enmity as they weep over the bodies of Romeo and Juliet.

There are many readings of *Layla and Majnun*, but most Islamic scholars consider it to be an allegorical tale, in which Majnun's longing corresponds with the soul's longing for union with God.

The idea that love might offer a glimpse of the eternal was originally proposed by Plato; however, it wasn't an idea that found much favour among classical poets. Islamic poets, on the other hand, found it fascinating. From the twelfth century onwards a number of works appeared in which the spiritual sub-text of love poetry was made more transparent, perhaps the finest and most influential example being Ibn Arabi's *The Interpreter of Desire*.

While visiting Mecca, Ibn Arabi fell in love with the Imam's daughter – a young woman of great beauty. He described her in such a way as to suggest an angelic presence, barely connected to the material world: an embodiment of absolute values such as 'eternal wisdom' and 'truth'. Ibn Arabi's love for the Imam's daughter was, of necessity, unfulfilled and therefore painful, but his love was also revelatory. According to Ibn Arabi, earthly beauty is an intimation of heavenly beauty: the light that shines from a woman's eyes emanates from an eternal source.

A corollary of Ibn Arabi's mysticism is that separation

from the beloved becomes an experience akin to banishment from paradise. Every time a relationship ends, every time the course of true love is frustrated, one or both parties are driven from the Garden of Eden – and when a man leaves the Garden of Eden, he does so in the person of the majnun, the romantic fool.

The Islamic courtly tradition was introduced into Western culture by the troubadours, whose poetry preserved many features of Arab mysticism – particularly, a quasi-religious praise of female beauty. However, as this theme was reworked, it also began to change. Spiritual inaccessibility gradually evolved into alluring aloofness, which in turn became regal disdain (the latter reflecting a certain degree of misogyny). Thus, a recurring figure in troubadour poetry was the cold, cruel mistress.

The theme of inaccessibility was also explored in another way: the introduction of a female character, immensely desirable, but unavailable through marriage.

Even at this very early stage, the authenticity of love was being judged according to its difficulty (with respect to obstacles and impediments) and its irrationality. In troubadour poetry, we can recognise the cultural ancestry of modern concepts such as Lee's mania or Tennov's limerence: love that does not need liking – love that may even thrive in response to rejection or contempt. The troubadour's cruel mistress reappears again and again in literature in different guises: the enchantress, the femme fatale, the Belle Dame sans Merci. Long before psychologists began to study love in a systematic way, literature required a particular female type who would represent unhappy love.

The doctrine of romantic love (also known as *courtezia* or *amour courtois*) would have spread across Europe irrespective of royal patronage; however, the process was certainly accelerated by events at the court of Poitiers, where

William IX is reputed to have been 'the first troubadour' (on account of having written the earliest surviving examples of courtly verse in the Provençal language). It was also at Poitiers that William's granddaughter, Eleanor of Aquitaine, and her daughter, Marie de Champagne, encouraged celebrated poets such as Bernard de Ventadour and Chrétien de Troyes to compose works that exemplified courtly ideals. A narrative vehicle that was popular among the poets of Poitiers was Arthurian legend, which delivered a cast of characters whose relationships could be fully exploited to dramatise the frustrating dynamics of romantic love. Thus, Guinevere's beauty is beyond compare, and Lancelot – Arthur's most loyal servant – must fall hopelessly in love with the queen. (English readers are more familiar with this dynamic through Sir Thomas Malory's *Le Morte d'Arthur*.) In the poetry of Chrétien de Troyes, love – always complicated, but even more complicated by courtly conventions – is once again described as an illness: 'My illness is what I want. And my pain is my health . . . I suffer agreeably . . . I am sick with delight.'

One of the most extraordinary developments at Poitiers was the creation of an inner court – the Court of Love – where noblewomen would meet to pose questions about love and the proper conduct of lovers. Questions would then be disputed, juried and judged, according to the increasingly dogmatic principles of *courtezia*. Perhaps, in an effort to make the task of this inner court easier, Marie instructed a cleric, Andrew Capelanus (also known as Andrew the Chaplain), to write a formal book of statutes: a kind of lovers' charter.

Andrew began his task by consulting a classical authority – the *Ars Amatoria* (or *Art of Love*) by Ovid. It is difficult to imagine a more inappropriate work on which to base a 'respectable' canon. As with much to do with romantic love, history reveals cross-purposes, because for Ovid adoration is only a means to an end. Ovid adores, not because he can't help himself, but because by feigning adoration he is more likely to succeed in seduction. He is a cunning and manipulative strategist, who advises on everything from good 'chat-up' lines to how physical defects can be concealed by adopting special positions during intercourse. In an age of political correctness, he is still able to offend modern sensibilities. He recommends pretending to cry, making false promises, writing flattering verses (however insincere) and even coercion: 'Some force is permissible – women are often pleased by force.'

Ovid also advises the aspirant libertine to affect the symptoms of love sickness: 'All lovers should be pallid, it's chic to be pale;/ Only fools deny it, pale skins rarely fail.' Moreover, he observes that loss of appetite and worry 'make the young lover as thin as a rake'. Therefore, if wishing to attract the attention of women, one should: 'Look lean – it suggests passion.'

When Andrew Capelanus came to write his own work – *The Art of Courtly Love* – he did so by borrowing from Ovid. Thus, Ovid's cynical observations were used to shore up the romantic ideal. Love sickness – merely another weapon in Ovid's armamentarium – became fully established as a crucial sign of love's authenticity.

Capelanus described love as 'a certain inborn suffering' and suggested thirty-one rules of love. They include the following:

Rule 2   He who is not jealous cannot love.

Rule 9   No one can love unless he is impelled by the persuasion of love (also translated as: No one can love who is not driven to do so by the power of love).

Rule 13   When made public love rarely endures.

Rule 14   The easy attainment of love makes it of little value; difficulty of attainment makes it prized.

Rule 15   Every lover regularly turns pale in the presence of his beloved.

Rule 16   When a lover suddenly catches sight of his beloved his heart palpitates.

Rule 20   A man in love is always apprehensive (also translated as: A lover is always fearful).

Rule 21   Real jealousy always increases the feeling of love.

Rule 22   Jealousy, and therefore love, are increased when one suspects his beloved.

Rule 30   A true lover is constantly and without intermission possessed by the thought of his beloved (also translated as: The true lover is continuously obsessed with the image of his beloved).

Love and mental illness were closely linked according to the principles of Hippocratic medicine; however, Capelanus's principles seem to do much the same thing. At Poitiers it was decided that love – if true – must be disturbed and slightly perverse; it must be obsessive, compulsive, agitated, anxious, jealous, suspicious, clandestine, and frustrating.

There is still some debate concerning to what extent Capelanus meant his rules to be taken seriously. It is possible that *The Art of Courtly Love* was meant to be satirical – but if so, its satirical content was lost on contemporary and subsequent generations. *The Art of Courtly Love* was never viewed as a critique. It was always viewed as a manifesto.

Romantic love became an increasingly important feature

of literature in the late twelfth and thirteenth centuries. The *Lais* of Marie de France and de Lorris's *Romance of the Rose* are significant examples; however, the quintessential courtly romance of the middle ages must be *Tristan* – now more widely encountered in the opera house as Wagner's *Tristan and Isolde*.

Although *Tristan* does not feature King Arthur, it is an 'Arthurian' romance set in a landscape of castles, quests and dragons. An authenticated 'original' does not exist, but five versions have been handed down – the most famous being those of Béroul, Gottfried von Strassburg and Thomas.

Tristan is raised by his uncle, King Mark of Cornwall, and it falls upon him to escort King Mark's bride-to-be, the beautiful Princess Isolde, from her home in Ireland to the king's castle. While crossing the Irish Sea, they both mistakenly drink a love potion, and subsequently fall in love. The love potion – a potent symbol of love's madness – neatly excuses Tristan's betrayal of his uncle.

In Gottfried's version, the bemused Tristan complains: 'I do not know what has come over poor Isolde and me, but we have both of us gone mad in the briefest space of time, with unimaginable torment – we are dying of love . . .'

Tristan and Isolde (against their better judgement) become clandestine lovers and, in doing so, stir the gods of tragedy. Much of the ensuing drama concerns their attempts to avoid discovery, and eventually they must separate. Tristan is wounded by a poisoned spear and, as his life ebbs away, he calls for Isolde. She rushes to be with him, but arrives too late and can do nothing to save him. Clasping his dead body, she gives up her spirit and dies.

During the middle ages, romantic narrative's landscape of kings and queens, knights and ladies, heroism, bravery, destiny and magic became established in the Western imagination, and is familiar to children, appearing in numerous story-books. The idea of romantic love has penetrated so deep into our culture, that few people escape its influence before leaving the nursery. Unfortunately, a consequence of this is that many grow up assuming they will find fairy-tale happiness in the real world – an expectation that is rarely fulfilled. Moreover, it is curious that the main exemplars of courtly romance (which in a sense foster our fairy-tale aspirations) rarely end with a 'happy ever after', but with torment, tears and death.

The romantic themes of idealisation and forbidden (or non-consummated) love were taken to new extremes in Renaissance Italy. Poets such as Dante and Petrarch placed their muses on absurdly elevated pedestals. Dante's Beatrice, and Petrarch's Laura, are portrayed as models of perfection and purity. Moreover, the fact that both women died prematurely and then reappear in poetic visions, emphasises their divinity. There is some debate concerning the identity of Petrarch's Laura. She may have been Laure de Noves of Avignon (a married woman with children), or she may never have existed at all (being merely a poetic invention). Dante's Beatrice, on the other hand, was definitely a real person.

The extreme idealisation of Beatrice and Laura is partly attributable to Marianism. During the thirteenth century, Mary became increasingly important as a mediator between human beings and God. It was to Mary that the majority prayed for divine intercession. She was more 'human', and therefore approachable, than all three personifications of the Holy Trinity. Moreover, her curious (and paradoxical) position as the mother of God gave her considerable authority. For some time, the river of romantic literature was swollen by the tributary of Marianism. Women were worshipped with religious fervour, and sexual desire was wholly sublimated.

The story of Dante and Beatrice is principally recorded

in Dante's *The New Life* (a hybrid of autobiography and literary treatise). They met for the first time as children, when the poet accompanied his father to the house of Folco Portinari (Beatrice's father). Dante immediately fell in love with Beatrice and remained devoted to her (more or less) for the rest of his life. She was married to a banker from an early age, and so – in true courtly style – Dante was forced to admire her from a distance. He appropriated the Arthurian role of Lancelot, and championed his 'mistress', not with arms, but with poetry.

The Marian nature of Dante's love for Beatrice did not exempt him from the commonplace symptoms of love sickness. He complained of all the usual problems: expansive moods and depression, lightheadedness, obsession, anorexia, sleeplessness, paleness, trepidation and anguish. And Beatrice occupied such an elevated position in his universe that even the slightest suspicion of her disapproval was crushing. When she failed to return his greeting, Dante became extremely distressed:

> . . . I was overcome by such sorrow that I left my fellow men and went to a secluded place, where I could bathe the earth with my bitter tears. Then, when my weeping was almost exhausted, I took myself to my room, where I could lament without being overheard. There, while calling for mercy from the lady of courtesy, and crying 'Love, help your servant!', I fell asleep like a little child crying after it has been beaten.

If anything, the spiritual nature of Dante's love for Beatrice seemed to exaggerate the usual psychopathological resonances. Even his moments of rapture were tainted with the uncomfortable, manic energy of a religious fanatic. His eyes shine, and we question his sanity; we are not very far away from shaking fists, prophecy and revelation.

Perhaps the most compelling example of this arose during a period of sickness, when it suddenly occurred to Dante that Beatrice was mortal and might one day die: 'At this I was overcome by such delirium that I shut my eyes and started to thrash about like a fever patient.' He then entered a world of lurid hallucination: 'Then I saw the sun darken and the stars changed to such a colour that I thought they wept; birds dropped dead while flying through the air, and there were vast earthquakes.' We are reminded of the darkness that fell on the earth at the time of the crucifixion. For Dante, a presentiment of separation was not painful – it was the apocalypse.

At the age of twenty-four Beatrice did die, and predictably Dante was thrown into deep despair – even though, by then, he too was married. While grieving, he became temporarily infatuated with another woman; however, these feelings were completely expunged when Beatrice appeared to him in a heavenly vision. Dante was reminded of Beatrice's incomparable beauty and he subsequently committed himself to a life of continued adoration. He became, in effect, a votary.

Love is predicated on togetherness in a world where things must exist separately, and total separation – because of death – is an inevitable and unbearable truth that few lovers can keep from contemplating. In the history of romantic story telling, love and death are old companions. Great love stories are made all the more poignant by our certain knowledge that the couple are cavorting on the lip of an open grave.

In his scholarly treatise, *Love in the Western World*, the Swiss philosopher Denis de Rougemont wrote:

> Romance only comes into existence when love is fatal, frowned upon and doomed by life itself. What stirs lyrical poets to their finest flights is neither the delight of the senses nor the fruit-

ful contentment of the settled couple; not the satisfaction of
love, but its *passion*. And passion means suffering.

To live up to the romantic ideal, love must be fated. It
must be passionate, painful and ultimately doomed. It must
culminate in death and, if we are lucky, transfiguration.

But why?

Although death appears in love stories prior to the middle
ages, it does so in the service of tragedy. After the middle ages,
however, death is almost wholly in the service of love. The
outcome of a fated love story might still be tragic, but death's
function has changed. Essentially, it offers unlimited possibilities for idealisation.

The most extraordinary feature of Dante's *The New Life*
is the degree to which he idealises Beatrice. Until Dante,
almost all love poetry – however heady – recognised that
beauty fades. In the end, time must ruin even the loveliest
of faces. Yet, when it comes to Beatrice, Dante simply refuses
to concede any ground to time. Of course, Beatrice conveniently obliged him by dying young, and in the reliquary
of Dante's imagination, Beatrice's incorruptible body parts
were preserved like those of a medieval saint.

The romantic tradition has always demanded that the
beloved be, in some sense, beyond reach. Yearning, without satisfaction or release, was presumed to be ennobling.
Because romantic love is never supposed to be consummated, it never weakens, and continues to dignify the lover.
When the beloved dies, she exchanges an earthly marriage
for a numinous marriage. In death, she becomes completely
unattainable, and the yearning must then go on for ever.

Islamic mysticism, *courtezia* and Renaissance literature have
all added registers of meaning to the word 'romantic'; however, it has also been enriched by association with a more

recent, but nevertheless highly important, cultural development – the rise of Romanticism.

Strictly speaking, Romanticism is only tenuously connected with 'romantic love'. The Romantic movement began in Germany towards the end of the eighteenth century, and continued to be influential, by varying degrees, until the end of the nineteenth. It began as a reaction against the values and preoccupations of the Enlightenment. The great thinkers of the Enlightenment venerated reason, lived in cities, and were keen to instigate political change. Romantics, on the other hand, were fascinated by emotions, revered nature, and were far more interested in personal psychology than social reform.

The concerns of the Romantic movement were much wider than those of the troubadours or the Court of Love at Poitiers. Even so, in matters of love, there are several continuities that link the idea of romance with Romanticism. Indeed, the work which launched the Romantic movement was a love story which preserves many courtly themes. This was Goethe's 1774 novel, *The Sorrows of Young Werther*.

Werther, an artistic young man, falls in love with the beautiful Lotte. Unfortunately, she is already engaged to Albert, a gentleman renowned for his honesty and good character. While waiting for Albert to announce the wedding day, Werther learns that Lotte and Albert have already been married. Werther tries to divert himself, and for a while wanders aimlessly, but his yearning for Lotte does not diminish and he feels compelled to return.

Werther is consumed with jealousy: 'At times I cannot grasp that she can love another man, that she dare love another man, when I love her alone with such passion and devotion, and neither know nor have anything but her!' He sinks into black despair: 'Ah, have ever men before me been so miserable?'

While out walking on a wet, dreary day, he meets a madman 'scrabbling about the rocks' picking flowers for his 'sweetheart'. The madman's mother appears, and explains to Werther that her son has only recently been released from a madhouse, where he has been restrained in chains for a whole year. The following day, Werther discovers that the madman was previously a clerk employed by Lotte's father. He, too, had fallen in love with Lotte, and the revelation of his love had cost him first his position and then his sanity.

The encounter with the madman is a presentiment of Werther's own fate. He becomes progressively more disturbed, agitated and has hallucinatory dreams of making love to Lotte: 'My senses are confused, for a full week I have been unable to think straight, my eyes are full of tears.' His misery becomes intolerable – even to the solicitous Lotte – who perceptively suggests: 'I fear, I very much fear that what makes the desire to possess me so attractive is its very impossibility.'

Werther cannot be reasoned with. He desires an eternal connection with Lotte, and he begins to see how this might be achieved. He leaves instructions for his body to be buried in clothes that are 'sacred' (because Lotte has touched them), and places a pink ribbon – a gift from Lotte – in his pocket. While experiencing a kind of spiritual reprieve from mental anguish ('All around me is so silent, and my soul is calm') Werther shoots himself, and dies.

A romantic love triangle, an idealised woman, an episode of wandering, and a young man who edges towards his doom. The old courtly themes are very much in evidence; however, it is Werther's demise that seems to resonate most strongly with the mystical origins of romantic idealism. Ultimately, courtly love is about realising spiritual objectives: beauty is back-lit by a sun that sets in paradise.

The spiritual sub-text of Werther's love for Lotte surfaces

several times before his death. For example, at one point, he says of Lotte: 'She is sacred to me. All my desires are stilled in her presence. I never know what I am about when I am with her; it is as if my soul were throbbing in every nerve.' In another section, the possibility of a spiritual reunion is innocently raised by Lotte herself, when she discusses her religious convictions: 'There will be a life for us after death, Werther! . . . but will we find each other again? And know each other? What do you suppose? What do you say?'

The Romantics had a highly developed sense of the numinous. They believed in a universal soul – a mysterious 'fundament' behind visible nature. Moreover, they believed that an understanding of this deeper truth might be achieved through communion with nature, or the experience of altered states of consciousness, such as powerful emotions, dreams or madness.

In this sense, Romanticism returns romantic love to its cultural source. It returns us to the desert, where Islamic sages sought truth in beauty. We are again in the company of Majnun, whose love is so intense, so powerful, it punctures the celestial dome and fenestrates heaven.

Romanticism is the closest thing we have to a religious faith in a predominantly secular society. This is probably because love is frequently associated with intense experiences of rapture and ecstasy. When love's madness enters its manic phase, consciousness is raised. If love is consummated, sexual activity can intensify the experience even further – evoking what psychologists have called 'oceanic feelings'.

Love's rapture and transcendent states have much in common. Both achieve a sense of escape from the limitations of human identity by union with another being (either lover or God). The desired outcome is a kind of self-annihilation, in which personality, ordinarily overburdened with worldly concerns, is lost in a moment of pure, unadulterated bliss.

Almost all religions have a pseudo-erotic mystical tradition. Hindus practise sexual Tantra and Sufi poetry is fundamentally love poetry. Even Christianity has – to the considerable embarrassment of the Church itself – been unable to resist linking sex and spirituality. St Teresa of Avila, for example, evokes the female genitalia by describing a 'wound of love', and famously wrote about a vision in which she was penetrated by an angel carrying a golden spear with 'a point of fire'. For St Teresa, spiritual enlightenment is a process that begins when the soul falls in love with God, and ends with 'spiritual marriage'.

In *Revelations of Divine Love*, another medieval Christian mystic, Julian of Norwich, described oddly pornographic visions of Jesus Christ's bleeding body. The sensuous language she employs knowingly emphasises the carnal aspects of carnage. Thus, her 'revelation' is 'horrifying and dreadful, sweet and lovely'. Moreover, when Jesus speaks, he speaks in the person of a lover: 'It is I whom you love; it is I whom you delight in . . . it is I whom you long for, whom you desire.'

The division that exists between reason and emotion has created a curious predicament for Western humanity. We find it hard to believe in God, but at the same time, we still have the capacity to look at the natural world and feel something close to reverence and awe. Although we suspect that there is no God, we feel that there should be. We are still dissatisfied with the limitations of personal identity. This is evidenced by the continuing popularity of recreational drugs. In the absence of an alternative, many settle for a chemical Nirvana.

In the East, where spirituality is still very much a part of everyday life, less is expected of love between human beings. The spiritual instinct is satisfied by religious observances, meditation or scripture. In the West, however, where religion plays no real part in the lives of most people, we have replaced religion with love. We have become passionate pilgrims, seeking the transport and meanings of spiritual ecstasy in the religion of romance and the sacrament of sex.

Even if we have little knowledge of the cultural history of romance, we all – to a greater or lesser extent – subscribe to a broad set of 'romantic' expectations. The notion of romance has inveigled itself into every aspect of courtship, sex and love. We seek to create a 'romantic atmosphere' on a dinner date, we allow ourselves the indulgence of a 'holiday romance', or attempt to revive passion with a long-term partner by taking a 'romantic weekend break'.

The cultural history of 'romance' and various meanings of the word 'romantic' make it extremely difficult to define 'romantic love'. Academic psychology – usually quite pedantic about its terminology – has been unable to establish a consensus. Some psychologists use the term in accordance with its courtly origins, whereas others use it interchangeably with 'passionate love'. As a culture, we seem to have settled on the latter usage, viewing 'romantic love' and 'falling in love' as much the same thing.

It has already been argued that the fundamental features of romantic love are evolutionary in origin. Thus, courtship gives women time to evaluate the fitness of suitors; heroic acts are a form of male resource display; and an exclusive (or idealised) relationship is necessary for the formation of a strong pair-bond. Most contemporary evolutionary theorists would agree with Capelanus when he points out that the ease with which love can be won is inversely related to its value. In any social hierarchy, the more beautiful a woman is, the more difficult it will be for a man to win her affection. Beauty advertises good genes which, being at a premium, can be withheld for longer. A beautiful woman is never short of suitors. The inaccessibility of fairy-tale queens is perhaps the logical extension of this principle.

That we should find traces of evolutionary theory in story telling is unremarkable. Art has always served as an instrument of self-enquiry and self-definition. Therefore, it was inevitable that certain fundamental features of human behaviour should appear as conventions in romantic literature. The problem with the courtly tradition, however, is that during the course of its development, the romantic ideal became increasingly rigid and extreme; the imposition of arbitrary codes of conduct offered unlimited scope for self-contradiction and confusion.

The idea that psychopathology is related to conflict is an old one, and it is an explanatory principle that appears and reappears in the writings of numerous psychologists. Thus, individuals whose theories of psychopathology are extremely different – for example, Sigmund Freud and Ivan Pavlov – still have this much in common.

In the 1950s, Gregory Bateson and colleagues developed a new conflict-based theory of psychopathology which made use of a pivotal concept known as the 'double bind'. Essentially, Bateson suggested that severe psychological problems might be caused by 'mixed messages' – as, for example, when a mother repeatedly tells her son that she loves him, while turning her head away in disgust. The term double bind has also been used to describe 'catch-22' situations, where whatever choice is made, the outcome is undesirable.

The doctrine of romantic love has a double bind at its heart. It confuses the carnal and the spiritual. What started off as allegorical literature eventually became a code of conduct – and a completely impractical one at that. Arab mystical literature explored the correspondences between sexual desire and spiritual desire. However, as these threads were carried over the Pyrenees they became inextricably entangled – and much follows from this. The ever present tension between the carnal and spiritual produces a dynamic which generates layer upon layer of self-contradiction.

We expect another human being to make us feel complete, or fulfilled, yet these profound feelings of completion are usually only vouchsafed to the spiritually enlightened. We expect passionate love to last for ever – and even increase in intensity – but it is transitory; it almost always diminishes or turns into companionate love. We expect beauty to be resistant to the depredations of time, but all beauty fades. We like to think that we are being inexorably guided by supernatural forces towards one true love, but the most important factor in the formation of relationships (whether we like it or not) is chance, and in reality we fall in love promiscuously.

Worse still, the fabric of romance comes apart under the forces generated by its own contradictions. Women are worshipped as paradigms of purity, personifications of Marian virtue, but the foundations of adoration sink into a quagmire of lust and desire. Men make women into Madonnas, but cannot deny their sexual needs. Thus, they inevitably despoil paradise. In the later versions of 'Arthurian' legend (including those concerning Tristan), this is recognised by the introduction of a fatally adulterous relationship: Lancelot sleeps with Guinevere; Tristan sleeps with Isolde. As the courtly tradition evolved, more and more writers became preoccupied with adultery, rather than ennobling abstinence.

The impossible demands of romantic love have left a deep

impression on Western literature. As Denis de Rougemont has astutely observed: 'To judge by literature, adultery would seem to be one of the most remarkable of occupations in both Europe and America. Few are the novels that fail to allude to it . . . Without adultery, what would happen to imaginative writing?'

The fairy-tale, 'Once-upon-a-time' world of romantic love promises that we will live 'happy ever after', but romantic narrative is pure tragedy. Heroes vacillate between euphoria and melancholy, and then subside into states of morbid obsession. The name Tristan means child of sadness, and few romances end without first taking casualties. The confusion of the carnal and spiritual invites death into the bedroom and, ultimately, we join our voices with a vast choir and sing that great anthem of self-contradiction, the *liebestod*, the love death. Procreation and extinction accidentally join hands in the conceptual fog of romantic idealism, with devastating consequences.

Our romantic legacy is predicated on a Batesonian double bind, and its mixed messages incline us towards emotional instability. If evolutionary pressures have determined that love should drive us mad, then cultural pressures have created ideal conditions for its incubation.

In the early 1990s, a group of social scientists undertook a large cross-cultural study, in which they interviewed students from the USA, Italy, and the People's Republic of China about a variety of emotional experiences, including happiness, fear, anger, sadness and love. When the study was completed, it was found that there was remarkable agreement concerning all of the emotions, but with one exception – love. American and European subjects rated love very positively, and equated it with other positive experiences like joy and happiness. The Chinese subjects, however, were much more doubtful. In the Chinese language there are very few ideographs that correspond with the more positive love-related words found in English and Italian. Instead, love tends to be associated with more negative emotional states. For example, the Chinese subjects linked passionate love with ideographs which translate as 'infatuation', 'unrequited love', 'nostalgia' and 'sorrow'. When told of Western ideas about love, the Chinese subjects thought they were inaccurate and unrealistic.

These findings raise some interesting questions. Has the Western romantic tradition made us blind to love's madness? China has no equivalent tradition. In fact, during the Cultural Revolution, 'romantic love' was outlawed – considered by the communist elite to be a 'bourgeois' indulgence. Given this context, is it possible that the Chinese are better equipped to evaluate the pitfalls of passionate love? It would seem that for many Chinese students, they would as much want to fall in love as develop a psychiatric illness.

The ancient Greeks were troubled by passion – seeing it as a force that could easily overthrow reason and disturb the mind's equilibrium. In many respects, this view has been preserved in several Asian and Oriental cultures. To be romantic is to play with fire – the volatile, inner fire of Hippocratic and Islamic medicine. Although passion can be exciting, it is extremely unreliable – so unreliable, that Asian and Oriental cultures have rejected passion as the basis of marriage, subscribing instead to the more rational processes of 'arrangement'. The formation of a new family unit is considered to be of such great importance – not only to the bride, groom, their progeny and immediate family, but to the entire local community and wider society – that it cannot be based on love alone. There must be a deeper level of compatibility, embracing factors such as background, education and temperament, to ensure that the relationship will last.

The Chinese anthropologist Francis Hsu has suggested that Western and Eastern cultures differ with respect to social awareness and obligation. In the West, the individual – his or her personal identity – is considered to be much more important than his or her social role. In the East, however, this is entirely reversed. The individual's personal identity is considered less important than their ability to be a good son, daughter, husband or mother. Therefore, a successful marriage is more likely to arise from a pairing that takes the full social and cultural credentials of both parties into account.

The romantic tradition represents the antithesis of this kind of thinking – and reaches its most extreme expression in elopement. From a Western perspective, the instinctive response to elopement is positive. Yet, the eloping couple are usually in the throes of love's madness, and remove themselves entirely from their social context. In doing so, they immediately lose the benefits of an existing support network (friends and family) and incur the costs of geographical displacement. They become disconnected, two mutually absorbed individuals who have relinquished social obligations and can no longer properly occupy a defined social role. Needless to say, a relationship that takes place in a social vacuum has fewer external forces holding it together.

It is interesting that this disregard for social context was always a feature of romantic writing. For example, the figure of the Majnun, being mad, is by necessity a social outcast, but in the romantic tradition, losing or risking everything for love, including one's mind, is almost expected. In the *Lais* of Marie de France (a collection of courtly tales written in the late twelfth century) the disconnection of lovers from their social context is even more conspicuous. French literature scholars Glynn Burgess and Keith Busby point out that:

> Marie concentrates on the individuality of her characters and is not very concerned with their integration into society. If society does not appreciate the lovers, then the lovers die or abandon society, and society is the poorer for it.

Perhaps as a consequence of this disenfranchisement, Marie's images of love are almost always painful. Again, Burgess and Busby write:

> If we take the *Lais* as a whole work, compared with other works of medieval literature, the characteristic of Marie's view of love seems to be an almost inevitable association with suffering.

The theme of the lover – or lovers – standing outside society, re-emerges intermittently throughout the entire history of romantic writing, and ultimately we find ourselves in the frozen wastes of Romantic poetry, where young men set off on winter journeys, meaning either never to return or to die. This represents yet another paradox. One of the main aims of the courtly tradition was to socialise love, to make it genteel and polite. Yet ultimately, romance is an anti-social phenomenon. It weakens social cohesion.

The Asian and Eastern belief that all of society has a stake in the success of love was curiously echoed by Erich Fromm in *The Art of Loving*. Fromm insisted that the principal problem of Western society is alienation. When we love, however, we should feel connected – and this sense of connection extends beyond the family to the social whole. Socially aware love – love that acknowledges its social context – is essential to the well-being of everyone.

For most people raised in the West, the concept of an arranged marriage – or policing love – seems distasteful, even repugnant. Yet, arranged marriage is practised by 60 per cent of the world's population – and approximately half of these couples claim that they stay together because of love (not romantic love, maybe, but something far more durable). In Britain and the US, where people still uphold the romantic ideal, nearly half of first marriages end in divorce, while those marriages that survive are often characterised by deep levels of dissatisfaction – particularly among women. The divorce rate for second and third marriages is even higher.

Love's madness usually strikes with the onset of adolescence. Subsequently, there is a high risk of pregnancy, impetuous marriage, or both. Statistics show that teenage marriages are very fragile, and a high percentage break down within only a few years. Teenage pregnancy (compared with pregnancy in early adulthood) is associated with premature birth, low birth weight, and death during childbirth. Teenage pregnancy also has social consequences. It will interrupt, or even terminate, a young woman's education, and the children of most teenage families are financially disadvantaged. The idea of risking everything for love is portrayed in the West as a noble undertaking, but subscribing to this doctrine frequently results in loneliness, hardship and poverty.

In stark contrast, the tradition of arranged marriage has a number of pragmatic advantages, rarely appreciated by dyed-in-the-wool romantics. The arranged marriage system is strongly associated with the idea of coercion, yet, in reality, Asian and Oriental cultures almost always allow the prospective bride and groom to exercise some choice, albeit limited. In India, the 'girl-seeing' ceremony has evolved specifically for this purpose. Typically, the young man's family will visit the young woman's family, and the young man is given a special seat. The young woman then enters the room, kneels, bows and leaves. Both are then in a position to decide whether they find each other attractive and wish to proceed further.

Although arranged marriages are treated with suspicion in the West, they represent a preference for many who have been raised in Asian and Eastern cultures. It is assumed that a 'good marriage' can only be achieved if couples are carefully matched, and then supported by their families. To base a marriage on passion is simply irresponsible, and likely to result in unhappiness. Surprisingly – for incurable romantics at least – contemporary research does not contradict this view.

Psychologists Paul Yelsma and Kuriakose Athappilly have studied relationship satisfaction levels of couples who married for love and those who married by arrangement. Those whose marriages were arranged show much higher levels of satisfaction than those who married for love. Other studies have produced a similar pattern of results.

Almost instinctively, the Occidental sensibility finds such results difficult to believe, but why shouldn't arranged marriages be superior to those that are based on a temporary madness? A long-term relationship – if it is to be happy – must be based on more than the tortured logic and inflated expectations of romantic idealism.

The Dalai Lama, examining romantic love from the cool, rational vantage of Buddhism, does not hesitate to identify it as a form of madness:

> When a couple has just met, seen each other on just a few occasions, they may be madly in love and very happy, but any decision about marriage made at that instant would be very shaky. Just as one can become, in some sense, insane from the power of intense anger or hatred, it is also possible for an individual to become in some sense insane by the power of passion and lust.

Romantic love springs from absurdities such as 'love at first sight'. It is preoccupied with superficial (and transient) characteristics such as physical beauty, and usually ends in confusion and frustration.

> ... sometimes you might even find situations where an individual could feel, 'Oh, my boyfriend or girlfriend is not really a good person, not a kind person, but still I feel attracted to him or her.'

According to the Dalai Lama, meaningful, satisfying and lasting relationships are not based on romantic idealism, but on mutual understanding, respect and compassion. True love is not instant. Love that strikes like a bolt of lightning is almost certainly suspect, as are the whirlwind romances that are the staple of romantic fiction. In essence, the Dalai Lama suggests that a commitment based on deep friendship is more likely to outlast a commitment based on desire. In contrast to the storm-tossed seas of romanticism, he offers an attractive alternative of still waters and lotus flowers – the relationship as sanctuary, a retreat from madness, rather than a manifestation of madness.

Perhaps, after more than a thousand years of disappointment, we can see the first signs of disaffection in the West – cultural trends that tacitly acknowledge the common-sense virtues of Asian and Oriental attitudes to love and marriage. Over the last fifty years, dating agencies have become increasingly popular, operating on similar principles to those that govern arranged marriages. The only fundamental difference is that the initial matching takes place in a computer, rather than a group of human brains. Even seemingly esoteric rituals, like the 'girl-seeing' ceremony, have equivalents – for instance, the provision of a photograph or video.

Dating agencies are distinctly unromantic. They militate

against all the basic assumptions of romantic love. Yet, they are responsible for bringing a large number of people together in relationships that seem to be very successful.

The idea of arrangement does not preclude falling in love. Indeed, in Asian and other Eastern societies, it is assumed that a couple will fall in love and become passionate – but *after* the marriage has taken place. Thus, couples can experience love's madness safely, but know that when it passes, they will still have a robust and healthy relationship. Dating agencies seem to offer the same kind of security; couples can engage in the dangerous high-wire act of falling in love, comfortable in the knowledge that there is a safety net in place.

Disaffection with the failure of romantic love was dramatically demonstrated recently by American psychologist Robert Epstein, who, in addition to holding several academic posts, is also the editor-in-chief of *Psychology Today*. Having considered the merits of arranged marriages, Epstein wondered whether it would be possible to rehabilitate the concept for Western consumption. Consequently, in the June 2002 issue, he argued against romantic assumptions, and suggested that it might be possible to learn to love any suitable partner. He proposed a programme to test his hypothesis: the signing of a six-month exclusivity contract (to obviate the problem of parallel dating); commitment to intensive joint-counselling sessions; frequent 'getaways'; and participation in exercises designed to foster mutual love. Epstein suggested that such a programme – credible to Westerners – might achieve the same result as the arranged marriage system: reliable, meaningful and enduring love. More daringly, Epstein volunteered to be the first subject in his own experiment.

He expected the article to have little impact; however, the subsequent response was overwhelming. It aroused enormous media interest, and Epstein received hundreds of letters, e-mails and telephone calls from women eager to sign his contract.

It would seem that romantic love – which promises heaven on earth – has ultimately delivered something closer to despair.

5

Hallucinating Beauty

Being somewhat large and languishing and lazy,
Yet of a beauty that would drive you crazy.
                              Don Juan, Lord Byron

'The Judgement of Paris' is an episode in Greek mythology which dramatises the degree to which human beings venerate beauty. At the marriage feast of Peleus and Thetis, Eris (the personification of discord) threw a golden apple among the guests, inscribed with the provocative words 'For the most beautiful'. The apple (thereafter known as the apple of discord) was immediately claimed by three competing deities: Hera, Athena and Aphrodite. In order to settle the dispute, Paris – the most handsome of mortal men – was asked to intercede, but before he could make his judgement, each deity tried to advance her claim by tempting him with a reward. Hera offered him greatness, Athena success in war, and Aphrodite offered marriage to the most beautiful woman in the world. After some deliberation, Paris decided that Aphrodite – the goddess of love – should possess the apple. She honoured her promise and, with her help, Paris eventually abducted Helen of Troy (reputed to be the most beautiful woman in the world).

It was Paris's judgement, placing beauty above greatness

or military prowess, that ultimately caused the Trojan War. In Homer's *Iliad*, the city elders of Troy, on seeing Helen, whisper to one another: 'No wonder Achaians and Trojans have been fighting all these years for such a woman!' She is a 'divine creature come down from heaven'. In her presence, reason fails. It seems to them that Helen's beauty provides ample justification for a long and terrible war.

If love has the power to overthrow reason, then its most potent weapon is beauty. In any modern re-creation of Paris's dilemma, human beings seem compelled to imitate his judgement. Kings have abdicated, politicians have fallen and plutocrats have lost fortunes – all because of beauty.

The veneration of beauty is something that links the ancient world with the modern. Beauty is still associated with divinity, particularly in the West. Those who are beautiful become god-like. They achieve omnipresence through the media and omnipotence through wealth and influence. Contemporary culture has created a new Mount Olympus, the summit of which is populated by pop icons, sports heroes, supermodels and Hollywood megastars; and when these latter-day deities choose to descend, their presence among ordinary mortals induces hysteria – the screaming, weeping, hair-pulling and fainting of fans overwhelmed by their presence.

Beauty seems capable of creating instant desire, a deep, visceral yearning. The ease with which beauty bypasses reason is embarrassing, revealing as it does too many of our weaknesses. Beauty shocks us. A beautiful person can effortlessly elicit a sigh, and leave us swooning on the edge of an emotional precipice. Our lack of resistance is little short of indecent.

Alexander Liberman, formerly of *Vogue* magazine, once said: 'The good model is . . . involved in provoking the photographer – by her movement, her expression, her attitude – to fall in love momentarily and to capture this fleeting seduction.' When we encounter beauty – particularly outstanding beauty – we begin to fall in love.

In the eighteenth century, the Scottish philosopher David Hume wrote *A Treatise of Human Nature*. It is one of the great anatomies of the mind. In a section titled 'Of the amorous passion, or love betwixt the sexes', Hume attempts to deconstruct love.

> 'Tis plain, that this affection [love], in its most natural state, is deriv'd from the conjunction of three different impressions or passions, *viz*. The pleasing sensation arising from beauty; the bodily appetite for generation; and a generous kindness or good-will.

Love, then – according to Hume – is composed of three separate elements: an appreciation of beauty, sexual desire and amity (a system not too dissimilar to Sternberg's 'triangular' theory). Hume informs us that love can develop from any of these single elements. Thus: 'One who is inflam'd with lust, feels at least a momentary kindness towards the object of it, and at the same time fancies her more beautiful than ordinary.' However, more often than not, love proceeds first from physical attraction: '. . . the most common species of love is that which first arises from beauty, and afterwards diffuses itself into kindness and into the bodily appetite'.

Scientific research (and everyday experience) seems to support Hume. The starting point of most relationships involves both parties finding each other attractive. The longevity and success of a relationship might be influenced by other factors, but unless a couple are attracted to each other in the first place, these other factors will not come into play.

The most extraordinary (and perplexing) example of

Hume's model operating in the real world is 'love at first sight', and when it happens, physical attraction seems to trigger 'bodily appetite' and 'generous kindness' almost simultaneously. The phenomenon exemplifies the Greek concept of *theia mania* – love (as a form of madness) delivered like lightning from the gods. When people who claim to have fallen in love at first sight are interviewed, they frequently suggest that they 'just knew' the person who they fell in love with was 'the one' – the single human being on the planet they were destined to meet, and with whom they could find happiness. Moreover, such conclusions were often reached on the basis of appearance alone, before a single word had been exchanged. Over 60 per cent of men and women in the West believe in love at first sight – the majority of whom claim to have experienced it. Were it not for the fact that love at first sight is culturally sanctioned by romantic idealism, such thinking would almost certainly be viewed as delusional.

In literature, examples of love at first sight abound. When Romeo sees Juliet for the first time, he cries: 'O! She doth teach the torches to burn bright . . . Did my heart love till now?' When Werther sees Lotte, he declares: 'My entire soul was transfixed by her figure, her tone, her manner . . . I delighted in her dark eyes . . . how my entire soul was drawn to her young lips and fresh, bright cheeks . . .' Nearly a hundred years later, the very same impressions are repeated by Turgenev, when the young protagonist of *First Love*, Vladimir, stumbles across the coquette, Zinaida: 'I forgot everything; my eyes devoured the graceful figure, the lovely neck, the beautiful arms, the slightly dishevelled fair hair under the white kerchief – and the half closed, perceptive eye, the lashes, the soft cheek beneath them . . .'

Love at first sight is so intense, it usually leaves an afterimage – like the patterns of luminosity that linger following a glance at the sun. Dante – who on seeing the young Beatrice considered her to be the daughter of a Homeric god – described Beatrice's likeness 'remaining in me always', and Turgenev's Vladimir was haunted by Zinaida: 'The image of the young girl floated before me.'

These 'flashbulb' memories – pictures that seem to have been stamped into the visual cortex – are very similar to those reported by trauma victims. Psychologists believe that such memories are particularly well preserved, remaining very vivid, because they cannot be assimilated with the rest of experience by the brain. Put very simply, the traumatic experience is so overwhelming that the usual procedures that convert experience into memory break down. 'Flashbulb' memories cannot be properly integrated into the existing network of ordinary memories. Thus, they exist in an unmodified form, retaining a powerful emotional charge and being much more likely to intrude into awareness.

Sometimes, trauma victims report a phenomenon known as re-experiencing. The individual actually relives the trauma in the form of an hallucinatory 'flashback'. It is interesting that many individuals who report a powerful experience of love at first sight are also prone to hallucinatory visions of their beloved. The first memory of love refuses to settle in the unconscious; it constantly reawakens and invades the real world like a dream.

One of the most remarkable and detailed accounts of love at first sight can be found in the autobiography of the composer Hector Berlioz. On 11 September 1827, he attended the French premiere of Shakespeare's *Hamlet* at the Odéon in Paris. The role of Ophelia was played by a young Irish actress, Henrietta Smithson, with whom he fell instantly in love.

The consequences were devastating. Berlioz experienced

numerous symptoms that would, under any other circumstances, be taken as evidence of a quite severe mental illness:

> ... the shock was too great, and it was a long while before
> I recovered from it. I became possessed by an intense, over-
> powering sense of sadness, that in my then sickly, nervous
> state produced a mental condition adequately to describe
> which would take a great physiologist. I could not sleep, I
> lost my spirits, my favourite studies became distasteful to
> me; I could not work, and I spent my time wandering
> aimlessly about Paris and its environs. During that long
> period of suffering I can only recall four occasions on which
> I slept, and then it was heavy, death-like sleep produced by
> complete physical exhaustion. These were one night when
> I had thrown myself down on some sheaves in a field near
> Ville-Juif; one day in a meadow in the neighbourhood of
> Sceaux; once on the snow on the banks of the frozen Seine,
> near Neuilly; and lastly on a table in the Café du Cardinal
> at the corner of the Boulevard des Italiens and the Rue
> Richelieu, where I slept for five hours, to the terror of the
> garçons, who thought I was dead and were afraid to come
> near me.

Berlioz began to rally after his initial bout of love sickness, and decided to impress Miss Smithson by putting on
a concert of his works for full orchestra and choir at the
Paris Conservatoire. Although he succeeded in organising
the concert (which turned out to be a very substantial undertaking), the event escaped Henrietta's notice – a disap-
pointing (if rather predictable) outcome. Berlioz then began
writing to her, but he did not get a single reply. She found
Berlioz's letters disturbing, and subsequently gave her maid
strict orders to stop receiving them.

Undeterred, the next stage of Berlioz's campaign was to
attract Henrietta Smithson's attention by getting his name

to appear next to hers on the same play-bill. He learned that she was to perform two acts from *Romeo and Juliet* at the Opèra Comique, so he promptly approached the theatre manager and persuaded him to include one of his overtures in the programme.

Whatever Berlioz hoped to gain by executing his cunning plan was wholly negated by his subsequent loss of self-control. When he arrived for an orchestral rehearsal, the troupe of actors were just finishing theirs. Romeo was carrying Smithson – as Juliet – off the stage, and from this rather odd vantage, Henrietta looked directly into Berlioz's eyes. This was, of course, the first time that she had ever seen him. Having already expended so much energy trying to impress her, one would have thought that he would strike a romantic or dignified pose – that he would exploit the moment to the full – but this was not to be. Instead, he emitted a loud cry before dashing out into the street, wildly wringing his hands. He was unable to return for an hour.

Although this episode appears in Berlioz's autobiography, there is some doubt as to whether it really happened. He does not tell us which of his overtures was performed, and no reviews appeared in the usual journals. Subsequently, Berlioz scholars have suggested that these events more probably reflect the content of a dream – or hallucination. If so, then they constitute a remarkable example of how love at first sight can affect the mind – even more remarkable, perhaps, than if the described events were real.

The next day, Smithson was due to leave for Holland. By this time, Berlioz (by accident, so he claimed) had taken lodgings opposite hers on the Rue Richelieu. He had been lying on his bed until three in the afternoon, and finally rose to look out of the window. The moment he chose coincided with Smithson's departure, and he was able to witness the object of his desire getting into a carriage, bound for Amsterdam. His reaction was characteristically over-wrought:

> No words can describe what I suffered; even Shakespeare has never painted the horrible gnawing at the heart, the sense of utter desolation, the worthlessness of life, the torture of one's throbbing pulses, and the wild confusion of one's mind, the disgust of life, and the impossibility of suicide . . . my mind was paralysed as my passion grew. I could only – suffer.

Berlioz was utterly devastated – so much so, that we must remind ourselves that he had still not spoken a single word to Henrietta Smithson. Nor, being French, had he understood a single word of her Shakespearian declarations on stage. Berlioz's strong feelings were predicated entirely on her beauty.

For more than two years, Berlioz heard nothing of Henrietta. During that time, he won a musical prize, wrote the Symphonie Fantastique (the movements of which romantically dramatised his infatuation for Smithson), narrowly survived being shipwrecked, met Felix Mendelssohn in Rome, and travelled around Italy – all of which failed to exorcise Smithson's memory. Indeed, on his return to Paris, he was still so obsessed with her that he took a room in her old lodging house. It was there that he learned again of her whereabouts. A servant told him that she was not only back in Paris, but she had only just vacated Berlioz's room – the night before his arrival. Berlioz suspected the operation of strange forces: '. . . a believer in magnetic influences, secret affinities, and mysterious promptings would certainly find in all this powerful argument in favour of his system'.

Subsequently, through a chain of acquaintances, Berlioz managed to ensure Henrietta's presence at a concert of his music, which included the Symphonie Fantastique.

Apparently, as the concert progressed, she realised that Berlioz was still passionately in love with her, and her heart melted. She consented to meet him, and within a matter of months they were married.

Sadly, Berlioz's expectations of conjugal bliss were never realised. The fantasy did not correspond with reality. In a relatively short space of time, Henrietta and Hector were making each other very unhappy. They argued. Henrietta started to drink heavily. She put on weight. Soon, Berlioz had stopped finding her quite so attractive. He neglected her and, in response, she became jealous – not without good reason. Berlioz became interested in younger women, and in due course he and Henrietta separated. After her death, he was forced to reflect on what he called their 'dead love'.

Berlioz was not so much a representative of the Romantic movement as the embodiment of romance itself. He lived his life like a romantic hero. Yet, in the end, he had to acknowledge that his passion was essentially shallow, a temporary madness. He lamented the fact that love – supposedly the greatest of all human emotions – could not triumph over even trivial adversities and hardship. In reality, domestic drudgery, financial problems and petty bickering proved too much for love – a deeply depressing thought for a man who had subscribed so wholeheartedly to the romantic ideal.

Yet how could it have been otherwise? Berlioz hardly knew his wife before they were married.

The narrative of the Symphonie Fantastique concerns a young artist who takes opium in a fit of amorous despair and enters a dreamscape, haunted by visions of his beautiful beloved. This was the woman whom Berlioz really fell in love with – a fantasy figure. It was inevitable that the woman he married – the real Henrietta Smithson – would be a disappointment.

Although Berlioz is an extreme example, his fate is shared by many. Under the influence of romantic idealism, intimate relationships have acquired enormous significance. Indeed, it is a basic tenet of romanticism that life cannot be satisfactory without someone special to love. Unfortunately, that special person might not materialise. Thus we are caught between need and reality, and if reality fails to deliver, we are perfectly capable of twisting it into shapes of our own choosing. Ordinary folk are transformed into brave knights and beautiful maidens, and everyday life is transformed as well, becoming like a film or fairy tale. Inevitably, however, reality reasserts itself. The vivid colours fade, and we find ourselves again in a monochrome world of flawed humanity, kitchen sinks, electricity bills and mortgage repayments.

When couples attend marital therapy, it is often the case that one party will ascribe his or her dissatisfaction to some kind of change in the other: 'He's not like he was when we were dating'; 'She's a different person now.' Typically, such assertions are used to legitimise scalding criticism: 'You're no fun any more'; 'You used to take much better care of yourself'; 'You've lost interest in sex' – but more often than not, the recipient of such criticism hasn't really changed at all. Rather, it is the critic's perception of them that has changed. Without love's magic, fairy-tale conventions are reversed, and even the most handsome prince can find himself croaking.

Dante was fortunate. His pseudo-religious visions of Beatrice were never tested against human imperfection. It was Berlioz's misfortune to have a wish come true. Romantic idealism rarely survives such a disaster.

Love at first sight – however implausible – is not an apocryphal phenomenon. Although it might not always result in the formation of a happy and successful relationship, it is certainly real, and occurs with considerable frequency (particularly among teenagers).

What then are the mechanisms that underlie it?

Any account of love at first sight must be speculative, due to insufficient research. Even so, it is still possible to generate some plausible hypotheses.

Firstly, love at first sight might be an example of what social psychologists call the 'halo effect'. Beauty is strongly associated with positive inferences and attributions. For example, in laboratory studies where people are asked to infer character traits from photographs, attractive people are always assumed to be more likeable. If we think someone has a beautiful face, then we automatically assume that they possess other attractive characteristics. Thus, they are easier to fall in love with.

Secondly, love at first sight might be explained by a more deeply rooted biological phenomenon known as 'imprinting'. This term is closely associated with the name of Konrad Lorenz, an ethologist who demonstrated that goslings would follow him and treat him as a 'mother figure' if he was the first thing they saw after hatching.

The idea of imprinting is closely associated with a critical or 'sensitive' period occurring just after birth. It would seem that for a limited time, goslings will form an instant and irreversible attachment to the most significant object in their environment. Ethologists have since observed critical periods in which parental bonding occurs in other birds and mammals. Human infants also have a similar critical period, although its effect on subsequent behaviour is more subtle.

The theoretical framework offered by imprinting suggests that love at first sight might be a vestigial effect of early learning experiences. Indeed, Lorenz claimed that imprinting experiences can influence mate choice in birds once they reach sexual maturity.

This idea is given considerable prominence in psycho-analysis. For example, Freud's Oedipus and Electra complexes permit parental characteristics to influence choice of partner. Jung also believed that this was possible, suggesting that: 'It is the strength of the bond with the parents that unconsciously influences the choice of partner, either positively or negatively.'

Modern scientific research has, to some extent, legitimised this view. In an experiment conducted at McMaster University in Ontario, it was found that subjects were more likely to trust unseen opponents in a game, when they were shown computer-generated pictures of opponents that had been morphed to look like themselves. The research team concluded that we are unconsciously attracted to faces that are similar to our own (which of course also generally resemble those of our parents).

Even more direct evidence has been collected by a team of scientists at the University of Chicago, who discovered that women prefer the smell of men whose genes match those of their father. This suggests that the mechanism underlying love at first sight might be olfactory – 'love at first sniff' might be a more apposite term! A criticism of 'Oedipal' theories of sexual attraction is that they make little sense from an evolutionary perspective. It is true that inbreeding with genetically similar partners increases the risk of birth abnormalities; however, outbreeding with completely different partners can also be problematic. Subsequently, it has been suggested that parental smells might guide sexually mature offspring towards partners with an intermediate (and possibly optimal) mix of genes.

Of course, smell is an important factor with respect to sexual attraction, irrespective of Oedipal theories. An alarming study published by George Preti and colleagues (of the Monell Chemical Senses Center in Philadelphia) has demonstrated that women exposed to scent collected from male arm-pit sweat (but masked by a stronger fragrance) report feeling less tense and more relaxed. One can easily see how evolutionary pressures might have led to such a development. Such a mechanism would not only make men seem more attractive (by association), but also engender compliance in mates. Evolution – typically amoral – seems to have provided predatory males with a natural variant of the 'date rape' drug Rohypnol.

It is plausible that love at first sight might represent the influence of a critical period in early childhood. However, it might also reflect the occurrence of a second critical period in adolescence. Most people experience falling in love at first sight between the ages of sixteen and twenty. Therefore, it might be the case that sexual maturity coincides with a critical period during which individuals – particularly young men – are prone to form strong emotional attachments. This would clearly make a great deal of sense from an evolutionary point of view.

Another idea that can be borrowed from ethology to explain love at first sight concerns stimuli that trigger (or release) instinctual behaviours. In a series of classic studies by ethologist Niko Tinbergen, it was shown that during its reproductive cycle, the male stickleback will exhibit specific responses to very precise physical characteristics known as 'sign stimuli' – presentation of the red throat of a rival is all that is necessary to provoke aggression; similarly, the swollen belly of a female (ripe with eggs) is all that is necessary to provoke courtship. Simple stimuli triggering instinctual responses are also found in more sophisticated animals such as primates. For example, sexual receptivity in female baboons is associated with swollen rear parts, which trigger sexual interest in males.

In experimental situations where sign stimuli are artificially exaggerated – becoming supernormal stimuli – there is a commensurate increase in the magnitude of the associated response. For instance, a female oyster-catcher will choose to incubate an artificial giant egg in preference to her genuine (but much smaller) eggs. The giant egg triggers an excessive brooding response. Again, similar principles seem to be operating during the courtship behaviour of some primates. Sexually receptive female baboons whose rear parts become superlarge receive far more attention from males. They begin breeding at a younger age, breed more frequently, and also have more offspring.

Love at first sight might be an attachment response triggered by features that function in a way similar to sign stimuli: features that we more commonly describe as tokens of beauty. Fortunately the human brain is more sophisticated than that of a stickleback or baboon – a woman with a beautiful pair of eyes will not necessarily cause every man she meets to fall in love with her. However, where a potential partner has a specific sensitivity to beautiful eyes, a strong attachment response might be elicited; the ancient stimulus-response circuits in the brain become active, overriding rational thought.

An ethological framework also implies that if an individual has a feature that qualifies as a supernormal sign stimulus, then he or she will be able to provoke an attachment response, even in those who would ordinarily be resistant to its effects. This might account for the success of many pop divas and film stars who possess a particularly attractive feature – which is often made even more attractive by surgical enhancement. The resulting body part, or body parts, become supernormal sign stimuli, eliciting powerful feelings of attachment. Devoted fans often describe committing themselves to an idol after experiencing something which seems to be a very close relative of love at first sight.

Ordinary individuals – less well endowed – can still attempt to capitalise on the same mechanism by applying make-up (a tradition that extends back to prehistory). The popularity of this strategy is reflected in the value of the worldwide cosmetic and toiletries industry, which is now close to 50 billion dollars. In *My Life for Beauty*, Helena Rubenstein, the doyenne of the cosmetics industry, helpfully suggested: 'There are no ugly women, only lazy ones.' It is not by chance that such a vast number of women choose to turn their eyes, lips and hair into supernormal sign stimuli by applying make-up and colour. They do it because it works!

The structures and mechanisms that mediate attachment behaviour are perhaps some of the most ancient in the brain. They were there long before evolution gave us the power to think rationally. Thus, in this sense, beauty makes its appeal to the instinctual, unthinking, unconscious parts of the brain. It should be no surprise, therefore, that when people fall in love at first sight, they cannot explain what is happening to them, and routinely opt for post-hoc gener-alisations that conform to the cultural expectations of romantic idealism: their love is fated, destined, and legit-imised by its sheer madness.

Beauty – we are told – is in the eye of the beholder; an aphorism which suggests that everyone, no matter what they look like, has the potential to be viewed as beautiful. Unfortunately, scientific research shows the opposite to be true. Most people have a very clear idea about who is, and who isn't, beautiful, and the extent to which men and women (the world over) agree on this issue is quite extraordinary.

The average human being can evaluate how beautiful a face is in under 150 milliseconds. Even if given much longer to make the same judgement, most people will not be inclined to change their minds. The brain is sensitive to feature arrangements to within one millimetre. Thus, the tiniest modifications to a computer-generated facial image can result in a shift of opinion with respect to attractiveness ratings. At three months, a human infant will gaze for longer at an attractive face than an unattractive face. Remarkably, when presented with faces from different races (to which the infant has never been exposed) the effect still holds.

Such findings suggest that we have an innate (and highly refined) aesthetic instinct that allows us to position others (as well as ourselves) in a theoretical beauty hierarchy. In effect, we are all born with a 'beauty sense' – a sense as real as our sense of touch or of smell.

There are numerous cautionary disquisitions and tales which exhort us to judge people by their character, rather than their appearance – true beauty is not skin-deep, true beauty comes from within – but this sentiment, however laudable, seems to have little impact on human behaviour. Superficial physical beauty is consistently valued above almost all other attributes; and for many, it is a necessary condition for love.

How, then, do we determine who is, and who isn't, beautiful? What do we see in a beautiful face?

Clearly, the constituent elements of the human face are extremely important. Lovers never tire of staring into each other's eyes; the mouth and lips have been much celebrated by poets – often attracting laboured comparison with cherries and rosebuds; and firm, clear skin is universally praised. However, the aesthetic success of the total ensemble depends on a single, fundamental rule – the rule of symmetry.

The fact that symmetrical faces are judged to be beautiful was first discovered by the nineteenth-century scientist Sir Francis Galton, a cousin of Charles Darwin. Using composite photography, Galton found that the single face which emerges from the combined images of several faces is almost always aesthetically pleasing. The photographs that emerged from his laboratory are still quite striking: androgynous, expressionless, yet beautiful faces that hang in the blurred mist of their complex method of composition.

But why should a combination of many faces create beauty, rather than just chaotic ugliness?

Essentially, composite photography disposes of idiosyncratic features. The more a feature deviates from the average face, the weaker its impression will be on the final image. Deviations are lost in the blur, while shared qualities and dimensions are strengthened. The result is a perfectly symmetrical face.

Ovid, in his mercilessly honest *Ars Amatoria*, noted that: 'Night turns any woman into a goddess.' Generations of lovers have since confirmed the accuracy of his observation. Soft lighting has become an obligatory requirement for those embarking on a new relationship. All faces – both male and female – are flattered by the night, because idiosyncrasies vanish in shadow. We become less unique and closer to an ideal average. Inevitably, we appear more symmetrical – and thus more beautiful.

The human head is an extraordinary accomplishment. Evolutionary pressures have compressed most of the human sensory apparatus into a very small space indeed. Our major sense organs are conveniently located at the front of the head, so that we can preview new environments before we actually enter them. The sensory organs are also very close to the brain, permitting the swift transmission of information. An efficient perceptual system has obvious advantages with respect to survival.

Given that the perceptual system is so complex, it is a difficult thing to construct. As a consequence, a great deal can go wrong. A poor genetic heritage is much more likely to affect the head than simpler body parts such as a thigh or knee. When we look at another person's face, we are looking directly at the place where genetic mutations – however small – are going to be most conspicuous. The more mutations there are in a person's genome, the more likely it is that his or her face will show abnormalities – especially asymmetries.

The face is also likely to betray other forms of genetic weakness, such as a poor immune system which is unable to resist potentially disfiguring diseases (a major problem for our ancestors who shared their environment with numerous parasitic organisms).

There is a proverb which states: A good face is a letter of recommendation. In the context of evolutionary theory, it is difficult to imagine a more accurate remark. Facial symmetry is the best and most reliable indication of fitness. Thus, our 'beauty sense' is really a form of genetic radar. When we see someone who is beautiful, we can be confident that their genes – if we mated with them – would more or less ensure the survival of our genes into the next generation. As usual, evolution achieves its objectives with a deft touch. When men and women are attracted to each other, they are not thinking of fitness, genetic mutations, or reproductive success. They merely find each other attractive. Yet, there has always been an awareness of the connection between health and beauty. Anticipating evolutionary psychology by over two hundred years, the eighteenth-century English poet William Shenstone wrote: 'Health is beauty, and the most perfect health is the most perfect beauty.' Today, we can revise Shenstone's observation for the twenty-first century, and declare: The genome is beauty, and the most perfect genome is the most perfect beauty.

Although facial symmetry is important from an evolutionary perspective, so too is body symmetry.

A recent study conducted in Canada found that body

symmetry in men is strongly associated with sexual success. The more symmetrical a man is, the more he will be perceived as beautiful, and the more sexual partners he will have. Another study, conducted by psychologist Randy Thornhill in New Mexico, found that the female partners of symmetrical men experience 40 per cent more orgasms during sexual intercourse. It is well known that the muscular contractions that occur during orgasm facilitate the passage of sperm towards the cervix, so it would seem that evolution has equipped women with an automatic mechanism that will increase fertility when copulation occurs with a beautiful – and therefore genetically fit – male. Still more remarkable is research conducted by the biologist John Manning who, using very precise measurements, discovered that women become more symmetrical (with respect to ears and fingers) when they ovulate. Evolutionary pressures have ensured that subtle physical changes make a woman more attractive when she is most fertile.

Recently, even more compelling evidence for the relationship between beauty and reproductive fitness was published by a research team based at the University of Valencia in Spain. It was found that facial attractiveness in men (as rated by two large groups of women) was positively correlated with sperm quality. Attractive men tend to produce sperm that are superior on measures of morphology and motility. In other words, their sperm are built better and are gifted swimmers!

A symmetrical body is perceived as beautiful by both men and women. However, gender-specific beauty appears to be determined by shape – and clearly, the ideal shape for a woman is not the ideal shape for a man (and vice versa).

In 1993, evolutionary psychologist Devendra Singh undertook a pioneering study, examining the extent to which a woman's figure can influence the degree to which men judge her to be attractive. He was particularly interested in 'curviness', which he measured using the waist-to-hip ratio (calculated by simply dividing waist size by hip size). The waist-to-hip ratio for young, healthy women is between 0.67 and 0.8. For men, it is between 0.89 and 0.95. The lower the waist-to-hip ratio, the more curviform the figure. Singh discovered that men asked to judge images of women in which the waist-to-hip ratio was systematically varied, reliably preferred images with lower waist-to-hip ratios. Moreover, as long as the waist-to-hip ratio was low, women were judged desirable irrespective of their overall body weight.

Singh has argued that the much celebrated hour-glass figure is a powerful evolutionary signal, strongly associated with health and fertility. Only fertile women have low waist-to-hip ratios. Prepubescent girls and postmenopausal women have waist-to-hip ratios similar to men. Moreover, in the ancestral environment, the hour-glass figure could only be maintained by females with surplus fat – that is, healthy females who were fit enough to gather or compete for food. Sickly or weak women would not be able to sustain large breasts and buttocks. They would also very likely be infertile. In addition, women with broad hips are – on average – better equipped for childbirth, and therefore more likely to facilitate the safe transmission of genes into the next generation.

The hour-glass figure has been associated with beauty in many different cultures and at many different times. Eleventh-century Indian sculptors depicted Hindu goddesses (such as Parvati) with waist-to-hip ratios of 0.3. Their sexy figures are so exaggerated, they have an almost cartoon-like quality. Curiously, we see much the same effect in computer-generated representations of heroines in games and animation vehicles. Low waist-to-hip ratios were achieved in the nineteenth century with corsets and bustle skirts – and tightly corded basques are still de rigueur among the centrefolds in the 'soft porn' industry. Even some dolls – think of Barbie – have a low waist-to-hip ratio.

Since publication, Singh's findings have attracted considerable interest and have provoked a fair amount of controversy. Psychologist Martin Tovee and colleagues, for example, claim that female attractiveness is more closely associated with the body mass index (BMI) than the waist-to-hip ratio. The body mass index is calculated by dividing weight (in kilograms) by height (in metres) squared. Individuals who have BMIs in the range of 20–25 are generally considered to have a healthy weight for their height. BMIs of less than 20, or over 30, are associated with health problems that can affect fertility or produce complications during labour. Thus, although Tovee and colleagues have challenged Singh's specific hypothesis, they still interpret their results within an evolutionary framework: female beauty can be understood in terms of an optimal BMI, which signifies fitness and promises reproductive success.

Tovee's research group have also investigated the physical parameters which determine beauty in the male body. Indeed, so precise was their investigation that in 1999 they were able to publish the following formula in the *Lancet*:

$$y = 2.776 \, x_1 \, 0.0607 \, x_2 \, 13.007 \, x_3 \, 16.796$$

The term y predicts attractiveness, where x_1, x_2 and x_3 are BMI, BMI squared, and waist-to-chest ratio (a measure of upper body shape) respectively.

Essentially, what this formula means, is that women find attractive men who possess 'inverted triangle' torsos (a narrow waist combined with broad chest and shoulders). Again, we can see the influence of evolutionary pressures. The inverted triangle shape in men is strongly associated with muscle development and physical strength. Needless to say, in the ancestral environment a male with these characteristics would be very desirable. His physique would not only suggest health, but the ability to defend against predation, ascend the social hierarchy, and provide for his mate and family.

Beauty has always been viewed as something mysterious, intangible, a semi-divine property not amenable to scientific investigation. Yet, the mathematical rules that determine beauty are gradually being understood. It may be that eventually we will be able to capture the essence of beauty in an algorithm (much the same way as physicists capture universal truths in elegant equations) – and perhaps such an algorithm could be the basis of a computer-generated image that would represent the ultimate face or body. We would then have created an image of absolute beauty – a contemporary Helen of Troy, as potent as myth. She will look out at us from cyberspace and hearts will break.

It has already been suggested that computer-generated characters – free from biological limits – develop physical features that reflect an evolutionary sub-text. The best example of this is Lara Croft, heroine of the computer game *Tombraider*. The fact that she has become a pin-up demonstrates the power of evolutionary signals. They can penetrate into the deepest regions of the brain, and trigger the neurochemistry of love. Lara Croft's impossible figure, with its astonishingly low waist-to-hip ratio, completely short-circuits rationality. Intelligent young men desire her, even though she is, in essence, a cartoon. Her large eyes, full lips, wasp-like waist, and perfect symmetry are supernormal sign stimuli. They operate beyond reason, possessed as they are with a raw power that has been fermenting for several billion years – that is, for as long as organisms have been reproducing sexually.

The drift towards supernormal sign stimuli is most evident in characters like Lara Croft, but the trend has been with us for many years. Women with impossibly long legs, for example, have been a mainstay in hosiery adverts for decades. By exploiting light, perspective, or simply tampering with the photographic image, it is possible to exaggerate desirable features, creating an appearance which is never encountered in the real world.

Computer technology adds a further dimension, insofar as previously static images can now move. Fictional characters blur the boundary that separates dream from reality. We are reminded of the ancient Greek legend of Pygmalion – sculptor and King of Cyprus – who made his statue of Galatea so beautiful, he could not resist falling in love with her. He begged Aphrodite to have mercy on his predicament, and the goddess intervened by bringing the statue to life. We too possess Aphrodite's magic. We too can make Galatea walk.

Sexual selection is the process which leads to the exaggeration of preferred characteristics – the best-known example being the peacock's tail discussed earlier. Needless to say, the timescale over which sexual selection modifies physiology can be calculated in hundreds of thousands, or even millions, of years. Modern technology allows us to observe selection pressures operating over a timescale of months, or even weeks. Thus, in the virtual environments of the pop video and computer game, evolutionary processes are accelerated. Eyes become larger and legs longer at the touch of a button. We have created images of beauty that have out-paced sexual selection. When you see the morphed body of a pop diva, or the perfect symmetry of Lara Croft, you are seeing the future. You are seeing where evolution will get to – given time.

But can we wait? Western society demands instant gratification – and we have the technology to realise our evolutionary dreams.

Formerly, only those who were disfigured consulted a cosmetic surgeon. Now, even the beautiful will have cosmetic surgery to enhance their big eyes, full lips or generous cleavage. Having created hallucinatory images of beauty that act as supernormal sign stimuli, we are now reproducing them in reality. The most beautiful people in the world no longer measure themselves against competition in the normal population, or even their peer group, but the semi-fantastic physiognomies of our evolutionary future.

In the ancestral environment, men and women lived in relatively small groups. Therefore, the chance of encountering a person of exceptional beauty was very low. Moreover, pre-eminence was achieved by being judged as beautiful relative to other members of the local tribe – a few hundred at most. Today, we are surrounded by images of exceptional beauty. It has been demonstrated that men express greater levels of dissatisfaction with their partners after being shown images of beautiful women. By saturating the media with images of exceptional beauty, we are cultivating a culture of dissatisfaction and disappointment.

If exceptional beauty can provoke love, then the whole of society is – to a greater or lesser extent – lovesick. Every time we see supernormal beauty, our emotional 'horizontal hold' slips a little and we descend a few frames into melancholy. We have become an unrequited society, permanently yearning for the unattainable. In a curious cultural re-creation of courtly mysticism, idealised beauty torments us – not from heaven, but from every glossy magazine, roadside hoarding and television screen.

Evolutionary theory explains why we value beauty so highly; however, the explanation evolutionary theory offers is troubled by a fundamental contradiction. Evolutionary pressures have shaped us in order to optimise reproductive success, but these same pressures – by selecting for a refined beauty sense – might actually reduce the number of pair-bonds that could potentially be achieved in a given population. Put more simply, we could become too choosy for our own good.

Exacting aesthetic standards must, by their very nature, limit opportunities for reproduction. An individual who will only mate with an outstandingly beautiful partner will have more difficulty reproducing than someone who is less fussy. A corollary of this is that if a sufficient number of individuals chose to be celibate, rather than mate with an imperfect partner, then the species would very probably become extinct. Clearly, this has not happened and there is little evidence to suggest that such an outcome is even a remote possibility.

Human beings have a highly refined beauty sense, but, at the same time, this doesn't stop them from mating with imperfect partners. Indeed, if anything, the mating behaviour of humans has a distinct tendency to pull in the opposite direction. Imperfections are frequently overlooked, and lovers are almost invariably generous with compliments. This strongly suggests the operation of some other principle or mechanism.

As Hume observed, although it is more common for beauty to trigger sexual desire and amity, the opposite is also possible. When a man desires a woman, or enjoys a woman's company, he typically 'fancies her more beautiful than ordinary'. Implicit in Hume's analysis is a circular relationship between the parts of love – a circular relationship that is guaranteed to increase love's intensity. Desire will encourage amity, which in turn will lead to a more favourable judgement of beauty, which in turn will heighten desire, and so on. Each revolution produces an escalation of 'amorous passion', and the beloved appears more and more beautiful.

Evolution may have endowed us with a highly refined beauty sense, but it has also endowed us with a Humean mechanism that transforms the appearance of those we love. Thus, although we are instinctively attracted to the most beautiful people in our environment, we are never in any real danger of choosing celibacy in lieu of perfection.

Robert Burton, in one of the quirkiest passages of *The Anatomy of Melancholy*, reflected at length on love's power to affect aesthetic judgements. 'Every lover,' says Burton, 'admires his mistress, though she be very deformed of herself, ill-favoured, wrinkled, pimpled, pale, red, yellow.' He then continues his list, adding numerous unsightly physical attributes:

> goggle-eyed, blear-eyed, or with staring eyes, she looks like a squis'd cat . . . sparrow-mouthed, Persian hook-nosed, have a sharp fox-nose, a red nose, China flat.

And simply cannot stop:

> a nose like a promontory, gubber-tushed, rotten teeth . . . a witch's beard, her breath stink all over the room . . . a vast virago, or an ugly tit, a slug, a fat fustilugs . . . whom thou couldst not fancy for a world, but hatest, loathest, and wouldst have spit in her face, or blow thy nose in her bosom.

Towards the end of his litany, Burton has worked himself into a frenzy – 'a slut, a scold, a rank, rammy, filthy, beastly quean, dishonest peradventure' – but having exhausted himself, and all possible permutations of insult, he notes that:

> for all this . . . he [the lover] takes no notice of any such errors or imperfections of body or mind . . . he had rather have her than any woman in the world.

Although other students of love sickness had observed that love is blind, before Burton no one had described the consequences with such relish.

Like the fabled philosopher's stone, love can work a transformative miracle, albeit a subjective one. But a subjective miracle is all that Darwinian principles require. As long as we think that our partner is beautiful, this will be sufficient to achieve evolutionary objectives. The pair-bond will be sustained and vulnerable progeny will be raised safely.

In the nineteenth century, the writer Stendhal proposed a theory of love after being rejected by Mathilde Dembowski, a 28-year-old Milanese woman. Stendhal's theory was published as *De l'Amour* (*On Love*) in 1822, and represents one of the first 'modern' attempts to understand the psychology of love. It can be regarded as modern because it gives a central role to perceptual distortion – a phenomenon that only received proper academic consideration in the twentieth century.

Stendhal's account of love's progress is complex, including seven separate stages. However, the most important of these are two stages of 'crystallisation' – a term which possessed a special, technical meaning for Stendhal. He uses it to mean something close to adoration or idealisation, and chose the word because his thinking was influenced by knowledge of a simple natural phenomenon:

> Leave a lover with his thoughts for twenty-four hours, and this is what will happen:
>
> At the salt mines of Salzburg, they throw a leafless wintry bough into one of the abandoned workings. Two or three months later they haul it out covered with a shining deposit of crystals. The smallest twig, no bigger than a tom-tit's claw, is studded with a galaxy of scintillating diamonds. The original branch is no longer recognizable.

> What I have called crystallization is a mental process which draws from everything that happens new proofs of the perfection of the loved one.

Thus, crystallisation describes a psychological process – largely imaginative – that can transform an ordinary human being into an object of profound, even transcendent, beauty. Stendhal identified three separate but interrelated features of crystallisation: the perfect image of the beloved, the imagined rapture of being loved by a perfect being, and fear of rejection. Thus, idealisation cannot occur in the absence of anxiety.

Stendhal stressed, repeatedly, how love influences perception moreover, these new perceptions cannot be corrected by reason: 'From the moment he falls in love even the wisest man no longer sees anything *as it really is*.' This is exactly the position shared by many psychoanalysts, who believe that idealisation is achieved by defence mechanisms that distort reality. A straightforward example of this is 'projection'. The strong desire to possess a perfect partner might lead an individual to project desirable characteristics on to the 'blank screen' of a suitable candidate. However, the result is a form of narcissism – a playing-out of egocentric fantasies that will very probably prove emotionally unsatisfying. The beloved becomes something closer to a self-induced hallucination than a living, breathing person. Ultimately, reality will reassert itself, the idealised image will evaporate, and the disappointed lover will claim that his or her beloved has changed.

Another psychoanalytic idea relevant to the phenomenon of projective idealisation is Jung's notion of the archetypes. An archetype is a kind of organising principle or template in the unconscious, influencing how we think and feel. Among the archetypes, Jung identified the *anima* (in men) and the *animus* (in women). The *anima* influences the expression of female characteristics in men, and the *animus* influences the expression of male characteristics in women. However, the *anima* and *animus* can also influence how men and women perceive each other. The *anima* and *animus* have a tendency to assume idealised forms that appear in the mythology and art of all civilisations, such as earth mother or warrior.

Jung believed that he fell in love with his wife, Emma, under the influence of archetypal forces. At the age of twenty-one, he called at the house of the Rauschbach family. There, he saw a pretty girl of fourteen, standing at the top of a staircase. They said nothing to each other. Yet, Jung immediately turned to his companion and said, with absolute certainty, that this girl was his future wife. His companion laughed, but seven years later, Jung and Emma Rauschbach were married.

Reflecting on his experience of love at first sight, Jung said:

> The archetype is a force. It has an autonomy and it can suddenly seize you . . . You see, you have a certain image in yourself without knowing it, of woman, of *the* woman. You see that girl, or at least a good imitation of your type and instantly you get a seizure and you are gone.

Sadly, Emma Rauschbach suffered the fate of most idealised women. The idealisation faded, and Jung became an incorrigible flirt and womaniser.

Evolutionary theory agrees with psychoanalysis concerning the fragility of idealised beauty. The illusion does not have to be a strong one because it is not needed for very long. Once love's madness has run its course – and the safety of genes is secured in the next generation – perceptual distortions are corrected. For many, the experience of love ending is something of a rude awakening – a fact mischievously recognised by John Barrymore, who once defined love as 'the delightful interval between meeting a beautiful girl and discovering that she looks like a haddock'.

6

Obsession

'Only You'
Song title, The Platters

Obsession.

The word frequently stands alone, its singularity emphasising characteristics such as intensity and fixed interest. We are accustomed to seeing it on perfume bottles, CDs and dust jackets, usually in a stark script against a dark background. Obsession is never comfortable. It is always disconcerting – tinged, however slightly, with the chroma of psychopathology. On a film poster 'a tale of obsession' promises something strange, even sinister. We are invited to enter a mental universe that has collapsed around its core, a mind that has closed in on itself.

The symptoms of love are many and varied, but it has been argued that obsession is the most fundamental – the primary psychological disturbance from which all other disturbances follow. Originally, this view was espoused by early medical giants such as Galen and Ibn Sina, who believed that the humoral imbalances associated with love sickness were precipitated by preoccupation with the beloved. To some extent, this is still a legitimate view. Thoughts and images of the beloved almost invariably precede (and maintain) extreme emotional states such as melancholy and rapture. Similarly, obsession seems to be the primary cause of several 'physical' symptoms: insomnia and restlessness are almost invariably associated with obsessional thinking.

Obsession produces a psychiatric domino effect – the serial collapse of circuit panels in the brain. Once obsessional preoccupation has been triggered, new complications are introduced, one after another.

The etymological root of the word 'obsession' is the Latin *obsidere*, which means 'to besiege'. It reflects a fundamental feature of obsessional experience – feeling trapped. This is very much apparent in the literature of love, which often employs metaphors of entrapment and incarceration. People are made 'slaves' to love or become love's 'prisoner', hearts are 'captured' and 'held hostage'. Obsessional thoughts are so powerful, the individual feels robbed of personal freedom. He or she is no longer at liberty to exercise basic choices – even the most basic choice of all: what to think about. It is easy to see why many medieval scholars concluded that obsessional thinking was a symptom of possession.

The darker implications of the word 'obsession' are part of a legacy that can be traced – in the West – back to the fifteenth century, an age when psychopathology and demonology were much the same thing. Supernatural accounts of mental illness have always existed (doctors and priests are traditional enemies – vying with each other for the same clientele), but in the medieval world, the Church had begun to assert its authority. Obsessional phenomena were of particular interest to it, because they seemed to lend themselves so readily to a supernatural interpretation (as late as the seventeenth century, obsession was still being confused with possession). Under the watchful eye of a suspicious and pious clergy, ardent lovers – with their predilection for excess – were in a precarious position. Historical records suggest that of the many individuals who were identified as being possessed, a sizeable number were very probably just in love.

Supernatural accounts of mental illness became particularly influential during the late middle ages. Although demons were understood to be the principal culprits, they were always assumed to be in the service of witches. Thus, the cause of mental illness was deemed to be maleficium – witches' malice (a view that almost certainly reflects institutionalised misogyny in the Church). As soon as this idea gained general acceptance, it provided an excellent excuse for the cruel persecution of women across Europe. Witch-hunts may have accounted for up to 200,000 deaths by execution (particularly by burning).

Much of the blame for these atrocities must be apportioned to (the inappropriately named) Pope Innocent VIII. It was he who instructed his envoys, the Dominicans James Sprenger and Heinrich Kramer, to research and write an inquisitors' manual, the infamous *Malleus Maleficarum* (or *Witches' Hammer*) of 1486. Although the *Malleus Maleficarum* was primarily a tool for inquisitors, it is now of medical interest, insofar as the 'signs' which Sprenger and Kramer ascribe to maleficium are also widely recognised as the symptoms of mental illness. Thus, to medical historians, the *Malleus Maleficarum* can also be read as a mental-health census. Among the various infirmities of the mind that Sprenger and Kramer describe, such as 'obsession and frenzy', can be found references to 'philocaption' – inordinate or excessive love.

Sprenger and Kramer suggest that philocaption has three separate causes, one natural and two supernatural. The natural cause is 'lack of control of the eyes' (by which they really mean sexual interest). The supernatural causes are the 'temptation of devils' and 'the spells of necromancers and witches'.

It is clear from their description that philocaption was an 'obsessional' illness. They present case studies of besotted lovers, some of whom became fixated on total strangers. In this respect, philocaption bore a striking resemblance to love at first sight. It also had a compulsive element, because afflicted individuals often felt an irresistible urge to follow those with whom they had fallen in love.

Obviously, Sprenger and Kramer are more preoccupied with the supernatural rather than natural causes of philocaption, and warn the reader of witches who: 'can infect the minds of men with an inordinate love of strange women, and so inflame their hearts that by no shame or punishment, by no words or actions can they be forced to desist from such love'. It is interesting that even when discussing the supernatural causes of philocaption, they cannot avoid using medical language: witches 'infect' rather than influence the minds of men.

Sprenger and Kramer's 'treatment' advice suggests that obsessional love has always been regarded as a thorny problem. When caused by supernatural agencies, philocaption required special procedures, above and beyond exorcism (which alone was not considered a strong enough remedy). They recommend that the afflicted individual should invoke his guardian angel on a daily basis, confess, and visit the shrines of the saints (especially the Blessed Virgin). Without employing these additional steps, the prognosis was poor.

Obsessional love is so intense, so unnerving, it commands the respect of inquisitors.

The term 'obsession' was not claimed as a formal medical term until 1799; and since then, doctors have had considerable difficulty establishing the parameters of obsessional psychopathology. Thus, over the last two hundred years, obsessional illness has appeared in many diagnostic guises, such as monomania, psychasthenia, fixed ideas and forced deliberations, to name but a few. The picture is complicated even further because obsessional thinking often appears in patients whose primary diagnosis is not 'obsessional' – for instance, individuals with depression frequently ruminate on a specific theme to the exclusion of everything else. Given the ubiquity of obsessional thinking, psychiatrists frequently employ the term obsession in much the same way as the layman: that is, to describe a kind of thinking (associated with everything from stamp-collecting to fanaticism) characterised by a single or specific preoccupation.

In contemporary diagnostic systems, obsessional thinking (and compulsive behaviour) are most closely associated with the diagnosis of Obsessive Compulsive Disorder (OCD). Typically, the affected individual experiences recurrent thoughts, images or impulses which engender a state of anxiety (or discomfort). The individual then tries to reduce anxiety levels by engaging in certain behaviours which are usually accompanied by a sense of compulsion. The best-known examples of this are washing and checking. In the former, the individual is preoccupied by thoughts of contamination, and reduces anxiety by frequent hand-washing, while in the latter the individual is preoccupied by doubts about past actions (such as closing a front door) and reduces anxiety by returning to check, often several times. In addition, OCD can be associated with a range of other problems which include: insistence on order or symmetry (lining up possessions), hoarding (being unable to throw away worthless objects), and superstitious thinking (for example, overestimating the significance of lucky or unlucky numbers). Once compulsive behaviours are established, they usually become ritualistic – they must be performed in a certain way or to a certain arbitrary standard in order to produce a reduction in anxiety. Failure to meet these arbitrary criteria (which are often very involved) will necessitate further repetition. Rituals are not always observable. They might be performed internally, in the form of, say, working through a series of lucky numbers or images.

Some patients with OCD also experience unwanted, intrusive thoughts and images, which usually dramatise hypothetical events wholly repugnant to the sufferer. For example, an extremely humane individual might be tormented by mental images of causing physical harm to others. Attempts to banish such images by suppressing them usually only succeed in increasing their frequency.

A sub-group of patients with OCD are sometimes described as 'pure obsessionals', 'ruminators', or individuals with 'morbid preoccupations'. They complain of unpleasant thoughts and extreme worry, all of which concern a single theme such as the inevitability of death.

To what extent, then, do correspondences exist between OCD and obsession in the context of love?

The most obvious similarity is that patients with OCD and people who have fallen in love seem unable to govern the contents of their own minds. Thoughts and images that enter awareness cannot be dismissed. Although for lovers this experience is at first enjoyable, it soon becomes problematic. Patients with OCD often find it difficult to engage in everyday tasks as they are always being distracted by internal 'activity', which can prove very disabling. The same is true of lovers.

In Gabriel García Márquez's exquisite novel of romance and old age, *Love in the Time of Cholera*, we are warned that once obsession takes hold of a mind, it may do so in perpetuity:

Fiorentino Ariza, on the other hand, had not stopped thinking about her for a single moment since Fermina Daza had rejected him out of hand after a long and troubled love affair fifty-one years, nine months, and four days ago. He did not have to keep a running tally, drawing a line for each day on the walls of his cell, because not a day passed that something did not happen to remind him of her.

The pitiful state of Márquez's fictional hero is complemented by real case studies. In *Love's Executioner*, the psychoanalyst Irvin Yallom describes the case of Thelma, a seventy-year-old woman who, after having had a twenty-seven-day affair with a younger man, became completely obsessed with him. Long after the relationship had ended, the obsession persisted in the absence of any contact or encouragement. In an early psychotherapy session she confessed:

> For eight years I haven't stopped thinking about him. At seven in the morning I wonder if he's awake yet, and at eight I imagine him eating his oatmeal (he loves oatmeal – he grew up on a Nebraska farm). I keep looking for him when I walk down the street. I often mistakenly think I see him, and rush up to greet some stranger. I dream about him. I replay in my mind each of our meetings together during those twenty-seven days. In fact, most of my life goes on in these dreams – I scarcely note what's happening in the present. My life is being lived eight years ago.

Although the act of obsessing is the principal common territory shared by lovers and patients with OCD, there are many more similarities.

Before going on dates, lovers often engage in extensive washing and cleaning rituals. In order to prepare, they will pay close attention to personal hygiene, spending as much time in the bathroom as many patients with contamination fears. Lovers often feel a strong compulsion to re-establish contact with their partner when separated. This can be quite overwhelming, crushing their resolve to 'play it cool'. Compulsions of this nature usually reduce anxiety and discomfort, but, as with clinical compulsions, such relief is relatively short-lived. The compulsion swiftly returns, often with greater intensity. Lovers ruminate, worrying excessively about the relationship not 'working out'. Moreover, anxieties might be made worse by the occurrence of disturbing intrusive thoughts and images, which typically relate to infidelity or the beloved's sexual history.

Lovers are highly superstitious. They routinely invest chance experiences with special significance. A song played in the background on a first date becomes 'our song' – a totem of love, able to draw a couple together when things are not going so well. Lovers have special restaurants, special tables and special wines, rituals that must be repeated on special days. They hoard valueless items – a champagne cork, a cigarette lighter, an old T-shirt. The idea of throwing such tokens of love away seems almost sacrilegious – a betrayal. Anyone who has ever been in love will have the equivalent of at least one shoebox in the attic in which the remains of a love hoard can be discovered. In *The Sorrows of Young Werther*, the eponymous hero describes a curious and unique attachment to an article of clothing:

> It cost me a wrench but in the end I decided not to wear the simple blue frock-coat I had on when I first danced with Lotte any more; it had become quite unpresentable. Still, I have had a new one made, exactly like the other, down to the collar and lapels, and the very same buff waistcoat and breeches as well.
>
> But it does not feel quite right. I do not know – I suppose in time I shall grow to like it better.

Goethe (through the person of Werther) clearly recognised how difficult it is for lovers to part with things associated with love. It is almost as though these tokens of association are perceived as a physical extension of the beloved – their possession provides a point of contact even in the beloved's absence.

One of the most bizarre features of OCD, closely associated with superstitious thinking, is a phenomenon known as thought-action-fusion. The term is used by psychologists and psychiatrists to denote a belief in the equivalence of thought and action: a belief that mental events can influence events in the real world. Typically, a patient with OCD will experience an unwanted thought about harm coming to a friend or relative, and then worry that the mere occurrence of such a thought will increase the likelihood of the 'bad thing' happening. The subsequent anxiety state is then reduced by the performance of a reparative ritual such as touching wood three times.

Lovers often experience something very similar to thought-action-fusion, usually in the form of intense wishes. In the very early stages of a relationship, a lover might try to make a chance encounter happen by simply thinking about it. Instead of having the thought 'I hope she's at the bus stop today', the lover might say to himself 'Be there, be there, be there.' Such phrases are often repeated, suggesting an underlying belief that continued effort is correlated with influence.

Almost all individuals suffering from OCD complain of excessive doubting. Indeed, so prevalent is doubting among OCD sufferers that nineteenth-century French psychiatrists knew it as *la manie du doute* (the doubting madness). OCD patients will doubt virtually everything: whether or not they are sufficiently clean, whether or not they have turned off an electrical appliance, whether or not their memories are reliable, whether or not they can trust their senses, and whether or not a ritual will be effective as a means of warding off danger.

Generalised doubting is also very much a feature of love – something acknowledged by Stendhal, who proposed 'doubt' as the sixth phase of his seven-stage theory of love. Like obsessional patients, lovers are always asking themselves questions: 'Do I look OK?', 'Should I have said that?', 'What did he mean?', 'Am I rushing things?', 'Should I text her?', 'Does he know how I feel?' Lovers – particularly insecure lovers – are often engaged in a continual process of self-interrogation.

The link between OCD and love is supported by some fascinating biochemical research undertaken by Italian psychiatrist Donatella Marazziti. When Marazziti began her investigations in the late 1990s, it had been known for some time that obsessional illness was linked to low levels of the neurotransmitter serotonin. Subsequently, Marazziti designed a study to establish if low levels of serotonin were also evident in individuals who professed to be in love.

Blood samples were taken from three groups: individuals claiming to have recently fallen in love, individuals suffering from an obsessional illness, and finally, individuals who were neither in love nor suffering from a psychiatric condition. The third, or normal, group showed the usual levels of serotonin; however, both the 'obsessional' and 'in-love' groups showed serotonin levels that had dropped by approximately 40 per cent.

One year later Marazziti re-examined a sub-set of the in-love group. Their serotonin levels had risen again to normal levels; however, when questioned about their relationships, it was discovered that more gentle feelings had replaced the fevered emotional state that characterised the first few months of being in love. Thus, it would seem that a return to normal levels of serotonin marks the beginnings of the transition from passionate to a more companionate form of love.

Because there are so many similarities between OCD and falling in love, it is tempting to suggest that the relationship is more than just coincidental. In Chapter 3, it was suggested that love might have obsessional properties for evolutionary reasons. An exclusive and persistent preoccupation with a chosen mate would certainly facilitate the formation of a successful pair-bond – that is, a pair-bond of sufficient strength to ensure that procreation takes place and that progeny enjoy the benefits of joint parental care. However, perhaps other obsessional phenomena are also of evolutionary significance. Perhaps they too once had a role to play with respect to reproductive success.

It is generally accepted that the principal manifestations of OCD represent behaviour patterns that may once have had survival value – for instance, early hominids who washed or groomed, and frequently checked their environment for danger, would have been less vulnerable to disease and predation – but in the ancestral environment, washing and checking were not only relevant with respect to survival, they were also relevant with respect to sexual reproduction. Parasitic infection was rife, and many of these infections were potentially disfiguring. In Chapter 5, it was suggested that symmetrical bodies and faces are perceived as more beautiful, because they advertise healthy genes (the kind of genes that could provide offspring with an effective immune system). However, the fastidiously clean would also be in a position to advertise good health. They too would be less vulnerable to parasitic infection, and they too would be able to advertise their advantage with physical symmetries. Of course, these two traits are not mutually exclusive. Presumably, those who possessed genes for a good immune system, as well as genes for fastidious cleanliness, benefited the most, attracting either more or healthier mates, and thus achieving maximum reproductive success.

A corollary of the above is that another obsessional symptom – sensitivity to symmetry – might also carry an evolutionary advantage. In a relatively healthy community, asymmetries might be quite subtle, and so only the most discerning individuals would be able to maximise their reproductive success by selecting the very healthiest mates from a closely matched peer group. This framework offers an explanation for the evolutionary origins of an intriguing psychiatric condition known as Body Dysmorphic Disorder.

Body Dysmorphic Disorder (BDD) is often described as an OCD-spectrum disorder, and may ultimately prove to be a variant of OCD. BDD patients have obsessions and compulsions, but their obsessions are typically concerned with an imagined or slight physical defect, and their compulsions tend to take the form of close and systematic self-examination. Patients with BDD are particularly sensitive to asymmetries. Indeed, they frequently complain of physical problems such as having one ear higher than the other or having a 'crooked' nose. These abnormalities are usually so subtle, they are often invisible to the examining doctor. Nevertheless, they are real (even if a magnifying glass is required to detect them). Presumably, the evolutionary 'fitness detector' in BDD patients is over-sensitive. BDD patients see themselves as unattractive (that is, unfit) and are subsequently prone to develop depression and problems with self-esteem. There is some evidence to suggest that BDD patients apply their exacting aesthetic standards not only to themselves, but to others and the world in general. Recent research conducted by British psychiatrist David Veale and colleagues shows that a high proportion of patients with BDD have either had an education in art and design, or work in that field.

Checking also has a role in ensuring reproductive success. From an evolutionary point of view, jealousy can be regarded as an adaptive emotion. It is a safeguard against the costs of infidelity. Ancestral males who did not 'check up' on their mates were easily cuckolded, and subsequently failed to transfer their genes into the next generation. Jealous males, however, would have been more confident concerning paternity, having 'checked up' more often. Intense suspicion, in both men and women, is almost always associated with excessive checking.

Finally, hoarding might also be an obsessional characteristic related to reproductive success. In its original form, hoarding might have been closer to 'nesting' or 'home-making'. Clearly, a disposition to collect and keep materials that could later be used to provide offspring with a warm, comfortable environment has obvious advantages with respect to their survival.

Obsessional traits were probably highly adaptive in the ancestral environment, particularly with respect to successful courtship and the maintenance of a secure pair-bond. When we fall in love, we obsess, wash, groom, self-inspect, check up, and begin to collect together a love hoard. We begin to exhibit symptoms that have much in common with OCD, yet, these symptoms may represent the activation of ancient behaviour patterns that served our ancestors well. It may be that the rituals of the lover and the rituals of the patient with OCD share not only the same characteristics, but the very same origin. When we stand in front of the bathroom mirror, before embarking on a first date – washing, scrubbing, plucking and scenting – we are, in fact, merely repeating a procedure that formerly involved the removal of crab lice and dust. In matters of love, we never stray very far from the plains of Africa.

* * *

Of the many compulsions associated with obsession, the compulsion to follow is perhaps the most strong. It is as though the image of the loved one, permanently suspended in the medium of awareness, proves too tantalising. It becomes a lure, a tease, irresistible bait. Even in absolute silence, an obsessed lover can still hear a siren call.

It would seem that obsession is never satisfied by imaginary union. Fantasies, however idyllic, tend to be experienced as tormenting; they merely emphasise geographical distance. Thus the obsessional lover is forced to seek out the 'real thing', the real beloved, the original physical form from which all fantasy images have been copied. In a curious way, obsession turns Platonic idealism on its head. The desired form is ultimately physical, not spiritual. In the mind of an obsessional, perfect beauty is located in the material world. Love is consummated not on some numinous plane, but on earth, where we can touch, and feel the beat of another's heart.

The desire to be with the loved one – to breathe the same air, to be warmed by the same sunlight – seems to override reason completely. The obsessional lover will frequently visit places where he or she might meet the beloved. Even when the chances of such a meeting are extremely small, the effort still feels justified. Sometimes, merely standing on a pavement, or walking along a road where the loved one had recently been, will suffice as a means of securing some sense of physical connection. Lovers are capable of travelling miles, to touch a tree or statue, if it was once anointed by the beloved's fingertips.

Dickens's eponymous hero David Copperfield, desperate for a glimpse of Dora: 'walked miles upon miles daily in the hope of seeing her . . . I walked about the streets where the best shops for ladies were. I haunted the Bazaar like an unquiet spirit, I fagged through the park again and again, long after I was quite knocked up.'

Shadowing the beloved is a perilous business. Among love's excesses, it is the one behaviour most likely to frighten or cause offence. Although for the lover, following is an act of devotion, for the object of affection, it can easily be construed as an unwelcome invasion of privacy, or even molestation – a fact that the besotted Stendhal ignored in 1819, with disastrous consequences.

His unrequited relationship with Mathilde Dembowski was always strained, but he succeeded in making matters considerably worse by following her to Volterra, where her two young sons were being educated. Stendhal, showing a spectacular lack of judgement, had disguised himself in an overcoat and dark-green glasses. While in view, he made a spontaneous and rash decision to remove his disguise, and was immediately recognised. Needless to say, he had no ready justification for his presence, and in perhaps one of the most misconceived attempts to avoid an uncomfortable confrontation ever, he pretended not to know Mathilde. Their exchange must have advanced the frontiers of embarrassment into uncharted regions.

The following day, Stendhal was unfortunate enough to run into Mathilde again. He swore that this time, their meeting had been a coincidence, but the circumstances were clearly suspicious. They had met on Mathilde's favourite meadow walk, which suggests that Stendhal had been observing her from afar and was well acquainted with her routine. Understandably, Mathilde was unimpressed, and reprimanded him severely.

Compulsive following was one of the cardinal symptoms of love sickness, as described by classical and Islamic doctors. Although the diagnosis of love sickness eventually lost medical currency, compulsive following actually survived the collapse of the humoral model, and continues to be a presence in contemporary diagnostic systems. Obsessional love, combined with compulsive following, is now described as erotomania or de Clérambault's syndrome.

The term erotomania was originally coined by Hippocrates, but other ancient authors, such as Plutarch (the first-century Greek biographer) and a Roman physician called Soranus, also refer to the condition. As we have already discovered, in the fifteenth century Sprenger and Kramer described an association between obsessional love and following, and in 1640, Jacques Ferrand wrote the first major work on the subject: *Erotomania or a Treatise, Discussing The Essence, Causes, Symptoms, Prognostiks and Cure of Lover or Erotique Melancholy*. During the nineteenth and early twentieth centuries, terms such as monomania and paranoia erotica were also employed to describe similar, if not identical, phenomena.

Unfortunately, the term erotomania appeared in medical texts for several thousand years without a precise definition, and early descriptions might reflect disorders of sexual appetite (for example, nymphomania), rather than the psychopathology of love. Problems of definition were rectified, however, after the publication in 1942 of G.G. de Clérambault's seminal work *Les psychoses passionnelles*, in which emphasis was decisively shifted away from the sexual arena. De Clérambault described five cases of erotomania in some detail (and referred to one other). In doing so, he established the emotional and behavioural parameters of the syndrome that eventually took his name.

The central feature of de Clérambault's syndrome is a delusion of love. The affected individual believes that another party, with whom they have had little or no contact, is in love with them. De Clérambault introduced two technical terms – subject and object – to describe the deluded individual and the other party concerned. This convention will be adopted here for ease of expression.

The subject is usually (but by no means always) a female, and the object tends to occupy a more elevated or respected social position. Indeed, the object might even be a public figure or celebrity of some kind. The subject almost always believes that it was the object who first fell in love, and the object who first declared love; however, the nature of this declaration might be too subtle for others to detect, or take the form of coded messages which only the subject can understand.

When subject and object know each other, the subject will usually invest too much meaning in the object's everyday behaviour – thus a simple courtesy might be viewed as 'special treatment'. When subject and object are not known to each other – for example, if the object is a celebrity – the subject is more likely to identify coded messages in the media. An innocuous newspaper photograph of the object will seem, to the subject, to be full of coded messages. For instance, the object will be wearing a particular tie-pin or brooch, to signify his or her continuing love for the subject. The process by which the subject learns of the object's intentions is not, of course, explicable by conventional means. Thus, the subject often assumes a pseudo-mystical connection with the object.

Once the subject has labelled the object's behaviour as amorous, he or she will reciprocate. If rejected, the subject will then generate reasons to explain (or excuse) the object's behaviour. Often, these explanations can become fiendishly complex, but ultimately they allow the subject to continue believing that the object is in love with them. This is an effective form of defence, rendering any rejection, however explicit or extreme, entirely impotent.

Apart from the core delusion of love, de Clérambault patients function normally in every other respect. They do not exhibit more severe signs of mental illness such as hallucinations, nor is it usual for them to suffer from other delusions. The onset of de Clérambault's syndrome is sudden, and once established, the course of the illness may be chronic.

Of de Clérambault's original case studies, his most celebrated patient was a 53-year-old designer and dressmaker in France, who believed that King George V was in love with her. She had sustained this belief for ten years, and became convinced that sailors and tourists were his emissaries, sent by the king to declare his love. Eventually, her obsession resulted in a compulsion to seek him out.

> She persistently pursued King George V from 1918 onwards, paying several visits to England. She frequently waited for him outside Buckingham Palace. She once saw a curtain move in one of the palace windows and interpreted this as a signal from the King. She claimed that all Londoners knew of his love for her, but alleged that he prevented her from finding lodgings in London, made her miss her hotel bookings, and was responsible for the loss of her baggage containing money and portraits of him. Such doubts as she had never persisted for long. She vividly summarized her passion for him. 'The King might hate me, but he can never forget. I could never be indifferent to him, nor he to me . . . It is in vain that he hurts me. He is the most distinguished of men . . . I was attracted to him from the depths of my heart. I wish to live under the same Heaven as he and in the midst of his subjects. If I have offended him I have suffered in my heart.'

In recent years, the term 'de Clérambault's syndrome' has been superseded again by 'erotomania'. However, as a result of de Clérambault's influence, the concept of erotomania itself has been transformed – being clearly understood now as a disturbance of emotional attachment rather than sexual desire.

Erotomania appears in DSM-IV as a sub-type of delusional disorder. Other sub-types include delusions of persecution (being cheated, spied on, or poisoned) and delusions of grandiosity (such as being an unrecognised genius). The essential feature of all sub-types of delusional disorder is the presence of a non-bizarre delusion which appears in the context of a relatively normal personality. Non-bizarre delusions are so called because they concern situations or events that can actually happen in real life, such as falling in love, being persecuted, or possessing a conspicuous talent. The content of bizarre delusions, on the other hand, typically reflects situations or events that do not happen in real life, such as being in telepathic communication with Martians.

Erotomania, as described in DSM-IV, shares many features with the syndrome described by de Clérambault – a delusional belief in the object's love, preoccupation with higher-status objects, general harassment (through telephone calls, letters, gifts, visits, surveillance) and 'stalking'. DSM-IV also respects the gender bias observed by de Clérambault, stating that erotomania is a predominantly female problem, although cases that come into conflict with the law tend to be male. Men are usually arrested on account of persistent following or because of misguided efforts to rescue the object from imagined danger. In the USA, women are four times more likely to be followed than men – and in the UK twice as likely.

In DSM-IV, the erotic features of erotomania have been de-emphasised: the authors unambiguously state that 'The delusion often concerns idealised romantic love and spiritual union rather than sexual attraction.' Thus, love – as experienced by the erotomaniac – has much in common with the transcendent forms of love described by Plato and Ibn Arabi. Indeed, erotomania seems to exemplify many of the basic tenets of romantic love: the fact that the subject chooses a high-status object encourages idealisation; the object, being unattainable, obviates sexual consummation and ennobles desire; and excessive demonstrations of affection (including acts of daring and rescue) correspond closely with courtly expectations – quests, bravery, and the defence of honour. The erotomaniac inhabits the culturally familiar world of knights, haughty queens, sublimated passion and spiritual aspirations. The erotomaniac straddles the boundary between literature and medicine, romance and psychiatry.

Psychoanalysts have suggested that the fundamental cause of erotomania is a fear of sexual union. The afflicted individual chooses an impossible lover – a lover completely beyond his or her social reach – which makes such a choice entirely safe. Sex is so unlikely, the erotomaniac is free to indulge in fantasies of romantic love without ever incurring the risk of genuine intimacy.

Erotomania and romanticism have also been linked together by psychoanalysts as forms of narcissism. It has already been suggested that many psychoanalysts construe romantic love as a narcissistic projection. The lover sees what he or she wants in the beloved, rather than a real person. Unconsciously, the erotomaniac might be performing a similar manoeuvre. Delusional conviction in another's love might be a form of excessive self-love simply attributed to an external source.

Erotomania and de Clérambault's syndrome are understood to be delusional disorders. As such, they represent relatively serious forms of psychiatric illness. However, the line that separates normal and abnormal mental states is often difficult to define. This is particularly true when delusions are classed as non-bizarre. Although contemporary psychiatry fosters the notion that beliefs can be neatly classified into normal and abnormal forms, the distinction is more readily accomplished in theory than practice. There seems to be a continuum linking the opposite poles of normal and abnormal behaviour, along which degrees of normality shade into degrees of abnormality. It is thus extremely difficult to establish and define points of transition.

When does the ordinary preoccupation of the lover for the beloved become obsessional? When do obsessions become delusions? At what point, exactly, do the culturally endorsed excesses of romance become psychopathology? It is extremely difficult to provide precise answers to such questions, so psychiatrists can only be fully confident of making a diagnosis in cases where abnormality is relatively obvious.

David Enoch and Hadrian Ball describe an extraordinary case of de Clérambault's syndrome in which the patient – a 33-year-old woman – became obsessed with the songwriter and former Beatle, Paul McCartney. The woman claimed that she had met McCartney at the age of eighteen, at which time she had requested his autograph. However, in typical de Clérambault fashion, she believed this incident to be of more significance to McCartney than herself. She alleged that McCartney had become obsessed with her, and had made various overtures. She reported, for example, that McCartney had instructed an artist to visit her house in order to procure a portrait.

The woman believed that she and McCartney had subsequently enjoyed a short-lived affair which lasted until she was nineteen. Thereafter, however, she reported that McCartney's presence in her life became a nuisance, and eventually an invasion. Enoch and Ball summarise the woman's account of these developments:

> Her feelings towards him then changed because he had plagued and dominated her life. She stated that he did this because he is obsessed with her and wishes to marry her. She believed that he follows her wherever she goes and if unable

to do this, he sends his entourage or 'puppets' instead. She claimed that on several occasions she had been abducted by him, that he takes her to a hotel, shows her photographs that he has of her and forces her to have intercourse. McCartney's private physician then gives her an injection of some substance that makes her forget the experiences.

Although this patient was entirely lucid, and apparently presented herself well, it is clear that her account strongly suggests the presence of severe psychiatric disturbance. Presumably, the events she described were either the result of hallucinatory episodes, or a profound dysregulation of normal mental processes resulting in the creation of false memories. The strong theme of persecution also suggests paranoia. A significant number of cases, however, are not so readily classified as abnormal. In the absence of a implausible narrative (or other florid symptoms) it is extremely difficult to establish whether the phenomena we associate with falling in love have strayed far enough along our theoretical continuum to qualify as bona fide examples of abnormality.

Consider, for example, love at first sight. Enoch and Ball provide the following quotation from a twenty-year-old female de Clérambault patient who fell in love with a superior at work:

> As soon as he spoke to me I felt I had known him all my life, and it frightened me . . . this was the man I was intended to love – from that moment to this I have never been the same.

Now, compare this with a description of a similar experience reported by a non-psychiatric respondent who participated in a study of love at first sight, conducted by Professor Earl Naumann.

My mother and I walked into the church, and he walked up to seat us. He looked at me and I looked at him, and a chill went through my body. I think I was actually trembling. When he seated us, he gave me this long look. My mother turned to me and asked if I saw the way he looked at me. I just gasped and said 'Oh mom!' and sort of slid down in the pew. It was like lightning had just struck. I was thinking that I wanted to live with him and be his wife. I could have walked up to the altar and married him right then. In that 30 seconds, from the time that we walked into the church until we were seated, I knew he was the man for me.

Clearly, both Enoch and Ball's de Clérambault patient, and Naumann's non-psychiatric respondent, shared an identical experience. Both were instantly sure that they had met someone with whom they could spend the rest of their lives. Moreover, Naumann's respondent seems to be exhibiting the classic de Clérambault symptom of seeing the 'look of love' in the object's eyes first, before reciprocating. In a psychiatric clinic, such phenomena are described as psychopathological, but outside the clinic, they are described as romantic.

In many ways, patients with erotomania fulfil all our expectations of what a romantic lover should be. They are indefatigable. They are not discouraged by social or cultural differences. Their love is transcendent, mystical and fated. They believe that true love will conquer any obstacle. Moreover, even the most disturbing features of erotomania correspond, to a greater or lesser extent, with the experience of 'normal love'. The average person may not have 'stalked', exactly, but when in love, most have engaged in behaviour on the same spectrum – such as making sure that one is in the right place at the right time to increase the likelihood of a supposedly 'accidental' meeting – and when rejected, it is not uncommon to distort reality as a psychological defence

– 'She's been under a lot of stress lately. I'm sure she loves me really. I'll get back to her again in a few days.'

In Ian McEwan's compelling novel, *Enduring Love*, the author makes the point that psychopathological love can remain true – thus conforming to our romantic ideal – while so-called normal love falters. The protagonist's marriage is weakened under duress, but his homosexual de Clérambault admirer, Jed Parry, shows unswerving loyalty. Even when Jed is locked up in an asylum, the strength of his love is undiminished:

> I spend my days and nights in the company of shuffling, muttering, dribbling idiots, and the ones who aren't shuffling are restrained . . . I ought to be going under. Instead I feel more purpose than I've ever known in my life. I've never felt so free. . . I'm earning our happiness day by day and I don't care if it takes me a lifetime . . . I live for you. I love you. Thank you for loving me, thank you for accepting me, thank you for recognising what I am doing for our love.

Is it possible that what psychiatrists describe as a mental illness is, in fact, merely romantic love writ large? Perhaps the majority of erotomaniacs are simply romantic heroes who get 'no' for an answer. The condition is largely defined by the object's response, rather than the subject's mental state per se. When reciprocation occurs, forensic issues evaporate. By saying 'yes', instead of 'no', the object turns a sinister tale of obsession into a beautiful love story.

Erotomania (particularly as described in DSM-IV) raises complex issues relating to our attitudes to love. It also raises substantial ethical issues. To what extent is it appropriate to incarcerate individuals whose social transgressions stem from a set of strong beliefs about love – beliefs that are socially sanctioned and routinely celebrated in novels and films?

Perhaps these ethical tensions arise from a fundamental misconception. The psychopathology of love has survived in psychiatry textbooks because of an underlying assumption that love can be either normal or abnormal – healthy or 'sick'. The solution might be to acknowledge that no such distinction exists. Love – normal love – is largely indistinguishable from mental illness. By removing the distinction, we also remove the ethical dilemma.

An objection to this line of reasoning is that some forms of love do seem to be unequivocally abnormal. Over the past ten years or so, the media have taken a keen interest in stalking stories, especially when a celebrity is involved. These cases are often very disturbing, involving obsessed individuals who either threaten violence, or engage in acts of violence. However, it would be wrong to assume that such individuals are erotomaniacs. Their motivation may have little to do with romantic love.

Psychologist Paul Mullen and colleagues at Monash University in Victoria, Australia, have devised a typology of stalkers and specify five categories: rejected stalkers, intimacy seekers, incompetent suitors, resentful stalkers and predatory stalkers. Those who occupy the category of intimacy seekers are virtually identical to erotomaniacs, and on the whole are motivated by love. They simply want to be close to the object of their affections. Inevitably, they make a nuisance of themselves, but are a low risk with respect to aggression or violence.

If erotomania is simply romantic love writ large, then this suggests an intriguing possibility. Among the dusty volumes of academic psychiatry might be hidden some of the most heroic and romantic tales of love ever told: case studies of great lovers who were rejected, would not give up on love, and were subsequently pronounced insane.

* * *

Thomas Mann's *Death in Venice* was written in 1912. It is a troubling work, largely because of its homoerotic descriptions of a young boy, yet it is one of the most compelling explorations of the power of obsession in literature.

The narrative is spare. Aschenbach, a famous academic, travels to Venice where he sees a beautiful youth, Tadzio, with whom he becomes completely obsessed: he watches him, feels compelled to follow him, and thinks about him continuously. Aschenbach then contracts cholera and dies.

In spite of such an economic narrative, the text is extraordinarily haunting. Against the elegant backdrop of Venice's faded splendour, Aschenbach's yearning reaches levels of pitiful intensity.

It was Thomas Mann's intention to write a kind of morality tale, carefully documenting Aschenbach's loss of dignity, his descent into emotional chaos. However, all the way through, one senses a creeping lack of conviction that culminates in the final scene. It is ambiguous, suggesting death and transfiguration, redemption through suffering – in fact, the worst excesses of romantic idealism. Mann could not condemn Aschenbach's folly, because ultimately, Aschenbach's folly was his own. Like so many works of fiction, *Death in Venice* is rooted in reality. In May 1911, Thomas Mann had taken a short holiday in Venice with his wife and brother. There, he saw a beautiful ten-year-old Polish boy – the future Baron Moes – with whom he became obsessed. Later, his wife confirmed that Mann had become fascinated with the boy (although he had not followed him around in the manner of Aschenbach).

Death in Venice is also something of a confessional – an open psychotherapy session in which Mann tries to make sense of his own disturbing feelings. Indeed, it is easy to imagine the character of Aschenbach reclining in Freud's consulting room. He is an individual whose importunate love reminds us of real psychoanalytic cases such as the Wolf Man.

Aschenbach's Achilles heel is his susceptibility to beauty. Although, strictly speaking, he does not fall in love at first sight, the process of falling in love is certainly initiated the instant he sees Tadzio.

> With astonishment Aschenbach noticed that the boy was entirely beautiful. His countenance, pale and gracefully reserved, was surrounded by ringlets of honey-coloured hair, and with its straight nose, its enchanting mouth, its expression of sweet and divine gravity, it recalled Greek sculpture of the noblest period.

On the following day, when Aschenbach sees Tadzio again, he has already begun to idealise him.

> With a smile and a murmured word in his soft liquescent language, he took his seat, and now especially, as his profile was exactly turned to the watching Aschenbach, the latter was again amazed, indeed startled, by the truly god-like beauty of this human creature.

Aschenbach spends hours watching Tadzio – deriving exquisite pleasure from his every movement. However, this unseemly voyeurism is justified by Platonic mysticism; Tadzio's beauty evokes memories of absolute perfection; Aschenbach's desire – that is, Mann's desire – is ennobled by Truth.

> His eyes embraced that noble figure at the blue water's edge, and in rising ecstasy he felt he was gazing on Beauty itself, on Form as a thought of God, on the one and pure perfection that dwells in the spirit and of which a human similitude and likeness had been lightly and graciously set up for him to worship.

Mann is faithful to his original intention, insofar as he does show us Aschenbach's degradation. After Tadzio smiles at him, Aschenbach is totally overcome. We witness the ignominious spectacle of an old man collapsing into a seat, trembling, shuddering, and whispering 'I love you.' Mann acknowledges Aschenbach's pathetic situation: it is 'absurd, depraved, ludicrous'; but at the same time, he cannot resist adding 'and sacred nevertheless'. It is as though he is still trying to redeem Aschenbach, still trying to salvage his suspect desire from iniquity.

Aschenbach dies, slumped in a deck chair, watching Tadzio walking in the shallow waters of a beach, but at this point, we do not know whether the Tadzio he is watching is real or hallucinatory. Love has driven Aschenbach quite mad. Tadzio has become a semi-mystical being, an angel floating against a 'nebulous vastness'.

> But to him [Aschenbach] it was as if the pale and lovely soul-summoner out there were smiling to him, beckoning to him; as if he loosed his hand from his hip and pointed outwards, hovering ahead and onwards, into an immensity rich with unutterable expectation.

Surely, if we were to pick up a shell on this beach and raise it to our collective ear, we would not hear the sea but the soaring arcs of the *Liebestod*. In the figure of Aschenbach, Thomas Mann's obsession with a ten-year-old boy is sanitised by Greek philosophy and the veneration of beauty. Nevertheless, it is unlikely that Mann would have glimpsed heaven in a secluded Venetian apartment, in the company of a child, however beautiful. Such a scenario does not bring to mind images of 'an immensity rich with unutterable expectation', but of a sad, possibly sick man in his mid-thirties, about to inflict appalling emotional damage on an innocent victim.

Obsession is the mainstay of passionate love, but we must never forget its legacy of sinister associations. Every obsession conceals a sleeping demon – and it is stirred all too easily.

7

Too Close for Comfort

A woman can become a man's friend only in the following
stages – first an acquaintance, next a mistress, and then a
friend.

Uncle Vanya, Anton Chekhov

In attempting to deconstruct love, almost all theorists have
included in their scheme an element of love that corresponds with friendship. This observation has been relatively
consistent throughout history, and can be traced back to
Aristotle. In the eighteenth century, the philosopher David
Hume considered 'generous kindness' to be an essential
ingredient of love and, over two hundred years later,
Sternberg placed 'liking' at the apex of his triangular model.
That love and friendship overlap is frequently confirmed by
everyday experience. When men and women describe the
circumstances of their marriage, it is not uncommon to hear
them confess: 'I married my best friend.' Moreover, the most
successful and lasting marriages seem to be those in which
friendship – shared activities, interests and talking together
– plays an important role.

Since ancient times, there have been numerous attempts to
establish typologies of love, many of which identify several
sub-types, but it is possible that many of these sub-types are

redundant. They may, in fact, represent nothing more than variations of two fundamental forms: passionate (or romantic) love and companionate (or friendly) love.

In the 1970s, psychologists Elaine Hatfield and G.W. Walster defined companionate love as 'the affection we feel for those with whom our lives are deeply entwined'. Clearly, such a definition is somewhat broad – companionate love might be experienced between long-standing friends as well as lovers. Indeed, any relationship that is of sufficient length – permitting two lives to become deeply entwined – might be described as 'companionate'. However, in the context of research into love, the term 'companionate love' is usually reserved to describe the closeness that couples enjoy after passionate love has become less intense (or disappeared). Sternberg states: 'Most romantic relationships that . . . survive eventually turn into companionate love relationships: the passion begins to melt, but the intimacy remains.'

Although couples generally proceed from passionate to companionate love, most relationships are based on a degree of amity from the very beginning. Therefore, the progression from passionate to companionate love probably reflects a change of emphasis rather than a transition per se. In the early stages of a relationship, factors such as physical attractiveness and sexual interest seem to play a much more important role than friendship, but with the passing of time, this pattern of emphasis typically reverses.

As we have already established, passionate love is frequently irrational and compulsive. Companionate love, on the other hand, is rational and voluntary in nature. Companionate lovers maintain a continuing commitment to each other because they are compatible – not because they are overwhelmed with desire. Pain has no place in the language of companionate love. Whereas passionate love is intensified by misery and distress, companionate love is intensified only by shared pleasures.

Companionate love may not be dramatic, like passionate love, but it is certainly more solid and reliable. It is associated with deep feelings of closeness, attachment, loyalty, sharing, familiarity and intimacy.

The subdued but sympathetic qualities of companionate love were beautifully captured by T.S. Eliot in his poem, 'A Dedication to My Wife', in which he describes:

> The breathing in unison
> Of lovers whose bodies smell of each other
> Who think the same thoughts without need of speech
> And babble the same speech without need of meaning

Eliot goes on to describe the marital relationship as 'the rose-garden that is ours and ours only'. The biographical details of Eliot's life indicate that he was far from an ideal husband – yet, his poetry shows a curious sensitivity to the qualities of companionate love. Lesser poets, whose pyrotechnic verse displays reflect the heat and spectacle of passionate love, often fail to exploit the charming and muted affinities of conjugal fondness.

At first sight, it seems rather implausible that links can be made between companionate love and mental illness. Companionate love seems too restrained, too sensible. Yet, even after incendiary passions have been exhausted, the seeds of insanity can still take root in passion's ashes. Perhaps something of love's original madness always survives, albeit in a more subtle and diluted form.

But how are intimacy and psychopathology related? How can closeness promote madness?

Eliot's image of the rose garden provides a clue. It suggests somewhere secluded, somewhere removed from worldly traffic, a walled retreat. The psychopathology of companionate love is often associated with social withdrawal. It is as though the companionate couple enter Eliot's 'rose garden' – but then refuse to come out. They are happy to inhale the heavily scented air, hold hands and talk indefinitely.

The word intimacy is derived from the Latin *intimus*, meaning inner or inmost. Thus, when couples become intimate, they expose and share their ontological core. In many languages, equivalent words exist, some of which also emphasise notions of complicity and confidentiality: the French word *intime* also means secret, and the Spanish word *intimo* also means private.

In isolation, the boundary that separates each mind seems to dissolve and the conjugal union becomes intellectually and emotionally symbiotic. We have all encountered such couples, – they speak for each other, finish each other's sentences and wear identical clothing. They become nothing less than the psychological equivalent of Siamese twins – joined by the faculty of amity. Of course, passionate love can also blur ego boundaries – indeed, during sexual intercourse, passionate lovers often experience semi-mystical states of merging – but it is very unusual for such altered states to last. They tend to occur in the early, euphoric days of a relationship, and diminish as sex becomes less frequent. The interesting feature of companionate intimacy is that it can lead to a more or less permanent blurring of the ego boundary.

In his *Epistles on Friendship*, the tenth-century Persian calligrapher Abu Hayyan al-Tawhidi noted that closeness can produce a phenomenon whereby one soul appears to occupy two bodies. This observation seems particularly pertinent with respect to artistic representations of marriage, which typically show two people whose alarming similarity suggests a 'common soul'. In Gainsborough's *Mr and Mrs Andrews*, an aristocratic couple stare out of the canvas with almost identical enigmatic expressions, while in Grant Wood's famous *American Gothic*, we are presented with a farmer and his wife who might otherwise be mistaken for a pair of glum, puritanical twins. There are many other examples. Clearly, these similarities might be attributable to assortative mating (men and women choosing partners of similar attractiveness), but on the other hand, great artists seem to capture the effect of an additional process – a morphological consequence of diminishing individuality, of too much time spent in the rose garden.

Such artistic observations have recently gained empirical support. A team of psychologists based at Northwestern University in the USA found that dating couples became more similar in their emotional responses to laboratory tasks when assessed over the course of a year. Emotional convergence was also a good predictor of relationship longevity.

The idea that close couples represent two facets of the same being has recurred intermittently for millennia. Indeed, the concept dates back to a mythological account of the origins of humanity which appears in Plato's *Symposium*. According to Greek legend, human beings were once double-headed creatures with four legs and four arms, and divisible into three genders: male, female and hermaphrodite. As a punishment for human pride, Zeus decided to weaken the human race by cutting their bodies in two. Thereafter, each incomplete being yearned to be reunited with its other half, producing the three permutations of human sexual relationships – homosexual, lesbian and heterosexual:

> It is from this distant epoch, then, that we may date the innate love which human beings feel for one another, the love which restores us to our ancient state by attempting to weld two beings into one and to heal the wounds which humanity suffered.

The idea that we are born incomplete, and must find our 'other half', is extremely pervasive. Indeed, it has become something of an implicit assumption, influencing our understanding of love at almost every level. In the romantic canon, the idea of incompletion has inspired countless narratives in which separated lovers overcome obstacles because they are mysteriously drawn together. It is their destiny to be united and nothing will stop them. On a more mundane level, the term 'other half' or even 'better half' is often used colloquially to describe a wife or husband.

The Platonic myth, however, has troubling implications. It suggests that until we find a soulmate we are weak, wounded and unfinished. Moreover, there is nothing we can do to heal ourselves. We are entirely dependent on our 'other half'.

In his novella, *The Dying Animal*, Philip Roth takes issue with Platonic idealism. David, an ageing academic, has fallen in love with a voluptuous young beauty, and his friend George begs him to see reason:

> People think that in falling in love they make themselves whole? The Platonic union of souls? I think otherwise. I think you're whole before you begin. And the love fractures you. You're whole, and then you're cracked open. She was a foreign body introduced into your wholeness. And for a year and a half you struggled to incorporate it. You either get rid of it or incorporate it through self-distortion. And that's what you did and what drove you mad.

In reality, it is neither tenable nor psychologically healthy for two people to strive for Platonic union. As Roth suggests, a union of this kind can only ever be illusory – preserved by distortions of a magnitude we would only ordinarily find in the context of a mental illness. When a couple become too close, when ego boundaries blur, they do not achieve a transcendent state of wholeness, but rather, something far more sinister and strange: a delusional symbiosis.

The perils of Platonic union are not entirely unrecognised

in the general population. Indeed, one of the most popular readings at wedding ceremonies is an excerpt from Khalil Gibran's *The Prophet*, which includes a gentle warning: '. . . stand together, yet not too near together: For the pillars of the temple stand apart, And the oak tree and the cypress grow not in each other's shadow.'

Perhaps one of the most extraordinary examples of closeness leading to a breakdown of ego boundaries is a condition that psychiatrists call the couvade syndrome. It is a gender-specific problem, affecting only men with pregnant partners. Typically, the father-to-be complains of a range of physical symptoms, most of which are associated with either carrying a child or, more dramatically, giving birth. These symptoms rarely continue after the child has been born.

The word couvade was originally used by anthropologists to describe a practice observed in many so-called primitive societies. Among these peoples, it was customary for a father-to-be to retire for the duration of his wife's labour. During his confinement, he might engage in a symbolic birth, simulating parturient pain and being attended by a tribal doctor.

Although there is no equivalent of the couvade birth ritual in the West, couvade-type phenomena have been described in Europe from the seventeenth century onwards. For example, in 1627 the philosopher Francis Bacon wrote: 'There is an Opinion abroad (whether Idle or no I cannot say) that loving and kinde Husbands have a Sense of their Wives Breeding Childe by some Accident in their Owne Body.' And in 1677 Robert Plot, a Fellow of the Royal Society, observed: 'In the birth of man it is equally strange that pangs of women in the exclusion of the child have sometimes affected the Abdomen of the husband . . .'

Bacon's tone suggests that couvade phenomena were relatively rare – or at least sufficiently rare to justify scepticism. However, plays of the sixteenth and seventeenth centuries frequently describe or allude to couvade phenomena, suggesting that the problem was perhaps more prevalent than supposed by contemporary scholars. Sympathetic pregnancy and labour are mentioned in the dramas of luminaries such as Beaumont and Fletcher, and Thomas Middleton. In Act IV of William Wycherley's *The Country Wife*, we find the following:

> Hows'e'r the kind wife's belly comes to swell
> The husband breeds for her and first is ill.

Clearly, the couvade symptoms described by Elizabethan and Jacobean dramatists were not associated with a birthing ritual or custom. Therefore, they must have been early examples of the modern syndrome.

Symptoms include gastrointestinal disturbance such as loss of appetite, nausea (particularly in the form of morning sickness), indigestion, abdominal pain, constipation and diarrhoea. Pregnancy cravings (for unusual foods, or unusual combinations of food) are also frequently described. A more puzzling couvade symptom is toothache. This is not particularly associated with pregnancy, but is experienced with abnormal frequency by men experiencing sympathetic pains. The association may be, at least in part, attributable to cultural influences. In English folklore, toothache was considered one of the principal symptoms of love sickness. Indeed, in Norfolk, toothache is still sometimes described as 'the love pain'. The notion that love and toothache are related seems to have been common knowledge in Elizabethan England – for instance, in Shakespeare's *Much Ado About Nothing*, Benedick experiences toothache after falling in love with Beatrice – but even so, the associ-

ation between love and toothache is hardly common knowledge now. Thus, it remains somewhat intriguing as to why
many modern cases of couvade present with this symptom.

Several of the above – particularly morning sickness and
cravings – are dramatic examples of how the couvade
syndrome mimics pregnancy. However, these pale into
insignificance when compared with what is probably the
most alarming expression of sympathetic symptomatology
– abdominal swelling. Remarkably, the father-to-be under-
goes a physical metamorphosis, eventually acquiring the
distended appearance of a gravid female.

Enoch and Ball cite an extraordinary case of this kind. A
soldier who had married while on leave learned shortly after
returning to duty that his wife was pregnant. In due course,
she suffered from morning sickness and wrote to him, detail-
ing her symptoms. The young husband became anxious, and
was soon in need of medical attention himself.

> A 26-year-old Australian soldier was admitted while on
> active service to a military hospital with a swollen abdomen
> resembling that of fairly advanced pregnancy. While he
> suffered occasional 'dry' vomiting he had no pain or tender-
> ness. Investigations showed no evidence of intra-abdominal
> disease. On being anaesthetized his abdomen became quite
> flat and no mass or abnormality could be felt on deep palpa-
> tion. Once he had regained consciousness tumefaction
> returned.

As is usually the case with couvade syndrome, the
soldier's abdominal swelling subsided after his wife had
given birth.

How, then, can the symptoms of couvade syndrome be
explained?

From Hippocratic times, it has always been recognised
that the mind can influence the physical processes of the

body. Moreover, there have been periods in the history of psychiatry when psychosomatic illnesses have dominated the clinical scene. In the late nineteenth century hysteria was extremely common, and many sufferers complained of physical symptoms that had no organic cause. Such cases were famously examined by the likes of Pierre Janet, Josef Breuer and Sigmund Freud, who concluded that the physical symptoms of hysteria were caused by unconscious (and possibly repressed) memories. Typically, a semantic link could be made between a distressing event and the nature of the symptoms. For example, hysterical paralysis of the legs might occur when a patient attempted to enter a room associated with childhood trauma. Such a symptom could be construed as a kind of automatic defence, a way of stopping the patient entering an environment that might trigger painful (and possibly overwhelming) memories.

The couvade syndrome is very similar to hysteria: the patient suffers from physical symptoms that have a psychological rather than organic cause. However, in the case of couvade syndrome, the symptoms are not produced by an unconscious memory. Usually sufferers recognise that the symptoms are 'sympathetic' in nature (although there are occasional exceptions). Even so, the mechanisms that produce couvade-type symptoms probably operate at an unconscious level. Abdominal distension, for instance, might be achieved by swallowing air; yet, a couvade patient won't necessarily be aware that he is doing this.

Recently, there has been a trend towards explaining the couvade syndrome as a form of anxiety disorder. When people become anxious, they often experience gastrointestinal disturbance and an exacerbation of aches and pains (because of hormonal changes and muscular tension). Therefore, straightforward manifestations of couvade syndrome (abdominal pain, nausea etc.) might represent nothing more than the effects of excessive worrying. However, this explanation is only partial. Several couvade symptoms, such as food cravings and excessive abdominal swelling, are not generally associated with anxiety. Moreover, many couvade sufferers who exhibit quite severe physical symptoms show no obvious signs of anxiety and appear to be relatively relaxed.

Although the couvade syndrome is often described as a rare psychiatric condition, this may be misleading. Dramatic symptoms such as abdominal swelling are infrequent, but the rest of the syndrome is probably more common than textbooks suggest. The first controlled study of couvade-type phenomena was published in 1965 by Trethowen and Conlon, who subsequently suggested that as many as 11 per cent of men suffer from psychosomatic symptoms during their wives' pregnancies. The results of a further analysis led the authors to raise this figure to 20 per cent. Since the 1960s, many more studies have been conducted, and the general trend has been to revise these figures in an upward direction. Indeed, recent investigations have found that as many as 79 per cent of men experience sympathetic symptoms during their wives' pregnancies.

In the next few decades, continuing research might demonstrate that the couvade syndrome is very common indeed – the natural consequence of togetherness. When couples become very close, perhaps it is inevitable that ego boundaries will weaken and break down, creating extraordinary possibilities for phenomena that resemble psychopathology.

Many psychiatrists and psychologists believe that the couvade syndrome is fundamentally an example of over-identification. The husband experiences intense empathy, and wishes to ease his wife's suffering by sharing her burden. Unconscious processes come into operation, and his wish is translated into reality.

The couvade syndrome is a declaration of support and solidarity, compassion and care – companionate, rather than passionate feelings. Unlike romantic love, which is ultimately narcissistic, companionate love is genuinely altruistic. For all its laudable qualities, however, companionate love can still unhinge the mind. A twenty-first-century man can suddenly find himself engaging in magical thinking, and re-enacting the superstitious rituals of our most primitive ancestors: ego boundaries dissolve, and he must take to his bed – his belly aching with the kick of a phantom child.

Social psychologists have demonstrated that when groups of people are isolated, they become more extreme in terms of their beliefs. The classic real-life study of this kind was undertaken at Bennington, a women's college in the United States renowned for its espousal of liberal values. It was found that the longer students stayed at Bennington, the more liberal they became. In the absence of exposure to counter-arguments, the young ladies drifted further and further to the left. The Bennington effect is much more conspicuous in smaller groups, for instance within the context of committees or small religious congregations, where exposure to contradictory ideas and beliefs can be even more restricted.

The ultimate 'small group' comprises only two people. Therefore, one would expect isolated dyads to develop the most extreme forms of complicit belief – so much so, that the contact points where the shared belief system and reality touch might be few and far between. In the West, marriages are perhaps the most common form of isolated dyad.

When couples have spent a great deal of time together it is often the case that they egg each other on, reinforcing beliefs that become increasingly idiosyncratic. At first these beliefs might be described as eccentric; but if they remain completely unchecked, they can become delusional. This transition is particularly characteristic of isolated couples who see themselves increasingly at odds with their social context. They cultivate an 'us' and 'them' attitude, which can slowly evolve into a form of mild paranoia. Subsequently, the world is viewed with considerable suspicion.

When two people share the same delusional belief system, it is described as *folie à deux*. This term was originally coined in the nineteenth century, but the same phenomenon has been recorded since the seventeenth. It is now recognised in ICD-10 as Induced Delusional Disorder, and in DSM-IV as Shared Psychotic Disorder.

Folie à deux can arise in the context of any dyadic relationship – such as parent and child, siblings, or simply friends – but between husband and wife it is extremely common, superseded in frequency only by *folie à deux* between female siblings. Some 22 per cent of all documented cases have occurred in marriages, particularly those of long standing. Isolation increases the risk, and some studies suggest that couples may be vulnerable after retirement. Even so, *folie à deux* can affect couples of all ages.

Typically, *folie à deux* evolves asymmetrically. One member of a couple – usually the dominant personality – becomes delusional first, and the same delusion is subsequently adopted by his or her partner. The delusions can be about virtually anything – for example, that dust is being deposited under the bed by an intruder, or that a neighbour has hidden surveillance equipment in the bathroom – but they frequently reflect the preoccupations of people who live a relatively impoverished and closeted existence.

Intimacy is clearly an important factor in maintaining the problem. Thus, both parties, to a greater or lesser extent, are reinforcing the delusional system. This is clearly the case in some couples whose delusional symptoms weaken, and then disappear, when separated. Indeed, temporary separation is considered to be a necessary condition of treatment for some couples.

It is of considerable interest that *folie à deux* seems to be an increasingly prevalent problem. Over the past thirty years or so, more reports of it have been appearing in medical publications than ever before. This may reflect a greater awareness of the problem among psychiatrists, or alternatively, it may be a consequence of social change.

It is one of the great ironies of modern life that, as communications technology has improved, people are more and more able to live in isolation. The Internet, home entertainment systems, and home office technology permit many individuals to eschew human contact altogether. Moreover, in big cities, high levels of street crime have fostered a bunker mentality. It is now tempting to close the door firmly on the outside world. Such conditions are ideal for the development of *folie à deux* delusions. Again, we find ourselves in Eliot's 'rose garden', where intimacy allows two minds to share a single belief system.

Current estimates of the prevalence of *folie à deux* are very probably conservative. Couples who develop the disorder do not seek help; therefore, they are unlikely to be included in mental health surveys. In addition, the majority of *folie à deux* delusions are relatively harmless, never getting to the point where medical intervention is required. If a couple choose to believe that the man who owns the corner shop is really Elvis Presley, what does it matter? Indeed, many so-called healthy couples share beliefs that are equally dubious – although perhaps socially sanctioned under the rubrics of religion or cultural heritage.

Folie à deux delusions demonstrate how enabling close relationships can be. Couples can encourage each other to entertain and explore a wide range of daring hypotheses about themselves and the world around them. In the same way that children can fill a wet afternoon with imaginary battles and journeys, so it is that couples afflicted with *folie à deux* can enliven a pedestrian existence with intrigue and conspiracy. However, some of these possibilities may also be sinister, and one wonders to what extent suicide pacts, usually seen as a token of romantic idealism, are also the result of shared delusions – couples have become so close, that the imminent death of one must automatically imply the death of the other. Here again, we encounter the perils of Platonic mythology.

Folie à deux is regarded as one of the strangest phenomena in all of psychiatry, and serves to show that love, even in its gentle, companionate guise, can be reason's enemy.

8

The Green-ey'd Monster

O, beware, my Lord, of jealousy.
It is the green-ey'd monster which doth mock
The meat it feeds on.
                    Othello, William Shakespeare

Jealousy and love are inseparable. It is almost impossible to love without also desiring exclusive possession of the beloved. As such, jealousy is a necessary condition of love – its absence suggests indifference and impartiality: a level of detachment that we cannot reconcile with passion and desire. In his famous guide to the principles of courtly love, the second of Andrew Capelanus's thirty-one rules states: 'He who is not jealous cannot love.' We know that love is real when it casts a shadow.

Most contemporary theorists agree with Capelanus. Moreover, surveys show that approximately 50 per cent of the general population believe that jealousy is an inevitable consequence of falling in love.

The word jealousy is derived from the Greek *zelos*, meaning fervour, ardour, intense desire; however, its modern meaning owes more to French influence. The French word *jalousie* is used in much the same way as its English equivalent, but it also has another meaning – a

Venetian blind. Nils Rettersol, a Norwegian psychiatrist, has suggested that the two meanings of *jalousie* are very probably related, insofar as the horizontal slats of a Venetian blind provide ideal conditions for both observation and concealment: a suspicious husband might be able to spy on his unfaithful wife by peering through a *jalousie* without fear of discovery.

Jealousy is a complex emotional state, triggered by a real or imagined threat to an existing sexual relationship. It is described as complex, because it is a mixture of several emotions. The most commonly reported are anxiety, anger and depression. These more basic emotions can blend together, or be experienced separately, as the jealous person shifts his or her attention to different aspects of the 'jealous situation'. An early response to suspected infidelity might be anxiety; however, a shift of attention to the 'rival figure' will probably arouse anger, and a further shift to issues surrounding loss will probably result in depression. It should be recognised, however, that these three basic emotions – anxiety, anger and depression – are also supplemented by several other emotions, such as shame, humiliation or rage.

Like all emotional states, jealousy predisposes the individual to think and behave in certain ways. Thus, the affected individual will very likely ruminate about a range of topics associated with his or her situation, and attempt to prevent the demise of his or her relationship. Occasionally, positive strategies are employed, such as showering a partner with gifts; however, these tend to be the exception rather than the rule. Jealousy is more commonly associated with surveillance, confrontation, ultimatums, and even the use of violence. Needless to say, jealousy is almost always experienced as distressing.

Among the emotions, jealousy is generally understood

to be one of the most powerful. This is certainly reflected in Greek and Roman mythology – where even the gods are not immune to its influence – and no discussion of jealousy is complete without mention of Othello, whose dark, brooding and explosive presence is always felt patrolling the borders of imagination whenever the subject is raised.

But why is jealousy such a powerful emotion?

The answer to this question is very simple: because it is important. From an evolutionary perspective, the fate of our genes is determined, to a very significant extent, by the degree to which we experience jealousy.

In Chapter 3, it was suggested that evolutionary pressures have selected love – a necessary madness – to ensure reproductive success. The primary function of love is to cement sexual relationships for a period of several years, in order to ensure that the vulnerable human infant receives care from its mother, resources from its father, and protection from both. But love doesn't always work. Like most evolutionary 'solutions', it is imperfect. Love can be flawed or inconsistent.

Love's imperfection has important consequences for humans. We live in complex social hierarchies that are highly competitive, so one of the biggest threats to the survival of our genes in subsequent generations is not predation or disease, but other human beings. If love were 100 per cent effective, then we would not have to worry about sexual rivals. We could be completely confident of our partner's sexual fidelity. But love is not 100 per cent effective, and there is always a chance, however slim, that our partner will mate with someone else. Infidelity is a major threat to reproductive success, so evolution has selected a secondary strategy to deal with this problem: jealousy.

For the most part, reproductive success is probably best

accomplished when male and female humans form an exclusive pair-bond, and subsequently work together to ensure that their offspring thrive. However, this may still be suboptimal. A combination of apparent monogamy and judicious sexual opportunism might constitute the real reproductive ceiling.

Inevitably, in any competitive environment, the evolution of exploitative mechanisms will be accompanied by the evolution of safeguards or defences. Jealousy is a safeguard against love's imperfection. It is the means by which rivals protect their reproductive interests.

It has already been suggested that the optimal strategy for reproductive success differs between the sexes. Biological differences have a profound impact on sexual politics.

In general, men can afford to be more profligate with their genetic material than women. The human male need only spend a few seconds copulating, to increase his chances of reproductive success, and his reservoir of genetic material is virtually limitless. Although a casual, illicit coupling will not necessarily ensure that his genes will be represented in the next generation, it is probably worth the gamble: hardly any energy is expended, there is no significant cost, and the return is potentially enormous. If the illicit coupling produces a child, then a cuckold might obligingly ensure the survival of an errant male's genes in future generations. The cuckold will nurture, protect and raise the child, giving the errant male's genes a 'free ride'.

Women, on the other hand, are not equipped to optimise their reproductive success in quite the same way. To produce a single child, a woman must use one of only 400 eggs, endure pregnancy for nine months, and then survive a potentially life-threatening labour. Moreover, she cannot fob off her child on an unsuspecting female. A woman's parental investment is so great, it is in her interest to be highly selective, and to form a strong pair-bond with a committed male. By doing this, she can be more confident that her child will reach maturity and her genes will survive into subsequent generations. Indiscriminate sex offers women few advantages with respect to reproductive success.

These factors have been important in shaping human sexuality. They are believed to be the basis of a marked gender difference with respect to fidelity. On the whole, men are much more likely to be unfaithful than women. Yet, this difference is not absolute. It is merely an asymmetry.

It is unlikely that all women in the ancestral environment were models of moral propriety. Some of them must have been sexually promiscuous. If this were not the case, then male sexual jealousy would not have evolved. There wouldn't have been a need for it, and we would now live in a world where men enjoyed total sexual security, and only women experienced sexual jealousy. In fact, almost the opposite is true. In general, men seem to experience sexual jealousy far more keenly than women.

Why should this be the case?

Although a man can optimise his reproductive success by cuckolding another male, he does so within a social environment in which others are operating according to the very same principle. Thus, he too might be cuckolded. From a parental-investment point of view, this outcome is a total and unmitigated disaster. The male will not only waste his resources raising another man's child, he will also nullify his previous investments such as the time and energy spent competing for an attractive partner. He will also lose all indirect benefits, for example his partner's time and energy, now being expended on her own and his rival's genetic interests.

Women can never be placed in such a catastrophic position. Women can never waste their time and energy in the same way, for the simple reason that it is impossible for a woman to have a child who will not preserve her genetic legacy. Unlike the male, the female can be 100 per cent confident that the child she gives birth to is her own and not someone else's. She is always sure that she is investing in her own genes. This is probably why men feel sexual jealousy more keenly than women. They have so much more to lose.

Even so, the fact that male sexual jealousy exists strongly suggests that some ancestral females were unfaithful. The most compelling evidence for female infidelity in the ancestral environment comes from studies of sperm competition.

Not very long ago, it was thought that sperm could only survive in the reproductive tract for approximately twenty-four hours, but it has now been demonstrated that sperm remain viable for up to a week. Recently, it was found that the vaginal walls contain tiny cavities in which sperm can be stored for several days before subsequent release. Thus, if during the course of a week a woman has intercourse with two or more men, a situation may arise in which sperm from a variety of donors all compete to fertilise a single egg at the same time. This may be one of the reasons why the human male produces so many sperm: a large number will have a greater probability of overwhelming any competition.

Yet more evidence can be derived from the study of sperm morphology. Recent research has established that there are two types of sperm – each fulfilling a different function. The most common sperm are those that possess a conical head and a long sinewy tail. They are good swimmers and are clearly designed to reach the unfertilised egg as soon as possible. In addition, there are a small number of sperm with coiled tails. These so-called 'kamikaze sperm' are very poor swimmers, but excellent saboteurs. In laboratory studies, it has been shown that when sperm from two males are mixed, kamikaze sperm will wrap their tails around competing sperm, producing a state of joint immobilisation. In real life, both the kamikaze sperm and its strangulated companion would die. Kamikaze sperm would only have evolved in the ancestral environment if ancestral females were mating with several partners.

It is relatively easy to see why sexual opportunism is a good strategy for the human male – a modest investment stands to deliver a massive return – but what do women have to gain? Female parental investment is always greater than male parental investment, and whoever a woman has sex with, she will still have to carry the child, give birth to the child, and (for the most part) look after it. Her genes will never get a 'free ride'. Moreover, the female of the species, being physically weaker, is more likely to suffer costly consequences if her infidelity is discovered. She might be beaten by her mate, or even killed. She is also more likely to be expelled from her social group.

Men are extremely vigilant when it comes to female infidelity, a fact that is reflected in the Western literary canon. The Trojan War begins with Helen's affair with Paris; Elizabethan drama is completely obsessed with female honour; and many of the outstanding novels of the nineteenth and twentieth centuries are preoccupied with the psychology of unfaithful heroines: Madame Bovary, Anna Karenina, and Lady Chatterley to name but a few. This preoccupation with female infidelity reaches disturbing proportions in certain 'fundamentalist' countries, where mere suspicion can still lead to stoning or execution (with few questions asked).

So how does infidelity work for women? How can it be justified when discovery is associated with such high costs?

Firstly, in the ancestral environment, sexual infidelity may have been a method of securing additional – and sometimes essential – resources. During famine a gift of food from a male admirer might have been the critical factor determining whether a woman survived, or died of starvation. Related to this point is what evolutionary psychologists call 'mate insurance'. In the ancestral environment life expectancy was very short, so maintaining a discreet connection with a 'back-up' male was probably very sensible. Then, the death of a mate would not necessarily result in starvation (a consequence that would affect both the female and her children who unequivocally carry her genes).

The second advantage is genetic diversity. Mating with different partners ensures that offspring have a broad mix of genes. This provides insurance against environmental change. For example, if diet is suddenly restricted, then only those individuals who possess genes for a particular kind of digestive enzyme might thrive. By making sure that her children are genetically diverse, a female might increase the chances of her own genes surviving in subsequent generations.

As one would expect, these ancestral influences can still be detected in contemporary female behaviour. Research has shown that women are strongly motivated to have affairs if offered the prospect of additional resources – expensive meals, luxury goods and presents such as clothing. Also, when women decide to have illicit sex, they tend to choose partners who are conspicuously healthy (and thus possess good genes). Even more remarkable is the fact that women tend to have sex with their lovers at times when they are most likely to conceive. Again, as with all evolutionary mechanisms, this happens automatically. Women do not choose to have sex with their lovers when they are most fertile. Rather, evolutionary pressures have ensured that sexual desire coincides with fertility.

Clearly, both sexes are capable of infidelity and both sexes experience jealousy, but this does not mean that men and women get jealous in quite the same way.

Men tend to be more sexually opportunistic than women, and women tend to have a preference for dependable, resource-rich mates. The fundamental evolutionary threat for men is wasted investment, whereas the fundamental evolutionary threat for women is abandonment (which is equivalent to resource withdrawal). These factors have a profound influence on gender politics.

In a much cited study by psychologist David Buss and colleagues, men and women were asked which they would find most upsetting: discovering that a partner had enjoyed passionate sex with another person or discovering that a partner had formed a deep emotional attachment to another person. Men reliably find the former more upsetting, while women reliably find the latter more upsetting. This asymmetry is pan-cultural, and is as commonly observed in the USA and the Netherlands as it is in Japan, Korea and Zimbabwe. Because the fundamental evolutionary threat for men is wasted investment, men are more likely to experience sexual jealousy. Women, for whom the threat of abandonment is more salient, are more likely to experience emotional jealousy.

This does not mean that women are happy for their partners to be unfaithful. Women find sexual infidelity painful too; however, research shows that women are much more likely than men to forgive sexual transgressions.

We are all the descendants of jealous ancestors. Men who were not jealous wasted their time and energy on other men's genes – and subsequently their own genes died out. Women who were not jealous never ensured that their mates were around long enough to provide for their children – and their genes probably died out too. Jealousy is an adaptation, a coping mechanism that we inherit on account of its usefulness.

David Buss views jealousy as an essential element of human nature:

> Jealousy, according to this perspective, is not a sign of immaturity, but rather, a supremely important passion that helped our ancestors, and most likely continues to help us today, to cope with a host of real reproductive threats. Jealousy, for example, motivates us to ward off rivals with verbal threats and cold primate stares. It drives us to keep partners from straying with tactics such as escalating vigilance or showering a partner with affection. And it communicates commitment to a partner who may be wavering, serving an important purpose in the maintenance of love.

Thus, jealousy is love's bastion, love's defensive carapace: not a sign of emotional immaturity, or insecurity, but an evolutionary solution to the problems our ancestors faced – as do we today – in a sexually competitive environment. As Buss suggests, jealousy is 'supremely important'. If our genes are to survive in subsequent generations, we cannot afford to have a casual attitude with respect to sexual rivals. We cannot dither, reasoning that we are not quite sure, don't really know, or have insufficient evidence to act upon. Jealousy works on the 'better safe than sorry' principle. A false alarm is embarrassing, but negligence can lead to a reproductive catastrophe. Therefore, as with all important emotions, jealousy takes away our freedom. By the time we have thought things through, it might be too late. Like love, jealousy is urgent. It overthrows reason – and in doing so, also mimics mental illness. Jealousy can be savage and obsessive – an ugly, 'green-ey'd monster'.

Attempts to overcome jealousy in the context of alternative lifestyles have, on the whole, proved unsuccessful.

For the vast majority of those who experimented with open relationships and 'swinging' in the 1960s and 1970s, jealousy was a major stumbling block. Although there are some people who can share their partner's sexual favours with equanimity, such people tend to be in a small minority. Love demands exclusivity. For the average human being, sexual experimentation can only be accomplished comfortably in the absence of love. Liberal thinking is no match for our evolutionary demons.

Two intellectual giants whose power to think rationally was completely undermined by jealousy were Sigmund Freud and Leo Tolstoy. They represent particularly interesting cases, insofar as both might be counted among the most psychologically insightful men who have ever lived. In their very different ways, they probed human nature, and shared a deep understanding of the human mind and its workings. Moreover, both men indulged in extensive self-analysis. Tolstoy's diaries are full of self-observation, and Freud's formalised sessions of introspection were part of a process that led to the foundation of psychoanalysis. Yet, when threatened by a sexual rival – and only a perceived sexual rival at that – neither Freud nor Tolstoy had sufficient insight to contain their jealous feelings. Both were overcome by jealous rage.

Freud was a champion of reason. Indeed, it might be argued that some of the more outlandish features of psychoanalysis became widely accepted purely because of Freud's 'reasonableness'. He was described by friends and acquaintances as a quiet, detached, meticulous man, whose principal pleasures were scholarly and retiring. However, we don't have to rely on their second-hand accounts – his personality has left a deep impression on almost every page of his collected works. Typically, Freud persuades by the systematic presentation of arguments and evidence. He seems fully aware of any logical weaknesses, which he reassuringly addresses as his thesis develops. He is always cool, precise and impartial. This dispassionate tone was sustained throughout his writing career, suggesting a solid, dependable character – someone not easily agitated by emotions. On the whole, such an impression is not far from the truth. Freud was not impulsive, passionate, or daring, and, in spite of many ill-fated attempts to represent him as a romantic hero, the facts of his life are more easily reconciled with the personality we encounter in his writings. Freud was a bourgeois doctor who spent most of his life seeing patients and relaxing with his family. He was not the kind of person we associate with jealous rage.

Freud experienced his episode of jealousy while he was courting Martha Bernays, a woman who was young and, by the standards of his time, very desirable. The courtship itself was fraught with logistical problems, largely because of Freud's professional obligations. Of the four and a half years that passed between their first meeting and their marriage, three years were spent apart. Even so, the couple were still in regular communication, often writing to each other every day.

Falling in love can be a disconcerting experience – but for a man like Freud, it was particularly so. Love disturbed the safety of his dry, refined, intellectual world. His letters show that he yearned to be with Martha, and the intensity of his emotions actually frightened him. In the autumn of 1885, while he was studying in Paris, Freud ascended one of the Notre Dame Cathedral towers. He was desperately missing Martha, and afterwards informed her in a letter: 'One climbs up three hundred steps, it is very dark, very lonely, on every step I could have given you a kiss if you had been with me, and you would have reached the top quite out of breath and wild.' It is a simple, poetic image – but unexpected: ravishing by numbers. Freud recognised that he was feeling something close to madness – which he found deeply worrying. Perhaps he was also aware that love might stir up darker emotions – the kind of violent, destructive emotions that he associated with our primitive (even animal) ancestry.

Freud's brush with his own evolutionary legacy began shortly after his engagement to Martha. He discovered that she had written a letter to one of her former suitors, the artist Fritz Wahle. Martha had not written anything incendiary – merely an affirmation of friendship – yet, this letter seems to have played on Freud's mind, arousing suspicion, and causing him an inordinate amount of distress.

> When the memory of your letter to Fritz . . . comes back to me I lose all control of myself, and had I the power to destroy the whole world, ourselves included, to let it all start over again – even at the risk that it might not create Martha and myself – I would do so without hesitation.

Clearly, this is rage writ large. Freud's jealousy was so intense, his subsequent behaviour was entirely out of character. The quiet, retiring scholar became all the things that he wasn't: impulsive, passionate and daring. He confronted Wahle, and their meeting was one that came perilously close to violence. There was talk of shooting, tears were shed, and letters were destroyed. Also, Freud's jealous rage left him with a strong desire to control Martha and he began making unreasonable demands. He insisted that Martha should be less familiar with one of her cousins and refrain from calling him by his first name; she should weaken family attachments – particularly with respect to her mother and brother Eli – and in general, she should spurn the company of others, respecting Freud's exclusive claim on her attention. His demands were so unreasonable, they created tensions which lasted for many years.

In later life, Freud wrote much on jealousy, and posited three types of increasing severity: normal, neurotic and pathological. Reflecting on his own jealousy, Freud took the view that he had behaved normally. If this assessment is to be taken seriously, then we must assume that – in Freud's opinion – normal jealousy is a semi-delusional state. Martha gave her fiancé no real reason to suspect infidelity. She came from a strict Orthodox Jewish background, and did not question the wisdom of traditional values.

The union of Leo Tolstoy and Sonya Behrs has the dubious accolade of being perhaps the most unhappy of all literary marriages. This is probably because – in spite of considerable bad feeling – the couple stayed together for some forty-eight years. In the initial stages of the relationship, it was Sonya who suffered from episodes of jealousy; however, in time, she was superseded in this respect by her husband.

Tolstoy's episode of jealousy is extremely interesting, as it serves as one of the best examples of life imitating art.

In 1890, Tolstoy published his famous story, *The Kreutzer Sonata*. The protagonist, Pozdnyshev, is visited by an old acquaintance, the violinist Trukhachevsky. Trukhachevsky offers to play duets with Pozdnyshev's wife, and they become musical companions, meeting regularly to rehearse. Pozdnyshev becomes jealous, and suspects that their musical evenings are merely a cover for an increasingly intimate relationship: 'It was obvious that the piano playing was meant to drown their voices, and perhaps their kisses, too.' He comes to believe that he can read guilt in his wife's facial expressions and, accusing her of 'flirting', he is overcome by a jealous rage:

I had a horrible wish to beat her, to kill her, but knew I couldn't do it, and so in order to continue giving expression to my frenzied rage, I grabbed a paperweight from my writing desk, and with another shout of 'Go!', I hurled it to the floor, narrowly missing her.

Pozdnyshev attends a meeting in the provinces, but is plagued by images of his wife and Trukhachevsky making love. He tries to reason with himself, but fails. Unable to sleep, he decides to return home at five o'clock in the morning.

By the time Pozdnyshev arrives back in Moscow, it is midnight. On entering his house, the first thing he sees in the hallway is Trukhachevsky's coat. Quietly, he takes a steel poniard from its hanging place on the wall, and bursts in on his wife and Trukhachevsky, who are sharing a late meal after an evening of rehearsal. In the ensuing mêlée, Trukhachevsky escapes, but Pozdnyshev's wife is killed.

Many years later, Tolstoy found himself playing the part of Pozdnyshev, in a domestic love triangle that was nothing more than the product of his own imagination. Sonya had formed an entirely platonic relationship with the pianist and composer Taneyev. For no obvious reason, Tolstoy became consumed with jealousy. He was convinced that something was going on between Taneyev and his wife, which was the direct cause of many bitter quarrels. Sonya despaired, saying of her husband: '. . . all I ever get now is that mad jealous passion which drives all real affection out of my heart'. Fortunately, the Taneyev incident did not end with Sonya's murder, but the Tolstoy marriage, already profoundly unhappy, became completely lifeless. It is a measure of their unhappiness that, when Tolstoy was dying of pneumonia in a remote railway station, he refused to see his wife.

*   *   *

The relationship between jealousy and madness has been explored in literature from earliest times, but it wasn't until the twentieth century that psychopathological forms of jealousy were identified by the medical community. This isn't to say that doctors did not recognise jealousy as a dangerous passion. They certainly did. It was just that jealousy was simply counted among the symptoms of love sickness and other forms of melancholy. Jealousy was not recognised as a distinct entity.

In *The Anatomy of Melancholy*, Robert Burton wrote:

> Of all passions, as I have already proved, love is most violent, and of those bitter potions which this love-melancholy affords, this bastard jealousy is the greatest, as appears by those prodigious symptoms which it hath, and that it produceth.

According to Burton, jealousy shares some of the core symptoms of love melancholy: for example, fear and sorrow. However, jealousy thickens the existing emotional broth with a host of other symptoms, such as 'anxiety of mind, suspicion, aggravation' and 'restless thoughts'. He stresses that jealous preoccupations are all-consuming. The afflicted individual will not be able to concentrate on everyday events, and every aspect of life is affected. Jealousy is 'a gall corrupting the honey of our life, madness, vertigo'.

For Burton, the underlying physiological processes of jealousy and love melancholy are the same. The logic of the humoral model predisposes those who love to become love-sick. The hot, moist, sanguine stage of love burns black bile and evaporates the vital fluids. This in turn leads to the cold, dry melancholy stage, of which jealousy is a part.

Burton noted that old men (particularly when married to younger wives) are susceptible to jealousy on account of being 'cold and dry by nature'. Although Burton's biochemistry may have been wrong, his psychology is as accurate now as it was in the seventeenth century. Contemporary research into so-called May-December marriages shows that older husbands are frequently tormented by jealousy – which has been linked with spousal murder. International crime statistics show that between 20 and 30 per cent of spousal murders occur in marriages where the wife is ten or more years younger than the husband.

In the seventeenth century, the medical profession was not optimistic concerning the fate of those who experienced excessive jealousy. The illness could easily progress from suspicion, through several degrees of emotional disturbance, to madness. It was also believed that jealousy was strongly associated with violence and suicide. After the collapse of the humoral model, love melancholy gradually lost currency in medical circles – and with it, jealousy. The status of jealousy as a psychiatric illness became unclear. Of course, people continued to have fits of jealousy, behaving irrationally as a consequence, and this was well acknowledged by many students of human behaviour. For example, in *On Love*, Stendhal wrote: '. . . in these moments of jealousy one usually loses one's head'. Nevertheless, in the absence of an explanatory theoretical framework, psychiatrists were less inclined to diagnose jealousy.

Things changed, however, with the advent of the twentieth century. In the world of psychiatry, jealousy made a comeback, and it did so entirely independently of love sickness. While love melancholy remained an historical curiosity, jealousy seemed to have much greater contemporary relevance. This is probably because, at that time, neurologists and psychiatrists were becoming increasingly interested in paranoia (which often takes the form of groundless suspicion concerning the harmful intentions of others). Thus, jealousy seemed to be a special case of paranoid delusional thinking.

The subsequent widespread acceptance of jealousy as a psychiatric illness is yet another example of diagnostic inconsistency. Numerous beliefs associated with love sickness could be described as delusional, but it was only 'jealous delusions' that were identified as psychopathological.

Between 1910 and the 1970s, numerous diagnostic terms were introduced into the psychiatric lexicon to describe psychopathological jealousy. These included: 'Othello syndrome', 'erotic jealousy syndrome', 'morbid jealousy', 'psychotic jealousy', 'paranoid jealousy', and 'delusional jealousy'. Today, psychopathological jealousy is recognised in both DSM-IV and ICD-10 under the heading of 'delusional disorder' – which can take several forms including erotomania. In DSM-IV the diagnosis of delusional disorder is qualified by the addition of specific terms (the full diagnosis for a jealous individual becoming 'delusional disorder – jealous type').

The core feature of psychopathological jealousy is a delusion of infidelity. However, in many respects, jealousy seems to be as closely related to Obsessive Compulsive Disorder as it is to paranoia. Like individuals who suffer from an obsessional illness, jealous individuals seem to have little control over the contents of their awareness. They experience unpleasant intrusive thoughts and images about their partners (usually involving a sexual rival) and ruminate excessively on jealous themes. It is as though the cognitive apparatus of love has been hijacked. The same psychological mechanisms that make it possible for lovers to obsess continuously about each other continue to operate, but now for a different reason. Pleasant fantasies are now replaced by disturbing ones. The obsession serves not to maintain a bond, but to remind the individual that such a bond might be easily broken.

Psychopathological jealousy also resembles OCD insofar as it is associated with a great deal of checking. The purpose of this checking is to find evidence that confirms the delusional belief. Thus, the affected individual will carefully inspect his or her partner's clothes, belongings, credit card statements, e-mails, and mobile telephone messages. Anything that cannot be accounted for will automatically be interpreted as confirmation that an affair is taking place. The evidence does not have to be compelling; a blonde hair found on a lapel, or a screwed-up bus ticket in a back pocket, will suffice. Affected individuals are also prone to claim that they have direct evidence that sexual intercourse has taken place. An innocuous stain on a bed sheet, for example, will often be misidentified as semen or a vaginal secretion. Partners are constantly interrogated, the purpose of which is to check, double-check, and cross-check a partner's 'story'. Any inconsistencies, however minor, are taken to be further proof of infidelity.

Jealousy is also strongly associated with irritability. This can quickly turn into a jealous rage and result in violence, particularly among those who drink excessively. As one might predict according to evolutionary theory, psychopathological jealousy is more prevalent among men than women, although this is probably because psychopathological jealousy has been defined in terms of sexual jealousy alone. If the diagnostic system was modified, such that it was more sensitive to the symptoms of emotional jealousy, then more women might receive the diagnosis.

It is interesting that patients diagnosed with psychopathological jealousy can rarely identify a specific rival. Even when they claim to have gathered a substantial amount of incriminating information, the rival often remains nothing more than a vague, shadowy figure. For men in particular, the rival is like an evolutionary archetype, an ancient symbol of all rivals: a stealthy predator who can steal sexual favours like an incubus.

Occasionally, however, affected individuals *can* identify a rival. This in itself is interesting, as again, the experience patients describe is like an inverted form of a phenomenon found when people fall in love. Many describe 'just knowing' that a particular person has had sex with a partner. Just like 'love at first sight', this knowledge has no factual basis, but is characterised by a sense of absolute certainty. The rival is identified with the supernatural swiftness that lovers employ to identify each other.

Although psychopathological jealousy is complicated by a plethora of associated symptoms, the essential determinant of the diagnosis is the presence of a delusion – the delusion of a partner's infidelity – and herein lies a fundamental diagnostic dilemma. Who can really say that this is a delusion? The only person who can answer this question – the partner – might be disinclined to tell the truth. Psychopathological jealousy is a context-dependent diagnosis, just like erotomania. With respect to erotomania, the same individual can be classed as either a delusional psychiatric patient or an indefatigable romantic, depending on the beloved's response. Similarly, psychopathological jealousy can become non-pathological in the time it takes for an errant partner to confess.

Jealousy is an evolutionary adaptation – part of love's necessary madness. Indeed, the necessity of jealousy is demonstrated virtually every day in the media. Celebrity affairs frequently make headline news, and errant lovers are constantly being caught out. Salacious gossip is rife. Sometimes, the kind of incriminating evidence that 'delusional' patients look for is just the kind of evidence that confirms infidelity in the real (rather than imagined) world. Innocuous stains can suddenly acquire real significance.

Think, for example, of former US President Bill Clinton, Monica Lewinski and that famous dress. In a society where marriage means little, and sexual mores are relaxed, the green-ey'd monster is frequently counted as a friend, rather than a foe.

Unfortunately, jealousy, perhaps more than any other emotion, is most likely to result in tragedy. Some 13 per cent of all murders involve spouses, and most of these are attributable to threatened, suspected or confirmed infidelity.

The evolutionary sub-text of jealousy is amply demonstrated by an important study conducted by Martin Daly and Margo Wilson, who examined some fifty-eight marital conflicts that led to murder in Detroit. As predicted by evolutionary theory, the murders were committed predominantly by men. Indeed, men were responsible for two-thirds. Of these, sixteen men killed their wives because of infidelity or suspected infidelity, and seventeen killed a rival or suspected rival. Only two men killed their wives for a reason other than jealousy – namely self-defence. Two gay men included in the sample also killed their partners because of infidelity. Women also murdered their husbands because of infidelity, but at a much lower rate and most did so in self-defence – after their husbands had accused them of infidelity and become violent. The same trends are pan-cultural, and can be observed in many different countries all over the world.

To some extent, the power of evolutionary forces is enshrined in the law. For centuries, 'crime of passion' ('provocation' in the UK) has been accepted as a defence (mostly, of course, for men). It has its origins in a medieval view of marriage which supposes that all men have a right to seek fatal revenge (as opposed to divorce) in recompense for loss of reputation. Recently, government ministers in the UK have been reviewing the provocation defence, as it clearly favours men rather than women. Even so, many objections to changes in the law are expected. Because men respond differently from women when they learn of a partner's infidelity, some are insistent that the law should take this into account. Removal of the provocation defence is perceived as unfair, and a failure to respect how gender differences affect behaviour.

But how does killing one's mate make sense from an evolutionary perspective? Killing a rival is understandable, but killing a partner is self-defeating. After the energy expenditure of courtship, murder ensures that there will be absolutely no return. It is impossible to achieve reproductive success with a dead spouse. Why, then, should evolution predispose men to murder their mate?

Daly and Wilson suggest that evolution does no such thing. Rather, spousal murder is a mistake – a 'slip-up' in a game of brinkmanship. Men use violence to control women – largely to keep them as sexual partners – but the strategy is not entirely effective. Women can resist violence or ignore it. Subsequently, men must use increasing levels of violence to pose a credible threat. Eventually, a critical threshold is crossed and the physical effects of violence cannot be accurately predicted. Thus, spousal murder is a 'slip-up', the unintentional result of an escalating battle in which greater force is met with greater resistance until uncontrolled violence leads to murder.

Jealousy is a curious paradox. When we love passionately, we love dangerously. The mathematics of murder underscore this irony. Statistically, if we are going to kill anyone at all, it is more likely to be the person we claim to love than almost any other.

This terrible fact was faced by O.J. Simpson, who was famously tried (and controversially acquitted) for the murder of his wife, Nicole Brown-Simpson. Simpson said:

'Let's say I committed this crime. Even if I did do this it would have to have been because I loved her very much, right?' One could not find a more succinct testimony concerning the close relationship between love and madness.

9

Addicted to Love

> Every form of addiction is bad, no matter whether the
> narcotic be alcohol or morphine or idealism.
>
> *Memories, Dreams, Reflections*, Carl Gustav Jung

In Shere Hite's 1987 survey, *Women and Love*, 69 per
cent of married women and 48 per cent of single women
had come to the decision that they neither liked, nor
trusted, being in love. The responses of these participants
showed that they experienced love as mostly distressing,
volatile and dangerous: 'Being in love can give pleasure,
even joy, but most of the time it's painful, unreal and uncer-
tain.' Although several respondents attributed this dissatisfaction to their own inadequacies or the selection of
inappropriate partners, just as many seemed to have come
to the conclusion that there was something wrong with the
actual state of being in love. Indeed, 17 per cent said that
they could no longer take love seriously, because being in
love was no different from being mentally unbalanced:
'Being "in love" is a neurosis'; 'I would define it as the
only socially acceptable psychosis'; 'at best a disease created
on the movie screen'.

These personal testimonies are complemented by an
extensive literature which emphasises the painful features of

love. Sales for books such as Robin Norwood's *Women Who Love Too Much* (and its legions of imitators) demonstrate an enduring appetite for writing which recognises that love can be unhappy and difficult. One of the most interesting features of this literature (largely produced for a female readership) is that in spite of all the pain and heartache associated with love, few can give it up. Love hurts – but this doesn't stop anyone trying to find it.

Many of the popular psychology books on love describe a mental state which seems to be a close cousin of Dorothy Tennov's limerence. According to Tennov, the limerent individual obsesses, idealises and shows high levels of emotional dependency. Typically, limerent individuals are unhappy – but they do not learn from their mistakes. They feel compelled to stay in unsatisfactory relationships, or seek out new relationships that prove equally unsatisfactory. Tennov concluded that limerence was an almost exclusively female trait.

The fact that so many individuals experience love as unpleasant, but nevertheless continue to pursue it, is clearly puzzling. On the whole, people do not continue to engage in behaviours that make them unhappy. The exception, of course, is when an individual suffers from a mental illness; and perhaps the best example of this phenomenon is when mental illness takes the form of an addiction.

There is some debate in academic circles concerning the extent to which addiction can be considered a true mental illness. Controversy hinges on a fundamental question: does substance abuse arise in certain people who are already predisposed to form addictions, or does substance abuse turn people into addicts? Irrespective of the ongoing debate, addiction is now treated as a mental illness, insofar as it appears in the two major diagnostic manuals that we have previously discussed, DSM-IV and ICD-10. Both include substantial sections devoted to 'substance-related disorders' and 'mental and behavioural disorders due to psychoactive substance use'.

The prevalence of addiction in Western culture has provided us with a powerful new metaphor for the experience of being in love – a metaphor that has proved irresistible to song-writers. Cole Porter's 'I Get a Kick Out of You', Roxy Music's 'Love is the Drug', and Robert Palmer's 'Addicted to Love' are particularly transparent examples. Some artists have exploited common resonances even further, by recording songs about addiction that actually sound (and read) like love songs, for instance, Eric Clapton's 'Cocaine' and The Stranglers' 'Golden Brown'.

There are certainly some striking similarities between love and addiction: addicts feel incomplete; they obsess, crave, and feel out of control; they experience severe mood disturbance (oscillating between euphoric 'highs' and desperate 'lows'); they become dependent and, when denied, suffer from a withdrawal syndrome; addicts accept that their behaviour is irrational, but feel compelled to continue. All of these characteristics are of course typical of lovers – particularly those described by Hite and Tennov. Love and addiction also show similarities with respect to the changing factors that maintain them over time. At first, addiction is maintained by pleasure, but the intensity of this pleasure gradually diminishes and the addiction is then maintained by the avoidance of pain. Addicts find that they are taking drugs not to feel good, but simply to stop feeling bad. It is interesting that the type of dependent, unsatisfactory love described in popular psychology books for women goes through a similar transition. Eventually, these relationships are maintained not by pleasure, but by the avoidance of the pain associated with separation.

To what extent can love really be considered an addiction? The concept of addiction automatically implies the existence of a substance, or substances, which an individual has become addicted to. When people talk about being addicted to love, they are perfectly aware that they are using a metaphor. The 'addiction' is to a person, or an experience, not a chemical. Yet, our use of the addiction metaphor is very revealing. It shows that although romantic idealism has encouraged us to think of love as a spiritual phenomenon, our experience of love inclines us towards reductionism.

When we cannot find the words to express why a relationship is succeeding or floundering, we are inclined to invoke the concept of 'chemistry'. The chemistry is either right, wrong, or entirely absent. The instinctive appropriation of this word acknowledges that love is a very physical experience; the pulse quickens, tears fall and butterflies are felt in the stomach. Ironically, love – our most elevated emotion – frequently reminds us that we are flesh and blood – a sentiment expressed in John Donne's poem 'The Extasie': 'Love's mysteries in soules doe grow, But yet the body is his book.'

The idea that love is induced (at least in part) by chemical reactions has an ancient provenance, and has been thoroughly exercised as a narrative device in Western story telling – Cupid's arrows, Tristan and Isolde's love potion, and the dew from love-in-idleness (which appears in Shakespeare's *A Midsummer Night's Dream*) serve as typical examples. However, the initial link between love and biochemistry was probably made in prehistoric times, with the discovery of aphrodisiacs. Archaeological evidence suggests that aphrodisiacs – or at least substances thought to be aphrodisiacs – were being used in Asia from 7000 BC onwards.

We associate the term aphrodisiac with exotic substances, such as mandragora, rhino horn or cantharides, but these substances have always been complemented by a range of ordinary foods thought to have an effect on libido. In *The Art of Love*, for example, Ovid advises the amorous to try savory juice, pepper mixed with nettle-seed, camomile blended with vintage wine, white onions from Megara, honey, eggs, pine nuts and the 'hot, sexy rocket from your garden plot'. Other foods frequently described as aphrodisiacs were probably selected on account of the ancient doctrine of signatures, which presumes a general correspondence between various 'forms' and their 'properties'. Thus, the open oyster – which looks like (and perhaps some would say even smells like) the female genitalia – has long been counted as an aphrodisiac. Many long-stalked mushrooms (resembling the erect penis) have also been identified as aphrodisiacs according to the same principle.

Although aphrodisiacs were often used in 'love potions', it was generally understood that they worked by increasing sexual desire. The idea that love (rather than mere sexual desire) might have a chemical basis was not properly consolidated until Hippocratic medicine had become universally accepted. Thereafter, love has always been viewed, at least in part, as a physical phenomenon.

The Hippocratic doctrine of humours served as the principal explanatory framework in medicine for over a thousand years, but when it fell from favour, it was soon replaced by other physical theories. By the middle of the twentieth century, scientists had demonstrated that sexual interest was influenced by the presence of chemical messengers, or hormones, in the blood. These discoveries revived the old Hippocratic idea that love could be understood in terms of physical processes in the body, but now, unlike their venerable predecessors, modern medical scientists could actually isolate the biological building blocks of love – complex molecules that tangled with the nervous system and inflamed desire.

According to Hippocratic principles, love is unstable and prone to progress towards psychopathology through two chemically different stages – the sanguine and the melancholy. Modern psychophysiologists have reached similar conclusions, suggesting that as superficial physical attraction develops into an emotional attachment, sex hormones become less important than bonding hormones. On a larger scale, the transition from passionate to companionate love is also presumed to reflect fundamental biochemical changes.

In the early 1980s, American psychiatrist Michael Liebowitz suggested that further clues to the underlying chemistry of love might be gleaned by identifying similarities between the different phases (or features) of love, and the effects of psychoactive substances. Such correspondences might indicate that the human body is capable of producing or synthesising chemicals that are similar in structure to recreational and prescription drugs. Thus, the initial rush of excitement associated with falling in love might be mediated by chemicals that resemble amphetamines and other stimulants (such as cocaine). Calm or positive states, on the other hand, might be mediated by chemicals that resemble narcotics (such as heroin, opium or morphine), tranquillisers (such as valium) and sedatives (such as barbiturates, alcohol and cannabis). In addition, Liebowitz suggested that the more transcendental experiences associated with love – an enhanced sense of beauty, timelessness and spiritual feelings – might be mediated by chemicals similar to psychedelics (such as LSD, mescaline and psilocybin).

If Liebowitz is right, and the human body is a kind of

natural pharmacy producing amphetamines, barbiturates and psychedelics, then this would go some way towards explaining why love is so frequently compared with addiction.

We all have the potential to become love junkies, and no one can escape the 'inner dealer'.

One of the most important chemicals to be released when prospective lovers meet is phenylethylamine (or PEA) – an amphetamine-like compound that raises mood and energy levels. Typically, it is complemented by the release of fear hormones such as adrenaline and noradrenaline which sharpen the senses. The potent cocktail of PEA and fight-flight hormones engenders a state of giddy excitement: an exhilarating 'rush'.

The existence of PEA not only explains why we crave love, but also why a romance interrupted in its early stages can be so distressing. Even though a couple may not have known each other long enough to achieve closeness, rejection can still be utterly devastating. When lovers are rejected, PEA levels suddenly drop and, like addicts, they immediately become depressed and agitated. Life is suddenly empty, dull and without purpose. The deep distress of the broken-hearted bears close comparison to the addict's 'crash' into the abstinent hell of 'cold turkey'.

In twentieth-century cinema and literature, the broken-hearted lover is often to be found in a café, eschewing nutrition in favour of endless cups of strong black coffee and a continuous chain of filterless cigarettes. Individuals who are unlucky in love often try to modify their mood by ingesting stimulants, and it might well be that they are unconsciously trying to compensate for the absence of PEA. A more recently discussed (but less stylish) response to rejection is binge eating – which, curiously, is even more understandable from a biochemical perspective. Chocolate contains stimulant chemicals that are very similar in structure to PEA; thus, chocolate bingeing might be a form of 'self-medication' which alleviates the symptoms of PEA withdrawal.

The word 'chocolate' has an ancient provenance, being derived from the Aztec chocolatl, meaning 'food of the gods'. Only the Aztec aristocracy – who would drink it from goblets of gold and eat it with spoons of tortoiseshell – were permitted to consume chocolate, which they also considered to be an aphrodisiac. The intervening five hundred years have done little to damage chocolate's reputation as a decadent, sensuous confection and one wonders whether this reputation has been sustained by genuine chemical links between chocolate, love and sex. In our culture, a shared cocoa before bedtime is a routine usually associated with advancing years and incipient insomnia. Yet, in reality, senior citizens might be serendipitously enjoying benefits above and beyond a good night's sleep.

PEA-like chemicals could also explain why lovers have traditionally always chosen chocolates as a gift (particularly when first dating). Eating chocolate might increase levels of amphetamine-like substances, intensifying love's natural high. However, it should be noted that the role of PEA with respect to love has been called into question by some critics, who suggest that PEA, when ingested as a constituent of food, may not be metabolised fast enough (or in sufficient quantities) to reach the brain.

In addition to the release of PEA, the early stages of a relationship are also associated with the release of fear hormones, and these too might have addictive properties. Although love and fear appear to occupy opposite ends of the emotional spectrum, they are in fact connected biochemically. In the 1890s, the perspicacious Victorian physician Sir Henry Finck observed that: 'Love can only be excited by strong and vivid emotion, and it is almost immaterial whether these emotions are agreeable or disagreeable.' Fear is a particularly good example of a 'disagreeable' emotion that contemporary research has found can 'excite' love.

There are a number of studies which show that elevated levels of physical arousal influence the perception of beauty. In the 1970s, for example, a research group in Vancouver arranged for two groups of men to walk across either an ordinary 'safe' bridge or a suspension bridge with low hand-rails that swung over a 230-foot drop – the latter being obviously more 'arousing' than the former. After completing the task, all experimental subjects were approached by an attractive research confederate who asked them to complete a questionnaire before providing them with her telephone number. Subjects were invited to give her a call if they wanted to discuss the experiment. The men who crossed the suspension bridge gave more sexualised answers on their questionnaires, and proved more likely to make a follow-up telephone call. It would seem that arousal – in the form of anxiety – made the attractive accomplice much more desirable.

Further evidence demonstrates that merely thinking we are aroused – even when we are not – is sufficient to alter our perception of beauty. In a classic laboratory study conducted by psychologist Stuart Valins, male college students were shown slides of *Playboy* models while being given false feedback of their heart rate. Some images were supposed to have increased their heart rate, while others were supposed to have had no effect. Subsequently, when asked to rate the slides for attractiveness, the experimental subjects displayed a preference for those whom they only thought had caused their heart rate to increase.

The fact that strong emotion (most notably fear) can encourage romance has been exploited by certain British theme parks who have reinvented the singles night, offering clients 'adrenaline dates' where the traditional candlelit dinner is replaced by a very untraditional selection of perilous white-knuckle rides.

Indirect evidence for the addictive properties of adrenaline can be drawn from several sources. Many individuals, for example, choose to participate in dangerous sports in order to experience a regular 'super-fix' of adrenaline, and clinical studies show that individuals who have been in life-threatening situations can paradoxically show increased levels of risk-taking behaviour such as driving too fast or getting into fights. It is almost as though they have developed a taste for fear.

Perhaps the most astonishing example of fear exciting love is the so-called Stockholm syndrome. On 23 August 1973, four Stockholm bank employees were taken hostage. They were held captive for six days by two ex-convicts who threatened to kill them, but also showed small acts of kindness. When the hostages were finally liberated by the police, all expressed considerable concern over the welfare of their captors. Eventually, two of the hostages formed relationships with their former captors and were engaged to be married.

Although the behaviour of the Stockholm hostages seemed bizarre at the time, subsequent research has shown the phenomenon is actually quite common. Such attachments have been formed by concentration camp prisoners, political prisoners, prisoners of war, cult members, pimp-controlled prostitutes, incest victims, battered women and victims of hijacking. Of course, many psychological factors contribute to the development of the Stockholm syndrome, but the most important factor seems to be intense fear. If chemicals like adrenaline are indeed addictive, it is easy to see how an attachment might develop between hostage and captor. The captor is, after all, the 'works', the means by which the addictive substance is introduced into the blood stream.

Among drugs of abuse, opium has acquired a certain cultural cachet. It is strongly associated with Romantic philosophy, Romantic poetry and the Romantic literary tradition. The practice of taking opium with alcohol (in the form of laudanum) became popular among artists of the late eighteenth and early nineteenth centuries, on account of its remarkable mind-altering properties. As well as being an analgesic, opium seemed to unfetter the imagination. In strange, dream-like states, Romantic poets experienced extraordinary inspirational visions. Opium also modified perceptual experience, delaying the flow of time and making the world more sensual. The relationship between opium and sensuality was reinforced in the opium dens of Victorian London, where a gentleman might not only 'chase the dragon', but also procure the services of a prostitute.

The idea that the human body itself might be capable of producing opium-like substances was first raised when psychologists turned their attention to the study of pain. Existing theories suggested that pain was the result of tissue damage, and therefore a relationship should exist between the severity of an injury and the amount of pain experienced. However, doctors had known for some time that this was simply untrue. For example, in combat situations, soldiers can suffer the most appalling injuries yet at the same time report little (or no) pain. This kind of observation suggested that under certain critical conditions the body might produce its own analgesia.

In the 1970s, scientists were excited by the discovery of naturally occurring opium-like substances – peptides – in the brain. These have since become better known as endorphins.

Initial investigations demonstrated that endorphins were almost certainly involved in the regulation of pain, and subsequent research has shown that they also modulate the release of sex hormones, the experience of pleasure, and appetite. The fact that endorphins are released during intercourse is well appreciated by many migraine sufferers, some of whom discover that sex is a kind of natural remedy for painful headaches.

Among the endorphins and endorphin-like chemicals that are released during intercourse, one has attracted a considerable amount of interest and controversy. This is the hormone known as oxytocin, an amino acid peptide. It is probably the only substance that comes anywhere close to being identified by scientists as the fundamental chemical constituent of love. If Cupid's arrows are dipped in anything, they are dipped in oxytocin.

The first study to arouse major interest in it was published in 1979, when C.A. Pedersen and J.R. Prange published a paper with the austere title: 'Induction of maternal behaviour in virgin rats after intracerebroventricular administration of oxytocin'. Pedersen and Prange had found that by injecting oxytocin directly into the ventricles (fluid-filled spaces) of the brain, 'virgin rats' could be made to behave like 'mother rats'. Oxytocin appeared to be a 'bonding' or attachment hormone – in essence, a hormone of love.

Subsequent studies of human beings have shown that almost all forms of bonding are associated with the release of oxytocin and endorphins. In *The Scientification of Love*, radical French obstetrician Michel Odent suggests that the very early stages of the mother-child relationship provide a model for all other forms of loving relationship, and that the experience of love is underpinned by a biochemistry that is likely to promote a form of addictive dependency.

It was . . . in 1979 that the maternal release of morphine-like hormones during labour and delivery was demonstrated, and the release of these endorphins is now well documented. In the early 1980s we learnt that the baby also releases its own endorphins in the birth process, both mother and baby are impregnated with opiates. The property of opiates to induce states of dependency is well known, so it is easy to anticipate how the beginning of a 'dependency' – an attachment – will be likely to develop.

Oxytocin is essential to the birth process and the physiology of attachment. It stimulates uterine contractions and triggers the 'milk ejection reflex'. Also, when the nipple is sucked, oxytocin levels rise. The intense pleasure that some women experience while breast-feeding is very probably caused by elevated levels of oxytocin. Many new mothers describe warm, 'floaty' sensations, that recollect the dreamy, suspended awareness of the opium addict. Elevated levels of oxytocin and endorphins in breast milk also account for the peculiar expression that creeps across a baby's face while feeding – most people immediately recognise it as the expression of someone who is 'stoned' or at least very seriously inebriated. It is in this altered state of consciousness that the bond between mother and child is secured.

Under the influence of the love hormone, mother and child can often stare into each other's eyes indefinitely – prefiguring the searching, mutual absorption of lovers.

In 'The Extasie', John Donne's besotted pair enter a trance-like state, linked by shared sight lines (or eye-beams):

> Our eye-beams twisted, and did thread
> Our eyes, upon one double string

Speechless, they remain fixed in this position for a whole day, while their souls advance along the 'double string' of sight – eventually meeting and merging together. Eyes cannot help but prompt thoughts of union. Laboratory research has shown that the more people profess to be in love, the more time they spend looking into each other's eyes. It is not by chance that time stands still for mothers, babies, lovers and opium addicts. It is because of brain chemistry.

Oxytocin plays a small part in increasing initial levels of sexual desire, but levels rise dramatically as couples become more intimate. Kissing and touching stimulate the release of yet more oxytocin, and levels peak with orgasm. During orgasm, a man will produce three to five times more oxytocin than normal, while a woman will produce even higher levels. In the same way that oxytocin cements the relationship between mother and child, its release during sexual intercourse may also serve to strengthen the emotional bond between lovers.

It is assumed that (along with the release of endorphins) oxytocin is responsible for the feelings of euphoria and intense pleasure that accompany intercourse and orgasm. In addition, the opiate marinade in which the brain is bathed must account – to a greater or lesser extent – for the semi-mystical states of union and merging that many lovers experience during intercourse.

The effects of oxytocin on memory are mixed and complex, but, in conjunction with another related hormone called vasopressin, oxytocin may have an important role to play in the generation and preservation of new memories. Thus, oxytocin may help consolidate the image of a lover in the neural machinery – a vivid image that will serve as a reminder of recent pleasures.

After accepting the proposal of Tsarevich Nicholas, Princess Alix of Hesse wrote to her fiancé: 'You are locked in my heart, the little key is lost and now you must stay there for ever.' Oxytocin may be the means by which pictures of those we love are locked in the metaphorical heart – and the little key may be nothing more than nine amino acids.

Elevated oxytocin levels might also explain why romantic evenings are recalled so vividly. The sights, sounds and smells that we associate with an important date seem to be impervious to decay. When we succumb to love's chemistry, the accidental touch of a finger, a subtle fragrance and an enigmatic smile can be faithfully preserved while all else fades.

Oxytocin is a hormone that has obvious evolutionary significance. It is instrumental in creating and maintaining romantic and maternal bonds. Thus, in the ancestral environment, its presence would have had a profound effect on reproductive success. By creating a set of mutual dependencies, the integrity of the family unit would have been sustained for longer periods, ensuring infant survival, and increasing the likelihood of gene transmission.

Although both men and women produce oxytocin, there is some evidence to suggest that oxytocin levels are somewhat higher in women. This is most marked when women are in their twenties, the decade in which they are also most fertile. Studies of oxytocin levels and sexual arousal also show that when women masturbate, they not only produce more oxytocin than men, but also levels which are liable to climb with each subsequent orgasm. This would suggest that young women may be slightly more prone than young men to form 'dependent' relationships. In effect, they are getting a bigger and better 'hit', which in turn might be associated with a bigger and more substantial withdrawal syndrome. This underlying difference in body chemistry might be responsible, at least in part, for the addictive patterns of loving described in the many popular psychology books for women.

This gender asymmetry would also make a certain degree of evolutionary sense. In the ancestral environment, it was far more important for females to retain their partners than the reverse. Biological inequalities (such as the numerical disparity between egg and sperm) meant that females had (and still do have) fewer opportunities to reproduce. Thus, for females, much more was 'hanging' on the survival of each child. So the sustained parental investment of a mate was absolutely essential. Without a male to provide, the vulnerable human infant would have difficulty surviving to adulthood. A chemical dependency on a mate would help ensure that females remained (and worked at) relationships, even if they proved unsatisfactory. Evolutionary pressures would select for tenacity, rather than personal happiness – in essence, for a woman who 'loves too much', a woman who might be 'clingy' even in a relationship characterised by abuse and unhappiness. It has already been suggested that evolutionary pressures may have rendered men more vulnerable to love's madness than women. However, once a relationship has been established, evolutionary pressures might reverse this pattern. In the longer term, perhaps it is women who are programmed to love beyond reason.

Oxytocin is the closest science has come to identifying the chemical substrate of love. As yet, nobody has experimented with the substance as a recreational drug, but such an experiment would be possible. Until recently, an oxytocin nasal spray was available in the USA, marketed as Syntocinon. It was intended for short-term use by new mothers experiencing problems with their milk-ejection reflex. The sprays are no longer available, but some pharmacists in the USA have been known to make them up on prescription. It is doubtful whether any of these have made it on to the streets – but the prospect is alive with possibilities. What would happen if subsequent generations of drug-users changed their pharmacological preference from LSD or E to O? What would a club look like, in which all of those who were formerly armed with poppers were equipped instead with Sintocinon sprays?

The phrase 'love is in the air' would take on a whole new meaning.

Another addictive substance often linked with love is alcohol. Obviously, the body does not produce its own alcohol, but biochemists have suggested that the effects of alcohol on neurotransmitter levels, and the neurochemistry of love, are very similar. At the level of experience, this observation is legitimised by the highest of authorities – the word of God as expressed in the Holy Bible.

The poems that make up 'The Song of Songs' represent the very first 'anthology' of connected love poetry. They were written down sometime after the fifth century BC, but their origins are much earlier. Indeed, the poems included in 'The Song of Songs' were probably preserved by an oral tradition that dates back at least another five hundred years. Although the poems are attributed to Solomon, the identity of the real author is unknown.

In 'The Song of Songs', two lovers speak verses, with each taking turns in an alternating sequence. Originally, the lovers were thought to be allegorical, representing God, the Israelites, or the Soul; however, modern scholars have abandoned this interpretation, and are now content to view the collection as a set of secular lyrics that celebrate passionate love.

One of the most conspicuous features of 'The Song of Songs' is the poet's use of bibulous language. The first speaker's senses are so overwhelmed by love, she is intoxicated by the experience, and expresses this clearly in the first few lines: 'For your love is better than wine.' Love, like alcohol, produces cravings, and the poet shuns restraint: '. . . drink: drink deeply, O lovers!' The verses become more and more impassioned, and the lovers describe each other as beings of almost supernatural beauty, with tormented, breathless repetitions: 'Behold, you are beautiful, my love; Behold, you are beautiful; Your eyes are doves. Behold, you are beautiful, my beloved, truly lovely.'

The words tumble out with the undisciplined urgency of insobriety. When the lovers kiss, the experience is so sublime, the sensorium becomes unreliable. Pleasure becomes hallucinatory: 'Your lips distil nectar, my bride; honey and milk are under your tongue.' But all of this luxurious melting and dissolving, pitching and tossing, proves too much. In despair, the female speaker cries, 'I am sick with love.'

If love makes us feel drunk, then the reverse is also true. Being drunk can also make us fall in love – or at least start the process. This effect seems to be mediated by the effect of alcohol on the perception of beauty. Most people have experienced the disconcerting phenomenon of suddenly finding friends, acquaintances or colleagues more attractive than usual after a few drinks. Moreover, many relationships are launched by a sexual indiscretion that takes place under the influence of alcohol.

The effect of alcohol on the perception of beauty is so common, a colloquial term has been created to describe it – 'beer goggles'. Recently, British psychologists Barry Jones and Ben Jones conducted the first empirical investigation into the 'beer-goggles effect', and found that four units of alcohol (the equivalent of two pints of lager or two and a half glasses of wine) are sufficient to increase estimates of attractiveness by 25 per cent. The authors of the study suggested that the 'beer-goggles effect' is produced because alcohol stimulates the nucleus accumbens, a structure in the brain thought to have a role in determining facial attractiveness.

In the middle ages, the learned recognised four stages of drunkenness which corresponded with the four humours: lion-drunk (or choleric), ape-drunk (or sanguine), mutton-drunk (or phlegmatic) and swine-drunk (or melancholic). Implicit in this conceptual system is the suggestion that it is possible to drink oneself into a state of love melancholy or love sickness. Even medieval scholars, it would seem, recognised the extraordinary consequences of donning a pair of 'beer goggles'.

Michael Liebowitz's suggestion, that there is much to be learned from correspondences between the effects of love and the effects of psychoactive substances, has proved very insightful, and there is a growing body of biochemical research that supports his view. However, the most compelling evidence linking love and addiction has come from a different source – brain-scanning studies.

On 5 September 2000, London-based neuroscientist Semir Zeki and his Swiss graduate student Andreas Bartels submitted a brief paper to the academic journal *NeuroReport*. It was called 'The neural basis of romantic love' – a title that former generations would have considered the stuff of fantasy. When the paper was published later the same year, it caused a sensation. For the first time ever, those parts of the brain that create the feeling of being in love had been identified.

Although brain-scanning technology is complex, the design of the experiment was very simple. Bartels and Zeki recruited eleven women and six men, all heterosexual, who professed to be 'truly, deeply and madly' in love with their partners. Eleven countries and several ethnic groups were represented in the sample, and the average length of relationship was 2.4 years. Each of the participants was given two brain scans: the first while they were looking at a photograph of their partner, and a second while looking at photographs of same-sex friends (with whom they were not in love). By comparing both sets of brain scans, it was possible to determine which areas of brain activity were exclusively associated with love.

When looking at their partners, those subjects who were in love showed brain activity in four main areas: the anterior cingulate cortex, the medial insula, the putamen and the caudate nucleus. Collectively, these structures are known to mediate a number of brain functions such as negative and positive emotions, self-awareness, and the assessment of other people's emotions and states of mind.

It is interesting that, having performed the ultimate act of reductionism, Bartels and Zeki could not resist the inclusion of a poetic reference in their otherwise coolly executed paper:

> By showing that a unique set of interconnected areas become active when humans view the face of someone who elicits a unique and characteristic set of emotions, we have shown that underlying one of the richest experiences of mankind is a functionally specialised system of the brain. It is perhaps surprising that so complex and overwhelming a sentiment should correlate differentially with activity in such restricted regions of the brain, and fascinating that the face that launched a thousand ships should have done so through such a limited expanse of cortex.

In addition, Bartels and Zeki make a further observation that seems to add a final and decisive confirmation with regards to love's addictive properties. They point out that in several other studies of cocaine- and opiate-induced euphoria, the very same areas of the brain show increased levels of activity. Thus, love and recreational drugs seem to affect the brain in exactly the same way.

It was suggested earlier that one of the characteristics shared by addicts and lovers is that they both obsess. The addict is always preoccupied by the next 'fix' or 'hit', while the lover is always preoccupied by the beloved. Such obsessions are associated with compulsive urges to seek out what is desired, be it a recreational drug or a person. It is of considerable interest, therefore, that the areas of brain activity that Bartels and Zeki associate with love are also those that other brain-scanning studies have found to be particularly active in patients suffering from Obsessive Compulsive Disorder. The anterior cingulate cortex and caudate nucleus are particularly active in patients with OCD, and several studies have found high levels of activity in the putamen and insula. As such, the Bartels and Zeki findings may add yet further support to the notion that love – even when euphoric – is like a mental illness.

Although all of Bartels and Zeki's experimental subjects considered themselves to be 'madly' in love, none were suffering from a recognised mental illness. Yet, the results of their brain scans clearly demonstrate that being in love and being mentally ill are biologically very similar states.

Since Bartels and Zeki's groundbreaking study, a further scanning investigation – relevant to the subject of love and addiction – has been conducted by Knut Kampe and colleagues. Sixteen volunteers (8 men and 8 women) rated forty images of unfamiliar faces while being brain-scanned. Irrespective of gender, when faces were rated as attractive, a part of the brain known as the ventral striatum was activated – a structure associated with the anticipation of pleasure, and again implicated in addiction. Interestingly, the ventral striatum was only activated when images were face-on, thus establishing direct eye contact.

Love Sick

When eyes meet across a crowded room, the pleasure centres of the brain glow with expectation. And who knows? Perhaps primal memories rise closer to the surface, reminding us that those eyes can stop time. The look of love is an invitation – an invitation to experience again the fathomless, opiate bliss of infancy.

10

What Becomes of the Broken-hearted?

... do not leave me in this abyss, where I cannot find you! Oh, God, it is unutterable! I cannot live without my life! I cannot live without my soul.

Wuthering Heights, Emily Brontë

Among the many historical figures who might be canonised as the patron saint of the broken-hearted, Lady Caroline Lamb must rank highly as a very competitive candidate. Her unrequited passion for the poet, Gordon Lord Byron, has been dissected in numerous biographies, re-imagined by novelists and celebrated in film. She has diverted the course of medieval Marianism, becoming a bedsitter icon for generations of rejected lovers. It is to her, rather than Mary, that the broken-hearted should now pray for intercession.

Caroline Lamb reinvented the romantic relationship for the modern world. Her story contains many of the old romantic themes – forbidden love, idealisation and impending doom – but it departs from tradition in two ways. Firstly, Lamb cast herself as the tragic lead, appropriating for women a role that had formerly always belonged to men;

and secondly, although her love was unhappy, it was never redemptive. Lamb operated beyond the reach of gender stereotypes and tidy moral certainties.

Benita Eisler (author of a scholarly biography of Byron) has observed: 'Lasting fewer than five months, Byron's affair with Lady Caroline Lamb is still the best-known episode of his life. Their passion – his brief, hers lifelong – came to define the canon of romantic love: scandalous, destructive, doomed, and inevitable.' It is extraordinary that such a brief relationship should skew not only our perception of Byron's biography, but also all subsequent representations of romance. The key to Lamb's great influence may be that she – more than any other person born after the Renaissance – reminded polite society that love and madness are inseparable. She turned her own suffering into a public event – and in doing so achieved immortality.

Caroline Lamb (or Caro as her contemporaries called her) had an unusual appearance. From childhood, she had attracted nicknames such as 'Ariel' and 'Sprite', and the images that we have of her confirm how appropriate these names were. In a well-known portrait by Sir Thomas Lawrence, she seems to be made of ectoplasm: a ghostly Caro is caught literally dissolving into the background. Yet her eyes are large and clear, smouldering with a passionate intensity.

In 1812, Caro was twenty-seven years old. She had been unhappily married for eight of them. Great love stories demand that conventions such as love at first sight should be observed. Caro not only met such demands, she surpassed them: she fell in love with Byron before she had even seen him, or even seen a sketch or miniature portrait of him. After reading Byron's *Childe Harold*, she declared that his appearance was irrelevant. She could love the author of *Childe Harold* whatever he looked like. Subsequently, she wrote an anonymous letter to him (thinly concealing her identity), and made it quite clear that she intended to start a love affair.

Caro's love for Byron was, at first, fully reciprocated. Byron paid her frequent visits and wrote to her incessantly. Some days he would write as many as ten letters. Moreover, Byron wanted to possess her exclusively and insisted that Caro give up waltzing – then the latest dance craze – because he could not bear to see her in another man's arms.

Having realised her ambition to make Byron her lover, Caro became obsessed with him. This resulted in some extraordinary lapses of etiquette. At public events, she could not stop herself from touching him, and when he was invited to events alone, she would wait outside with the coachmen until he came out. She would then follow him into his carriage without a chaperone. Such was her lack of discretion that Byron himself (no stranger to scandal) urged Caro to be more cautious, but if anything, her behaviour became even more provocative.

Caro kept his passions on the boil by making him jealous. She once sent him into a violent rage by refusing to swear that she loved him more than her husband. This, however, was a dangerous strategy to play with a man like Byron. He was already unnerved by her power over him, and, like many nonconformists, he had a deeply conservative side. He did not want to risk being ostracised by his peer group, and Caro's behaviour was exhausting everyone's patience. It was only possible to flout the rules for a limited period of time – thereafter, it would not be tolerated.

Byron began to withdraw – not a great deal, but enough to arouse Caro's suspicions. She became even more obsessed with him, and even more unwilling to compromise. She began to stalk him.

Disguising herself as a page-boy, she gained entry into

Byron's rooms, where she was later discovered rifling through his papers. Not long after, she repeated her ploy, and discovered Byron entertaining another woman.

Byron became confused. On the one hand, he was aware that Caro's obsessionality could, quite easily, destroy them both. On the other hand, he recognised a kindred spirit. Although he knew that their relationship must end, he found it almost impossible to disentangle himself. He would complain to others about her intolerable behaviour, and then write her reassuring letters or, even worse, arrange to meet her.

In the end, Byron attempted to resolve the situation by colluding with Caro's mother-in-law, Lady Melbourne, an influential woman with a reputation for ruthless scheming and manipulation. Her talent for weaving webs of intrigue was so well known, some called her 'the Spider'. It was almost as though, in order to free himself, Byron needed to betray Caro decisively. Part of the Spider's strategy was to marry Byron off to her niece, the virtuous Annabella Milbanke – but this would take time.

When Caro learned that Byron had enlisted the help of Lady Melbourne to extricate himself from the relationship, she responded with more harassment. Again, she disguised herself as a man, gained entry into Byron's rooms, and this time refused to leave. The following month, Caro sent Byron some of her pubic hair, with a request that the gesture be reciprocated.

Byron had had enough. He asked Lady Melbourne to rid him of Caro – by whatever means she had at her disposal. Caro was placed under surveillance by her family and her freedom was curtailed. She knew that Byron was betraying her, and her misery turned to anger which was expressed with characteristic theatricality. She had the silver buttons of her pages' uniforms inscribed with an adulterated version of the Byron family motto: 'Ne Crede Byron' ('Do not trust Byron'). Then, she stage-managed a bizarre piece of cathartic melodrama. She gathered together a group of young girls, dressed them in white, and instructed them to dance around a huge bonfire. While they did this, they recited curses, especially composed by Caro, and cast Byron's letters and poetry into the flames. As with most of Caro's histrionic displays, news of these events travelled fast. Subsequently, Byron (rather cruelly) took to calling Caro 'little Mania'. He feigned amusement, but really Caro's obsessionality was sufficiently extreme to disturb him. He would have been even more disturbed had he known that the letters she tossed into the flames were merely copies. She was still so much in love with him, she could not bear to destroy the originals.

Betrayed, humiliated and heartbroken, Caro simply refused to let Byron go. She wrote to him again, requesting a lock of his hair. He responded by sending her a lock of the hair of Lady Oxford – his new lover. To make his situation absolutely clear, the letter was sealed with Lady Oxford's coat of arms. This did nothing to dampen Caro's ardour. She responded by forging Byron's handwriting in order to get his publisher to release one of his portraits.

Byron was now finding Caro's presence in his life oppressive, but at the same time, his old ambivalence had never been entirely conquered. After all his efforts to distance himself from Caro, he began to contemplate seeing her again. Eisler believes that in many respects, Byron's love for Caro (like Caro's love for him) was pathological. Indeed, the language she employs is medical, rather than romantic: 'His thraldom to Caroline Lamb was a lingering disease, and no act of will, no love of another, could cure him. The illness had to run its course.'

Even though Caro's behaviour had been highly disturbed,

she was yet to reach her apogee. This was accomplished on the night of Lady Heathcote's waltz party. She had accepted an invitation, knowing that Byron would be there. Those who were privy to society gossip would have probably expected a scene of some kind, and Caro did not disappoint them. She delivered a coup of operatic dimensions.

Lady Melbourne's is the only surviving first-hand account. Caro and Byron exchanged a few frigid words. Then, in full view, Caro was seen mutilating herself with a broken glass and a pair of scissors. Almost immediately, she was covered in blood – a macabre travesty of Regency poise. Before anyone could intervene, she fainted, and was swiftly removed from the premises.

What had Byron said to provoke Caro? Apparently, very little. Writing to Lady Melbourne the following day, he explained what had passed between them: 'She took hold of my hand as I passed & pressed it against some sharp instrument – & said – "I mean to use this" – I answered – "Against me I presume" – & passed on.'

Caro did her very best to underplay the significance of what had happened. According to her, the self-inflicted wounds had been entirely accidental. She had been play-fully brandishing a knife, which had caused those around her to panic. She had been misunderstood. In the rush to seize the knife, she had been cut – that was all. It was a joke that had gone horribly wrong. But Caro was fooling nobody. From that night onwards, she was largely excluded from society.

Yet, bizarrely, from Caro's point of view, the evening of Lady Heathcote's waltz party was something of a success. Byron, fearing more of the same, decided that appeasement was now his only option. He agreed to write to her and, occasionally, they met.

Nevertheless, Byron was still trying to sever his emotional

links with Caro. He began an incestuous relationship with his half-sister, and continued to pursue Annabella Milbanke. In due course, his perverse attachment to Caro seemed, at last, to be petering out. She, too, seemed less troubled.

He was mistaken.

The 'disease' had not quite run its course.

On hearing rumours of Byron's colourful love life, Caro became intensely jealous. Seeking to avoid more high drama, Byron acted quickly, and admitted her to his rooms without argument. Afterwards, he denied renewing their sexual relationship, but Caro insisted that they became lovers again, albeit briefly. To what extent this renewed intimacy was real or imagined we will never know. However, at least psychologically, Caro seems to have achieved some kind of closure. She chose to construe their meetings as a fond farewell: two lovers, bruised by the intensity of their own passion, making peace before parting.

One year after Byron and Caro had officially ended their disastrous affair, Caro added a final flourish. Again, she started to appear in Byron's rooms (at all hours) and again, she was discovered raking through his papers, but these relatively modest intrusions really were her swansong. She never bothered Byron again.

It was Caroline Lamb, of course, who helped ensure Byron's celebrity by providing him with one of the most memorable epithets ever composed: 'Mad, bad, and dangerous to know' – but Caro's spectacular grief made it far more true of her than of him.

Lady Caroline Lamb is an extreme example of what can happen when people are rejected. Yet, we can sympathise with her misery. Only a tiny proportion of humanity escapes the pangs of unrequited love. Indeed, most people will have had some experience of unrequited love before reaching adulthood. The 'crushes' and infatuations of adolescence almost invariably lead to heartache, particularly when the individual (unaware of his or her place in the beauty hierarchy) falls in love with one who is unattainable. When we fall in love, we risk rejection – a fact that we learn relatively early.

Love is felt so intensely, it seems inconceivable that it will not always produce a response. Love is antiphonal. The words 'I love you' contain an implicit demand. They are incomplete without the answer: 'I love you too.' Implicit faith in romantic idealism makes us confident that if we proclaim our love loud enough, we will get an answer. As when calling across a valley, we assume that an echo will acknowledge our effort. But love does not obey physical laws. Sometimes we proclaim our love and there is no reply. Our words are killed by the dead acoustic of a cold heart and the ensuing silence is terrible.

The belief that true love will always be reciprocated is one of love's most enduring delusions. In Iris Murdoch's *A Severed Head*, one of the characters comes to realise this, and wistfully confesses: 'I was perhaps moreover a little the dupe of that illusion of lovers that the beloved object must, somehow, respond, that an extremity of love not only merits but compels some return.' Yet love, however extreme, does not compel 'some return' – and the more an individual believes in this 'illusion', the more confusing, the more devastating, the more utterly incomprehensible rejection will be.

The language of unrequited love tends towards the cataclysmic: worlds 'fall apart' and lives are 'crushed' or 'ruined'. When love is frustrated, there seems to be no purpose to life, no reason to 'carry on'. Love, even at its best, can be a painful, difficult experience, but when unrequited, love becomes toxic. Rejection can kill.

The countryside is full of high bridges, coastal paths and wind-scoured bluffs known locally as 'Lovers' Leap'. The desperation of disappointed lovers is engraved in the landscape – an indication that unrequited love has always had devastating consequences.

Robert Burton remarked on this phenomenon in the seventeenth century: 'It is well known in every village how many have either died for love, or voluntarily made away with themselves, that I need not much labour to prove it.' He goes on to cite literary examples, such as Dido and Medea, as well as real case histories like those of a young medical student who (for the love of a doctor's daughter) poisoned himself, and a barber in Frankfurt who cut his own throat because the woman he loved was betrothed to another. Suicide is never a rational act – there is always the possibility, however slim, that life will change for the better. Yet, for the rejected lover, reason has no currency. Thus, it can seem that death is preferable to life.

Suicide as a response to rejection has been recognised since the time of the ancient Greeks, but the modern precedent was not really established until the rise of Romanticism in the late eighteenth century. Love and death had always been linked in courtly romances, but the Church's indictment of 'self-slaughter' made the device unappealing to story tellers. By killing themselves, lovers negate their heroic qualities by simultaneously damning their souls for all time. Thus, the narrative requirement of death (to ensure perpetual union) is achieved, not by going against God's will, but with God's assistance (working as He does in mysterious ways). Lovers die by accident, in battle or by grief alone. In the *Tristan* of Thomas (written about 1160), on discovering her deceased lover, Ysolt simply yields up her soul.

> She takes him in her arms and then, lying full length, she kisses his face and lips and clasps him tightly to her. Then straining body to body, mouth to mouth, she at once renders up her spirit and of sorrow for her lover dies thus at his side.

After the Enlightenment, the Church's influence on story telling was weakened. Subsequently, the moral climate favoured the creation of a new kind of protagonist: one who was not damned, but dignified by suicide – a protagonist whose self-destruction could be construed as quietly heroic. He appears in fiction, for the first time, as Goethe's painfully sensitive anti-hero, Werther.

In *The Sorrows of Young Werther* Goethe made suicide – formerly an ungodly, psychopathological act – part of the romantic discourse. He legitimised suicide as an existential choice. The anonymous martyrs to love, who had met their end leaping off cliffs and headlands, could now be honoured as secular 'saints'. Suicide was ennobling, a confirmation of the highest ideal: that love is everything, and to live without love is not to live at all.

The Sorrows of Young Werther provided eighteenth-century society with a framework for the expression of difficult emotions. Indeed, in some ways, it can be understood as a protocol or 'manual' for those in the throes of unrequited love. Werther became a literary role model, and he is supposed to have precipitated an epidemic of suicides. This is probably an exaggeration, but he certainly had some influence in this respect. One young woman, for example, drowned herself in the River Ilm behind Goethe's garden, and another (deserted by her lover) killed herself with a copy of *The Sorrows of Young Werther* in her pocket. In due course, the problem came to the attention of various authorities. Leipzig city council banned the book, and in Denmark, a proposed translation was not allowed.

Much of the book's power can be attributed to its authenticity – it is like an eighteenth-century video diary – and it possesses this quality of gritty realism because it is largely autobiographical. It is a record of the thoughts and feelings that Goethe himself experienced after forming an unrequited attachment to Charlotte Buff, a nineteen-year-old woman who (like the fictional Lotte) was already engaged to be married. Goethe, of course, did not kill himself as a consequence; however, Werther's suicide is still rooted in reality, as it was inspired by the sad fate of Goethe's acquaintance, Wilhelm Jerusalem. Through *The Sorrows of Young Werther*, Jerusalem's suicide was to exert an enormous influence on the literary treatment of love. He opened the door through which countless Romantic heroes and heroines were to walk, culminating in the high tragedy of works such as Tolstoy's *Anna Karenina*.

Wilhelm Jerusalem studied law in Leipzig at the same time as Goethe, although he was in fact slightly older. He became the secretary of an ambassador, but devoted most of his free time to artistic and intellectual pursuits: namely painting, poetry and philosophy. He was greatly respected by his peers, and occasionally socialised with Goethe (but considered the author something of a lightweight).

Although Jerusalem may have not been impressed by Goethe, Goethe was certainly impressed by Jerusalem. Indeed, he seems to have made such an impression, that many of his characteristics and attributes were 'borrowed' for Goethe's greatest literary creation. For example, Werther's liking for blue frock-coats seems to have come from Jerusalem, as did his penchant for wandering. Indeed, Jerusalem had many of the attributes we now automatically associate with Romantic heroism. He was something of an outcast, had been cold-shouldered by high society, and was often to be found walking alone on moonlit nights.

Jerusalem fell in love with a married woman who rejected his advances. He was confronted by her jealous husband and forbidden to visit their house ever again. Although he did not show it, Jerusalem's heart was silently breaking. He spent the afternoon working through his papers, sorting out his debts and walking. In the evening, he made up a fire, asked his servant to bring him some wine, and wrote some letters. Later, he read a little.

The following morning he was discovered by his servant, still alive, though unconscious. Bloody tracks leading from the desk to the window showed that he had shot himself while seated, before dragging himself across the floor. At midday, he died. The same evening, he was buried, although without a priest in attendance.

Goethe was in no doubt what had killed Jerusalem. He had been a casualty of love. Reflecting on his death, he wrote: 'The poor fellow! I remember returning from a walk and meeting him in the moonlight, and saying to myself: he is in love. It was loneliness, God knows, that ate away his heart.'

Thus, Jerusalem's death provided Goethe with the denouement of Werther, a denouement that not only influenced generations of imitators, but also underscored the astonishing fact that love – when unrequited – can be a fatal affliction.

Why is unrequited love so destructive?

Clearly, beliefs about love and its overwhelming significance are an important factor. For the romantic idealist, there really is no point in living without love. The beloved is idealised – unique and irreplaceable. Thus, seeking love elsewhere is doomed to failure, and any surrogate love, being deficient, will only serve to emphasise what has been lost. Romantic idealism is also underpinned by the Platonic myth of the first humans – the quadrupedal hermaphrodites whose bodies were torn apart by Zeus as a punishment. We only have one 'other half'. Therefore, if that one special union is prevented, the primal wound will never heal. The romantic idealist is then presented with only limited possibilities: to live the rest of his or her life in pain, or to choose oblivion. In the throes of love's madness, with all its angst, torment and suffering, the latter might seem an attractive option – particularly during the nineteenth century, when widespread experimentation with opium resulted in 'oblivion' acquiring new connotations such as release, rest or eternal sleep.

The Platonic myth of origin has proved remarkably potent. It has been revisited and reworked time and time again during the course of Western literature. One of the great set pieces of the Romantic canon can be found in Emily Brontë's *Wuthering Heights*, in which Cathy compares her love for Linton with her love for Heathcliff. It is predicated on the Platonic notion that she and Heathcliff are essentially the same being:

> My love for Linton is like the foliage in the woods. Time will change it, I'm well aware, as winter changes the trees – my love for Heathcliff resembles the eternal rocks beneath – a source of little visible delight, but necessary. Nelly, I am Heathcliff – he's always, always in my mind – not as a pleasure, any more than I am always a pleasure to myself – but, as my own being.

To lose one's self is to die. Therefore, according to the Platonic doctrine, to lose one's true love is to lose one's self, and is also a kind of death. Losing love and losing life are much the same thing.

Freud believed that the feeling of merging that lovers experience – of being the same thing – is powerful because it resonates with primal memories. In infancy, the ego boundary between mother and child is less well defined. Thus, when lovers merge, they are, in a sense, regressing to a very early stage in their development. Freud suggested that the way lovers experience closeness is strongly influenced by unconscious memories of symbiosis. Although he considered human development from the time of birth onwards (he was one of the first doctors to consider the psychological effects of birth trauma) many of his followers speculated on yet earlier influences. For example, some schools of psychoanalysis explored the possibility that certain features of human experience (particularly transcendental or mystical experiences) might be related to prenatal memories. A corollary of this type of theorising is that, when lovers regress, the spiritual union they experience is a recollection of the womb, when mother and child were one.

The obstetrician Michel Odent describes the period before birth (and surrounding birth) as the 'primal period', and cites evidence demonstrating that the emotional state of a mother while pregnant will have long-term effects on the development of her child's personality. These effects extend well into adulthood, influencing characteristics such as sociability, aggressiveness and, more fundamentally, the capacity to love. Some studies have shown that a mother's mental state while pregnant will influence the personality of her child much more than her mental state in the year following the child's birth. In the context of these perfectly respectable empirical studies, the notion of prenatal memory, albeit unconscious, is easier to accept.

If the sense of 'one-ness' experienced by lovers resonates with early recollections of the symbiotic relationship between mother and child, then this may explain why rejection is experienced so intensely. The misery of unrequited love is, at least in part, the misery of a child rejected by its mother, or, even worse, the infant expelled from the comforting darkness of the womb into the cold, hard world of objects and glaring lights.

Long before psychoanalysts considered the relationship between early experiences and our response to rejection, poets had already made such a connection. Indeed, the very first significant 'named' love poet, Sappho, observed that the reaction of a spurned lover is similar to that of a spurned child:

> Afraid of losing you
> I ran fluttering
> Like a little girl
> After her mother

These links, made between early emotional development and adult behaviour, are pertinent with respect to one of the major theoretical frameworks in contemporary psychology: John Bowlby's 'attachment theory'. Bowlby's original work was concerned with the effects of maternal deprivation on mental health, and it was he who established that infants separated from their mothers at a critical phase in early development would be more at risk with respect to psychological problems in later life. For Bowlby, this critical phase was the first seven years of life.

Human beings are social animals. Therefore, one would expect the formation of attachments to play a special role in human affairs; the formation of a strong attachment bond is particularly important for the human infant, which is born helpless and remains vulnerable for many years after.

Bowlby suggested that human beings are equipped with a biologically rooted attachment system, selected by evolutionary pressures. Thus, human infants are born 'wired' to form strong attachments. Bowlby proposed that the principal purpose of the attachment system was to ensure survival. Clearly, infants who have formed strong attachments stand to benefit a great deal – an attached child is less vulnerable to predation, and is more likely to learn about the world by observing its parents.

Bowlby recognised that the attachment system was only one of many adaptive systems that operate to ensure our survival – the 'fight-flight' mechanism (or fear system) can be counted as another example – however, he maintained that the attachment system was the most fundamental. Indeed, all of the other survival systems, to a greater or lesser extent, depend on its primacy. This makes a great deal of sense from an evolutionary perspective. In the ancestral environment, an infant that failed to bond with its mother would get into trouble very quickly. If it didn't cry for attention, it might be neglected. If it did not root for the breast, it might not thrive. Therefore, all of the other survival systems must be preceded by the successful engagement of the attachment system.

Given that the attachment system is so fundamental, some psychologists have suggested that the neural mechanisms that subserve attachment in the infant also subserve love in the adult. This is supported by the existence of correspondences between infant attachment behaviour and the behaviour of romantically involved couples.

Psychologist Philip Shaver and colleagues have compiled an exhaustive survey of attachment behaviours that are complemented by parallel romantic behaviours. For example, infants who have established a secure attachment to their mothers feel safe, and are more likely to explore their environment. Similarly, when adults are confident that their love is reciprocated, they too feel safe, and are more likely to pursue diverse interests and pursuits. Conversely, when mothers are not available, or unresponsive, infants become anxious, preoccupied and cautious. Exactly the same pattern is observed in adults who doubt that their love is returned. Infants focus all of their attention on a single caregiver – usually the mother, or a mother figure. Romantic love is also, of necessity, always exclusive.

Even the minutiae of attachment behaviour are mirrored in the behaviour of romantically involved adults. For example, infants are fascinated by their mothers' appearance. Typically, mother and baby will stare into each other's eyes for extended periods of time, and possibly touch each other's faces. The same is true of lovers. Infants coo, sing, and engage in baby talk. Rather embarrassingly, lovers do much the same thing, often revisiting the nursery by making up pet names for each other and developing a private, infantile vocabulary. Such behaviour amused Robert Burton, whose seventeenth-century list of diminutives included: 'bird, mouse, lamb, puss, pigeon, pigsney, kid, honey, love, dove' and 'chicken' – some of which are still in use, behind closed doors, today.

Understanding romantic love from the perspective of evolutionary psychology and attachment theory is instructive for many reasons, but it is particularly useful when applied to unrequited love and rejection. As has already been suggested, rejection – or broken attachments – can evoke powerful feelings of infantile despair. These are primitive, overwhelming and likely to promote extremes of behaviour, some self-destructive.

Bowlby established that infants develop specific attachments between six and twelve months. Prior to six months, if an infant is handed to a stranger, it will not react. After six months, however, the infant will react with obvious distress. It will cling to its mother, cry, and when properly separated will struggle to free itself in order to get back to its mother. Bowlby described these behavioural changes as the protest response. If the infant's mother leaves altogether, protest is followed by despair – the infant becomes miserable, wretched and takes on an appearance not too dissimilar to that of a depressed adult. When separation is prolonged, the infant shows a further behavioural change, signalling a final transition from despair to detachment. The detached infant is a kind of emotional amputee. Unable to tolerate any more distress, it simply 'cuts off'. This sequence of behaviours – protest, despair and detachment – is reliably observed when small children are separated from their mothers.

Interestingly, these same three stages are frequently observed in rejected lovers. First, they respond with the equivalent of the protest response. They cry, become anxious, agitated, and struggle to re-establish some form of connection with the lost beloved. After repeated failures to thaw the beloved's heart, protest gives way to despair, and the unhappy lover exhibits all of the symptoms commonly associated with clinical depression. Finally, emotional exhaustion produces a state of detachment. This stage is by far the most dangerous with respect to suicide risk. It is well known that people in the advanced stages of depression often stop crying and may not show any obvious signs of distress. Although this might look like an adjustment for the better, in fact, it is usually the very opposite. The individual is simply numb inside, and no longer inclined to engage with the world.

Wilhelm Jerusalem seems to have been in a remarkably detached frame of mind at the time of his suicide. The way in which he sat at his desk, attended to his letters and drank a glass of wine – before shooting himself – suggests an abnormal level of emotional disengagement. It is interesting that Jerusalem – a model for the first Romantic anti-hero – set something of a precedent. Thereafter, Romantic art, literature and poetry showed a curious preoccupation with 'icy' stoicism. The Romantic canon champions the cause of spurned lovers who wander out across frozen wastes, meaning never to return; their inner frigidity complemented by the unforgiving immensity of a winter landscape.

Philip Shaver and colleagues have pointed out that if infantile attachment and romantic attachment are served by the same primitive neural systems, then we cannot expect lovers and rejected lovers to act rationally:

> We would say that the attachment system is more primitive than rationality, which is why both intense romantic love and intense grieving for a lost love seem uncontrollable and hence a bit 'crazy'. The system as a whole, however, does not seem crazy at all, given its important biological functions in both infancy and adulthood. It only looks crazy when its goals are unattainable.

Perhaps the most extreme example of irrational protest is observed in the context of bereavement. The attachment system is fully engaged in attempting to recover an attachment figure who has become completely unattainable. In grief, the protest response proceeds, irrespective of its obvious redundancy. Bereaved individuals often behave as though their partners are still present. They will listen for the sound of a turning key or a characteristic step. They may even prepare food or set a place at the table. At worst, a bereaved individual will go out searching for a loved one. Sadly, some may enjoy limited success, insofar as they actually find their loved one – but in the form of a visual hallucination.

The protest response in bereaved adults has many of the features of infantile thinking. The bereaved often behave as though they believe that they can will their partners back into existence. Such thinking revisits the magical world of childhood, where impossible wishes seem far from futile.

If adult love and infant attachment are mediated by the same ancient circuits in the brain, then we will be prone to address the adult problem of rejection with the emotional tools at the disposal of an infant. The trappings of adult sophistication fall away as the inner child screams its primal protest and tries to claw its way back to the security of an ancestral mother. When we are rejected, we feel as though we are losing everything – and in a way, we are.

In the ancestral environment, as today, a human infant without its mother would not survive for more than a matter of hours. Depression and detachment follow protest because, if your protest wasn't heard, you were as good as dead anyway.

For rejected lovers, whose neural circuits are still animated by ancient learning, there is not much more to be lost. A leap from a high place or a bullet in the head are methods by which it is possible to expedite the inevitable.

I I

A Many-splendored Thing

'Love is a Many-Splendored Thing',
Song title, Paul Francis Webster

As soon as human beings acquired the ability to write, they chose to write about love, and almost immediately, as they searched for words to describe the experience of being in love, they compared it to an illness – a mental illness. The ancient Egyptians did this, and so did the ancient Greeks. Roman elegists, Islamic scholars and the courtly poets of the medieval world also made much the same observation, and so, eventually, did Renaissance doctors, Elizabethan playwrights, novelists, psychoanalysts, psychiatrists, psychologists and brain scientists. Today, the tradition seems to be largely in the custody of the commercial music industry – reflecting an extraordinary global consensus. When recording artists sing of going 'crazy', or going 'out of my head', an international audience knows exactly what they mean. Everyone understands that they are singing about love, not psychiatry.

Although we like to think of love as fated, mysterious and transcendent, the reality of love is somewhat different. Love often 'looks' and feels like a mental illness. Broadly speaking, an individual in the throes of love is no less symptomatic than someone suffering from psychiatric conditions such as OCD, depression, mania, hypomania or manic depression. Moreover, the state of being in love can trigger behaviours associated with delusional disorders such as erotomania and morbid jealousy.

Even though love has been consistently described as a mental illness since the dawn of civilisation, a blunt statement to this effect is still somewhat disconcerting. As a culture, we are happy to recognise an association between love and mental illness, only providing it isn't taken too seriously. Perhaps this is why the link is now most frequently expounded, not in medical textbooks, but in popular songs. The overriding connotations of love are essentially positive, whereas those of mental illness are almost entirely negative. By not taking the links between love and mental illness too seriously, we can preserve an idealised view of love and, at the same time, distance ourselves from the somewhat frightening notion that few of us will escape an experience that is close to 'madness'.

Western society has always approached madness with excessive alarm. It has been viewed as a divine punishment, a manifestation of evil influence and, in modern times, a threat to the survival of civilisation.

Prejudice concerning mental illness runs deep and surfaces all too easily. Even though up to a third of Westerners can expect to experience some form of mental illness during the course of their lives, psychiatric problems are still viewed as embarrassing, shameful and a threat to public safety. Media and fictional representations of madness have generally not progressed very far beyond the precedent set by Hogarth in the eighteenth century. When the subject of mental illness is raised, somewhere, at the periphery of awareness, shadowy presences are grimacing, clawing the air and howling at the moon. We become prurient spectators in the dismal corridors of Bedlam.

Fortunately, since the time of Plato, this wholly negative view of mental illness has been intermittently challenged. Philosophers, physicians, social reformers, radical psychiatrists and, latterly, evolutionary psychologists have all suggested that mental illness might confer subtle advantages on the sufferer – or even on the entire species. Although we automatically interpret the phrase 'love is a mental illness' as pejorative, this reflects nothing more than our own socially conditioned attitudes. A legitimate alternative is to celebrate the fact that love is a mental illness – for a number of very good reasons.

The very fact that genes for mental illness have survived in the gene pool is of considerable interest to evolutionary psychologists. If mental illness is such a significant handicap, why haven't all of the genes that make us vulnerable to mental illness been eliminated by sexual or natural selection? And why is mental illness so very, very common? Our extraordinary susceptibility to psychiatric problems suggests that, in the ancestral environment at least, mental illness was in some way adaptive.

Clearly, genes for problems such as anxiety and fear played an extremely important role with respect to the survival of the species. Those of our ancestors who erred on the side of caution (and were quick to leave potentially dangerous situations) were more likely to escape predation, living long enough to reproduce and pass on their 'anxious genes' to the next generation. The consequences of this process are still with us today. Phobias for snakes and spiders are relatively common, even though such creatures are not a significant threat in the modern world. It would appear that human beings are born with a predisposition to fear snakes and spiders, because these were just the kind of venomous animals that our ancestors 'learned' (by natural selection) to avoid. Although ophidiophobia and arachnophobia are now classified as forms of mental illness (simple phobias in DSM-IV and ICD-10), in the ancestral environment, such sensitivities would have been associated with a clear advantage with respect to survival and subsequent reproductive success.

What of more severe forms of mental illness? It is relatively easy to see how a simple phobia might prove adaptive in the ancestral environment, but what of more complex problems such as schizophrenia? How could losing touch with reality ever be seen as an adaptive trait?

In their book, *Evolutionary Psychiatry*, Anthony Stevens and John Price suggest a novel hypothesis to explain why genes for schizophrenia might have survived in the gene pool. In the ancestral environment, the optimal size of a hunter-gatherer group would be somewhere between one hundred and 150 members. Once membership of the group exceeded 150, the cost of group membership might then begin to outweigh its benefits – the most obvious cost being insufficient food. Some members of the group would always go hungry. If, however, excess members formed independent splinter groups (closer to the optimal size), then everyone – in both the old and the new groups – would get fed. Unfortunately, human nature is conservative, and excess members would have been naturally reluctant to leave the relative safety of a large, established group. Stevens and Price have suggested that visionary, charismatic leaders – suffering from what we would now call schizophrenia – could have played a critical role in persuading the timorous to overcome their fears. Absolute conviction, grandiose plans, and hallucinatory visions of a better place are sometimes symptoms of schizophrenia, but they are also qualities that we associate with strong, far-sighted leadership. The 'ancestral schizophrenic' may have been a kind of tribal Moses, daring the discontented to follow him as he marched off towards the promised land.

From an evolutionary perspective, then, there are several reasons why genetic predispositions for particular mental illnesses might have survived in the gene pool. Thus, the idea of a functional – or beneficial – madness is deeply rooted in evolutionary thinking.

Although this approach to mental illness has had to wait for the growth of evolutionary psychology to receive scientific endorsement, it is not entirely without precedent. Before Hippocratic medicine, epilepsy was thought to be sacred; and later, Aristotle posited a link between conspicuous talent and melancholy. The Church attributed madness to demonic possession, but it also discreetly acknowledged 'madness of the cross' – spiritually enriching visions and hallucinations of the crucifixion. In folk tales, plays, and novels, fools and madmen repeatedly make astute observations, their nonsense tempered by a form of careless wisdom. In *The Praise of Folly*, Erasmus's 'foolish' heroine is highly perceptive, and the works of Shakespeare contain several Clowns and Fools (most notably in *King Lear* and *Twelfth Night*) whose 'knowingness' is disconcerting. Such characters are used to express the idea that in a mad world, only the mad are sane. As mental institutions became more famous – particularly London's Bedlam – this idea became an increasingly popular dramatic device. For instance, in John Fletcher's 1621 play, *The Pilgrim*, it is the custodians of madmen, appointed by a mad society, who are insane, not the long-suffering inmates. Since Fletcher's time, the asylum setting has been used to make the same point many times over, culminating in Ken Kesey's much praised novel, *One Flew over the Cuckoo's Nest*. Thus, as a culture, our collective prejudice concerning mental illness has never been complete. There has always been a niggling doubt about madness – a doubt eloquently expressed by the writer Edgar Allan Poe:

> Men have called me mad, but the question is not yet settled, whether madness is or is not the loftiest intelligence – whether much that is glorious – whether much that is profound – does not spring from disease of thought – from moods of mind exalted at the expense of the general intellect.

To what extent have these doubts led to the identification of appreciable advantages? Evolutionary psychologists have speculated about adaptivity in the ancestral environment and writers have praised naïve wisdom – but what does all this mean for the individual with mental illness? In what way is he or she 'better off' than someone who is supposed to be psychologically 'healthy'? Very little research has been undertaken into the positive consequences of mental illness, most probably because the scientific community (reflecting wider societal prejudices) has not expected to find any evidence supporting this view. Yet, early indications are that mental illness is associated with a very important advantage – and one that shows itself most obviously when people fall madly in love.

The idea that mental illness and 'talent' might be related has a long pedigree extending back to Aristotle; however, subsequent speculation failed to establish the exact nature of this relationship. Although there was a general consensus that reflective melancholics were great 'thinkers', the overall thesis was never really developed or refined. Nevertheless, throughout the nineteenth century, many European scholars began to write specifically on the relationship between mental illness and genius and, in due course, attention became more focused on the topic of artistic genius.

A Many-splendored Thing

It wasn't, however, until early in the twentieth century that one of the fathers of modern psychiatry – Emil Kraepelin – posited a special link between manic depression and artistic productivity:

> The volitional excitement which accompanies the disease may under certain circumstances set free powers which otherwise are constrained by all kinds of inhibition. Artistic activity namely may, by the untroubled surrender to momentary fancies of moods, and especially poetical activity by the facilitation of linguistic expression, experience a certain furtherance.

Many agreed with Kraepelin, but evidence for the relationship between manic depression and artistic productivity remained largely anecdotal for most of the ensuing century. A turning point, however, was the publication in 1993 of Kay Redfield Jamison's *Touched with Fire: Manic-depressive Illness and the Artistic Temperament*. Jamison was – and still is – a professor of psychiatry who herself suffers from manic depression, and was therefore particularly well placed to examine what is still (for some) a highly controversial area. Unlike those of her predecessors, Jamison's thesis was strengthened by research drawn from three sources: the psychiatric histories of acknowledged geniuses; the psychiatric histories of living artists; and the creative achievements of individuals known to be suffering from a mental illness. All of these sources confirmed anecdotal reports of a strong association between manic depression and artistic activity.

A disproportionate number of great artists seem to have suffered from manic depression, which encourages a very specific pattern of working. New ideas are contemplated during periods of melancholy, and are then translated into poems, paintings or symphonies during manic episodes (when energy levels are much higher). The composer Robert Schumann exemplifies this phenomenon. Inspection of his publications over the course of his life reveals an exact correspondence between mood state and productivity. For example, in 1833, when he attempted suicide, he produced two works. He was hypomanic throughout 1840, and subsequently produced twenty-four works. When depressed again in 1844, he produced nothing – but when hypomanic in 1849, he produced twenty-seven.

The most prolific artists seem to be able to ride their energy surges in much the same way as a surfer rides a wave. They are able to retain their balance as the swell gathers momentum and power. Then, they are equally well equipped to enjoy significant but diminishing motivational benefits as their descent carries them back towards the ruminative lagoon of melancholy. In attempting to determine the critical factors that link manic depression and creativity, Jamison makes much of the correspondences that exist between the manic (or hypomanic) brain, and the brain when engaged in the act of creation:

> Many of the changes in mood, thinking, and perception that characterize the mildly manic states – restlessness, ebullience, expansiveness, irritability, grandiosity, quickened and more finely tuned senses, intensity of emotional experiences, diversity of thought, and rapidity of associational processes – are highly characteristic of creative thought as well.

Mania appears to alter the brain's neurochemistry, such that the mind begins to display a kind of intellectual athleticism. It can run with new ideas and make unusual connections. Studies have found that during manic episodes, patients are more able to rhyme, pun and exploit sound associations. Their use of language becomes more daring and playful. As a result, a very high number of manic patients spontaneously start writing poetry. This effect is even observable in patients who have little or no prior interest in writing. When they are given word-association tests – in which the patient must respond to a given word (say, 'bread') with a self-generated associate (say, 'butter') – manic episodes produce a threefold increase in original responses. Yet more interesting is research which shows that mild manic episodes produce an improvement in intellectual ability that can be detected using IQ tests.

Of course, if a manic episode becomes too intense, creative and intellectual advantages will disappear. The welter of words, ideas and impressions will become overwhelming, producing a state of confused unintelligibility. To extend the surfing analogy, the mind loses its balance and tumbles out of control. However, this does not invalidate the general finding that manic illness seems to increase mental agility, albeit temporarily. Patients with manic depression whose mood is stabilised using lithium often complain that they feel 'flat' and less creative. Indeed, many manic-depressive patients for whom creativity is particularly important may fail to comply with their medication regimen for this reason. The great artists of the Romantic movement did something very similar. Individuals such as Byron and Berlioz almost certainly suffered from manic depression, yet neither made any attempt to live a tranquil life. Like many of their contemporaries, they chose instead to court emotional turmoil.

Although it is unlikely that all artists who lived and worked under the banner of Romanticism were manic-depressives, the vast majority still chose to live life at the extremes. Many may have been simply copying the antics of their artistic heroes, but others may have found that by leading a turbulent life, their creative powers were enhanced. The immoderate behaviour of artists has become a well-established cultural cliché, but its sustained popularity may be due to its very real effect on the brain. Artists have learned that by living life according to a repeating cycle of rapture and despair, an ordinary talent might be transformed into something that begins to look much more like genius.

The emotional rollercoaster of love is very similar to manic depression. Therefore, it is interesting that lovers, like manic-depressives, also become more creative. Even the most unimaginative individual, when in love, will become more expressive, perhaps using uncharacteristically passionate language. He or she might be tempted to pen a poem or lyric. The three guitar chords, learned in adolescence, and formerly reserved for dull moments on a Sunday afternoon, suddenly reveal their potential as the basis for a song. When in love, people will often make a Valentine's Day card, rather than buy one. Love seems to prefigure its ultimate aim of procreation by kindling generative urges.

Although authors such as Jamison have highlighted the relationship between manic depression and creativity, other commentators have suggested a similar association may exist with respect to obsessionality – the psychiatric phenomenon that we have already identified (along with depression and manic depression) as most pertinent to love. At first sight, this seems to be a less credible claim. Individuals with obsessional problems are generally thought to be rigid thinkers, supposedly lacking the mental flexibility considered essential for creativity. However, although individuals with obsessional problems can fixate on particular themes, these fixations frequently arise in the wake of some very agile reasoning. An individual with OCD who is obsessed with the idea of having been 'contaminated' may have 'worked out' a complicated (and often counter-intuitive) transmission pathway (such as patient to cup, cup to nurse,

nurse to child, child to toy, toy to seat, seat to newspaper, newspaper to me). The combination of flexible thinking, followed by fixation, is a reasonable description of the creative process. Once flexible thinking has produced some raw material, such as an innovative idea, the artist must then focus on that idea if it is to be made into a work of art. Again, as with manic depression, a disproportionate number of distinguished artists seems to have suffered from OCD – for example, Hans Christian Andersen, Henrik Ibsen, Honoré de Balzac and Charles Dickens, to name but a few.

The effect of love's madness on the creative faculty has been understood and celebrated in literature for centuries. Representations of lovers – particularly men – almost invariably involve the exercise of a poetic or musical gift. In the tale of Layla and Majnun (the ur-narrative from which many Western romances derive), Majnun's delirious, creative frenzy is portrayed as the principal symptom of his 'disease'; Tristan is described as a talented harpist and composer; and in the famous balcony scene of *Romeo and Juliet*, Romeo's love for Juliet unleashes cascades of poetry: 'But, soft! What light through yonder window breaks? It is the east, and Juliet is the sun!', 'With love's light wings did I o'erperch these walls; For stony limits cannot hold love out', 'How silver-sweet sound lovers' tongues by night, Like softest music to attending ears!' Several hundred years later, the balcony scene was still being exploited by Edmond Rostand, whose eponymous hero, Cyrano de Bergerac (hidden from view), seduces the beautiful Roxanne for young Christian with word-power alone: 'I love you, I'm overwhelmed, I love you to the point of madness! Your name is in my heart like a bell shaken by my constant trembling, ringing day and night: Roxanne, Roxanne, Roxanne!'

In *The Anatomy of Melancholy*, Robert Burton was acutely aware of love's ability to inspire. Indeed, he noted that many artistic (as well as scientific) achievements seemed to be 'for love's sake', and with due deference to an earlier authority wrote: 'As Nevisanus the lawyer holds, there never was an excellent poet that invented good fables, or made laudable verses, which was not in love himself; had he not taken a quill from Cupid's wings, he could never have written so amorously as he did.'

Burton believed that the relationship between love and creativity was so close, the degree to which a nation indulged its passions could be inferred from the quality of its art. Without a trace of envy, the splendidly phlegmatic Burton asked his readers: 'Why are Italians at this day generally so good poets and painters?' For which he had a simple and straightforward answer: 'Because every man of any fashion amongst them hath his mistress.'

Being lovesick is the only experience the average person gets of madness – but it is also the only experience the average person gets of being creative. Although love is painful, it awakens dormant capabilities. When we fall in love, all of us, to a greater or lesser extent, are 'touched with fire'.

Evolutionary pressures have determined that love should be experienced as a kind of madness, and those same pressures seem to have determined that this madness should be creative. Why should this be? Why does love's madness overthrow reason, and simultaneously make lovers burst into song? Why do lovers versify and sing in their madness?

By 1871, if Charles Darwin had been asked that question, he would have been able to give the enquirer a perfectly respectable answer. According to evolutionary theory, differences (both physical and psychological) between men and women can be attributed to sexual selection – the process by which the sexes shape each other by favouring mates with particular characteristics. The more obvious the difference, the more confident we can be that it is the result of sexual selection. For example, the physical characteristics associated with strength have been favoured by females when choosing male mates for nearly two million years: thus, the male is typically much larger than the female. Evolutionary theorists have traditionally collected evidence for the operation of sexual selection by examining the physical differences between the sexes; however, more recently, with the advent of evolutionary psychology, much interest has been shown in the psychological differences between men and women. A new reader, encountering many recent books or articles that touch upon the subject, could easily form the impression that the study of gender psychology from an evolutionary perspective is an entirely new development. However, Darwin was fascinated by gender psychology, and wrote about it in his 1871 bestseller, *The Descent of Man and Selection in Relation to Sex*. This important work was largely dismissed by Darwin's colleagues, and for much of the twentieth century it was somewhat overshadowed by *The Origin of Species*. In *The Descent of Man*, Darwin identified sexual selection as the mechanism by which the minds of men and women become differentially endowed. His observations do not make comfortable reading for those who subscribe to political correctness – and the average feminist will find them plain offensive. According to Darwin, in some domains of cultural activity, women appear to be conspicuously inferior to men. Such a marked disparity almost certainly implicates sexual selection, which in turn raises some intriguing possibilities concerning the nature of courtship in the ancestral environment.

Although you might be forgiven for thinking that Darwin was a male chauvinist, you would be very wrong. He was not, by any stretch of the imagination, the equivalent of a contemporary sexist. He had his fair share of Victorian prejudices, but he possessed the greatest respect for women. In spite of his famous comment about a wife being 'better than a dog', his respect deepened throughout the course of his life. He considered his wife Emma, not only his equal, but his superior in virtually everything – a claim that even Emma found a little embarrassing, knowing perfectly well that her husband was a genius of colossal stature. Perhaps it was because Darwin respected women, and believed women to be the intellectual equals of men, that he found disparities of achievement between the sexes so surprising – particularly within the arts.

In the *Descent of Man* he wrote:

> If two lists were made of the most eminent men and women in poetry, painting, sculpture, music (inclusive both of composition and performance), history, science, and philosophy, with half-a-dozen names under each subject, the two lists would not bear comparison . . .

Darwin was correct then – and he remains correct today. Even if we take into account the fact that historically women have always been disadvantaged because of social inequality, the disparity of artistic and scientific achievement that divides the sexes is quite extraordinary. From an evolutionary perspective, this strongly suggests that male talent has been shaped by sexual selection. Men might appear to be more gifted than women, but this is only because women have 'made' them that way! If women in the ancestral environment hadn't expressed a distinct preference for gifted mates, such a disparity would never have arisen in the first place.

> With social animals, the young males have to pass through many a contest before they win a female . . . But to avoid enemies or to attack them with success, to capture wild

animals, and to fashion weapons, requires the aid of the higher mental faculties, namely, observation, reason, invention, or imagination. These faculties will thus have been continually put to the test and selected during manhood; they will, moreover, have been strengthened by use during the same period of life. Consequently . . . we might expect that they would at least tend to be transmitted chiefly to the male offspring at the corresponding period of manhood.

In essence, Darwin was suggesting that invention and imagination may have been as important for survival in the ancestral environment as strength and speed. Thus, among the favoured attributes of men could be counted not only broad chests and narrow waists, large biceps and bulging thighs, but a powerful brain – the presence of which could be glimpsed through the transparency of an agile mind, a mind equipped to imagine future states of being, so that hunts could be planned and threats avoided; a mind equipped to envisage a drier cave, or a place where a fire might be kept burning safely, but that was also capable of imagining a new spear or a sharper axe-head, and that would reveal its power by producing things – tools, artifacts, cave-drawings – in effect, a creative mind.

The idea that creativity was (and still is) a feature of the male courtship display has been given a thorough exposition by psychologist Geoffrey Miller in *The Mating Mind*, a work that successfully redresses the widespread neglect of Darwin's theory of sexual selection. Although sexual selection is a concept of equivalent importance to natural selection (particularly with respect to understanding human evolution), the former has been given much less consideration by evolutionary theorists.

Miller reiterates Darwin's observation concerning the conspicuous difference between men and women with respect to producing works of art. He points out that: 'sexually mature males have produced almost all of the publicly displayed art throughout human history'. Such a marked disparity declares the unmistakable influence of sexual selection: 'Males produce about an order of magnitude more art, music and literature . . . than women, and they produce it mostly in young adulthood. This suggests that . . . the production of art, music and literature functions primarily as a courtship display.'

We find facial symmetry attractive, because the growth of perfectly balanced features is difficult to achieve and therefore sensitive to genetic abnormalities. Creativity may function in much the same way. Not everyone can use words adroitly, sing a melody, or faithfully reproduce images of the world, because to do so requires skill – and skill, like physical beauty, signals the presence of good genes. According to Miller, creativity in human males is the equivalent of a peacock's tail – an impressive resource display designed to make females swoon. When a man sings a love song, he is, in fact, opening a fan of opulent, shimmering feathers. Whatever the music, whatever the words, all men sing only one song, and it goes like this: 'My genes are good – mate with me, not my rival.'

Although human beings can mate all year round, it is interesting that romance has always been linked with the spring. Classical verses, medieval lyrics and Hollywood movies insist that love is a largely vernal phenomenon. Interestingly, psychologists have found that certain cognitive abilities in men – such as visual and spatial intelligence – become enhanced as the days lengthen. Perhaps romance has been associated with spring because that is when men are best equipped to engage in an intellectual resource display.

Darwin was thankful that the heritability of mental traits

in humans was kept within limits by certain biological checks. 'It is, indeed, fortunate,' he wrote, 'that the law of equal transmission of characters to both sexes prevails with mammals; otherwise it is probable that man would have become as superior in mental endowment to woman, as the peacock is in ornamental plumage to the peahen.' However, Darwin need not have worried on this count. As Geoffrey Miller has pointed out, if creativity is an ingredient of the male resource display, then females must necessarily remain the intellectual peers of men. A resource display that simply went over the heads of its target audience would be entirely wasted. Male creativity has only played a part in the dynamics of sexual selection because – at some level – women have recognised its value.

When we fall in love, when we vacillate between rapture and despair, we shake off the psychic shackles that bind our personalities. Our creative potential is released, and suddenly there are words to express our feelings. Because evolutionary pressures have determined that it is men who engage in resource display, and women who choose, love's madness must necessarily affect men more than women (a fact that is dramatised in romantic literature and confirmed by psychological research). It is men who must 'perform'. Given the relationship between manic depression and creativity, the man who falls madly in love will deliver a more impressive performance than his 'saner' rival – thus increasing the likelihood of achieving reproductive success.

The most frequent complaint that women voice concerning men is that men are uncommunicative. Men simply don't talk, especially about their emotions. Yet, in the throes of love's madness, even a silent man will find something to say: the most pedestrian vocabulary will discover its latent poetic possibilities in a love letter. Driven by obsession, and shaken out of complacency by dramatic mood swings, men unknowingly fulfil their evolutionary destiny.

Some of the greatest love poetry ever written can be viewed as evolutionary rhetoric: men persuading women to have sex. John Donne's 'Elegie: To his Mistress Going to Bed' and Andrew Marvell's 'To his Coy Mistress' are particularly good examples. Both poets wheedle, sweet-talk, coax, cajole, appease, and flatter – using strategies that most contemporary female readers recognise immediately.

'Had we but World enough, and Time,' says Marvell, 'This coyness, Lady, were no crime.' But 'Time's wingèd Chariot' is 'hurrying near'. Life is short – he says – tomorrow may never come. Like any young man trying to get his girlfriend to 'stay the night', Marvell will try any argument – and if the philosophical approach doesn't work, there's always the fallback position of promising sexual satisfaction:

> Let us roll all our Strength, and all
> Our sweetness, up into one Ball:
> And tear our Pleasures with rough strife,
> Thorough the Iron gates of Life.

In the remote ancestral environment, perhaps even before the development of language, interesting and engaging vocalisations may have represented man's first faltering attempts at the art of seduction. Vocal expression, when charged with feeling, becomes song – and the love song is perhaps the most effective means of achieving reciprocation. Love's madness, by intensifying feelings, elevates language to the condition of music, and thus equips would-be lovers with an incomparably useful tool. In *The Expression of the Emotions in Man and Animals*, Darwin recognised how evolutionary pressures have ensured that song – essentially a resource display – can also weaken female resistance.

Music has a wonderful power ... of recalling in a vague and indefinite manner, those strong emotions which were felt during long-past ages, when, as is probable, our early progenitors courted each other by the aid of vocal tones. And as several of our strongest emotions – grief, great joy, love, and sympathy – lead to the free secretion of tears, it is not surprising that music should be apt to cause our eyes to become suffused with tears, especially when we are already softened by any of the tenderer feelings.

Today, because of technology, we hear music every day, and we have become rather inured to its power. If, however, for whatever reason, we cannot listen to music for even a short time, subsequent exposure immediately reminds us of its remarkable potency. A mediocre melody and an obvious chord change might be all that is required to make us cry.

Those of our ancestors who sang beautiful love songs would have had a distinct advantage over those who were tone-deaf. This is as true now as it was on the African savannah. Women love singers. Frank Sinatra, Elvis Presley and Mick Jagger were all considered by their respective generations to be the most sexually desirable men on the planet. None are arresting examples of classical beauty, yet any shortfall in appearance seems to have been amply compensated for by vocal prowess. As ever, Shakespeare understood this phenomenon perfectly, when he informed us that music is the 'food of love'. A sexy voice and a pleasing arrangement of pitches can melt the coldest heart.

In the modern world, it is no longer essential to sing love songs – we can let others do it for us. A CD is just as likely to produce the desired effect of manipulating emotions. This no doubt explains why the use of discreet background music has become an essential feature of contemporary seduction.

It is interesting to note that artists, and particularly musicians, are always feared when they are sexual rivals. Freud, during his uncharacteristic episode of jealousy while courting Martha Bernays, wrote: 'I think there is a general enmity between artists and those engaged in the details of scientific work. We know that they possess in their art a master key to open with ease all female hearts.' From an evolutionary perspective, he was very probably right. Creative artists are constantly advertising their desirable genomes, and at the same time, softening female defences.

Yet, we are all descended from ancestors who successfully reproduced. Not all of them were naturally gifted, but all of them were capable of falling in love, and in their manic, rapturous moments, words would have tumbled out to fill the silence: new words, persuasive words, words that began to vibrate with passion, as inhibitions dissolved in the heat of desire. Seized by love's madness, some would have burst into song. The very first love songs that melted hearts ensured reproductive success, and account for our presence here today.

The implications of sexual selection are, when followed to a logical conclusion, quite astonishing. Ultimately, every great cultural achievement, every great intellectual accomplishment, every great work of art, has come into being because of our extraordinary creativity. And this gift – usually attributed to divine provenance – has been shaped by the dynamics of love. Men are inclined to exercise this gift more often than women, but women have it too. It might even be the case that, being the gender who must rank competing suitors, women have an even more advanced aesthetic sensibility.

Sexual selection has shaped the mind, and the mind has shaped our world. Miller underscores this point when he asserts:

. . . Greek mathematics, Buddhist wisdom, British evolutionary biology, and Californian computer games. These achievements are not side-effects of having big brains that can learn anything, but of having minds full of courtship adaptations that can be retrained and redirected to invent new ideas even when we are not in love.

Love drives us mad. Yet, it is a curiously enabling madness. Love can potentiate hitherto untapped reserves of creativity, and this creativity is often linked with the desire to excel and impress. This combination is extraordinarily powerful, and has had a profound effect on our development as a species.

In *The Ascent of Man*, the scientist and author Jacob Bronowski subtly acknowledges the intimate relationship between great human achievements and love. After discussing the evolutionary mechanism of sexual selection, Bronowski invites us (with little comment) to inspect a two-page photographic gallery of great scientists. All are men of genius. Yet, none of these colossi are shown alone – all are accompanied by their partners. Thus, we find James Watson seated on a sofa, holding the hand of his future wife (some three hours before their wedding); at his holiday villa in Pont Gisquet, Louis Pasteur sits under a tree, dictating to Marie; Albert and Elsa Einstein smile for the camera as they arrive in New York; Max and Hedwig Born pose together on a beach; and so on. Bronowski's gallery is curiously affecting, because of its implied sub-text: the entire human project is a joint activity, predicated on love.

The medical metaphor – linking love and mental illness – automatically suggests the prospect of cure. Indeed, as soon as doctors started diagnosing love, their professional instincts compelled them to experiment with treatments.

Although 'love magic' – the manufacture of love potions and antidotes – was practised in ancient Greece, it wasn't until the tenth century that the Iranian physician Ibn Sina published the first comprehensive description of love sickness ('ishq) and the strategies that might be employed to cure it.

Even though he was guided by the Hippocratic or humoral model, his approach to treatment was remarkably modern. Today he would be described as a holistic practitioner. Ibn Sina recognised that there was a close relationship between mind and body, and subsequently endorsed both physical and psychological treatments.

The physical treatments that Ibn Sina recommended were clearly informed by his Hippocratic orientation. For instance, love sickness was thought to improve under a regimen of frequent moisturising. Burning passion was supposed to desiccate the body, so moisturising was a method of replacing vital fluids. Similarly, the humoral model provided him with a rationale for many other treatment recommendations such as regular 'evacuations' and 'good food'.

Ibn Sina's psychological and behavioural strategies, however, were less influenced by dogmatic adherence to the humoral model. They were also remarkably coherent. One can see why these techniques might have worked.

The principal symptom of love sickness is obsession with the beloved. Therefore, Ibn Sina suggests that the lovesick individual might benefit from distraction. This can be achieved by engaging in demanding tasks (he gives the example of hunting) or intellectual activities such as disputations and quarrels. This advice seems perfectly reasonable. Obsessions are now understood to be self-perpetuating in the manner of a vicious circle. Thus, anything that might interrupt the process of obsessing is potentially helpful. It is also possible that engaging in cerebral activities such as disputations might confer a secondary advantage: namely, the exercise of the patient's faculty of reason – the faculty most overwhelmed by love's madness.

The treating physician is also encouraged by Ibn Sina to rebuke the lovesick patient and to raise doubts about the beloved's character. The purpose of this manoeuvre is to undermine idealisation. He states: 'The image that he [the lover] has within himself is nothing but a delusion.' Thus, the patient's mind contains a mental picture of his beloved that is sublimely enhanced. By attacking the idealised image, Ibn Sina is clearly seeking to weaken one of the most significant factors sustaining love's madness.

Techniques such as challenging beliefs and correcting perceptual biases are a key element of cognitive therapy – perhaps the most successful and widely practised of all the twentieth-century 'talking cures'. It is extraordinary that a similar approach was being practised by doctors in medieval Iran.

Ibn Sina's attempt to modify the idealised image did not end with rebukes and challenges. Indeed, his therapy contained a rather radical experiential component requiring the services of a cooperative elderly accomplice. An 'old woman' would be asked to dress up in clothes that reminded the lovesick patient of his beloved. She would then perform the tenth-century equivalent of a lap-dance (presenting her body parts in 'a shameless parody'). Clearly, such a sobering spectacle must have reminded lovesick patients that all beauty fades, and that today's objects of sexual interest are simply tomorrow's objects of revulsion.

Like idealisation, raw sexual desire was recognised as an important factor in the maintenance of love sickness. Thus, Ibn Sina urged his lovesick patients to have frequent sex with 'slave girls' – the underlying principle being that the dissipation of sexual energy saps passion (a principle that most women are all too familiar with, knowing that the sexually sated male is rarely romantic, largely uncommunicative, and inordinately fond of stertorous sleep).

Six hundred years after Ibn Sina, Robert Burton also considered the treatment of love. Burton repeated Ibn Sina's advice on diet and added that alcohol should also be avoided. As we now have experimental evidence showing that imbibing alcohol produces a positive bias with respect to the evaluation of beauty, Burton's injunction is very probably sound.

As with Ibn Sina, the focus of Burton's approach is to attack the idealised image of the beloved; however, his method – 'counsel and persuasion' – brings us even closer to contemporary talking cures. Indeed, he provides the aspirant therapist with specific arguments that can be used as weapons in the campaign against idealisation – for example: '. . . every day detracts from her person, and this beauty is *bonum fragile*, a mere flash, a Venice glass, quickly broken'. He develops his theme, stressing how beauty is swiftly ruined by illness and accident: '. . . a little sickness, a fever, small pox, wound scar, loss of an eye or limb, a violent passion, a distemperature of heat or cold, mars all in an instant'.

Burton suggests that love's madness might be avoided altogether by nipping it in the bud. Thus, he urges us 'to withstand the beginnings'. This is a perceptive statement, recognising that engagement in the process of falling in love intensifies the experience. To some extent, people in the West are following Burton's advice all the time. The supernormal beauty of media celebrities might trigger the process of falling in love – but few adults allow themselves to entertain the idea that they will one day form a relationship with a famous actor or actress. Recognition of the impossibility of such relationships seems to halt the process of falling in love, arresting it at the stage of sexual interest.

Love sickness and love melancholy no longer feature in modern diagnostic manuals. Nevertheless, contemporary psychotherapists still find themselves confronting the problems of love in clinical settings. For example, a patient presenting with depression might be experiencing low mood because of unrequited love; one of the parties in a couple referred for marital therapy might show an addictive pattern of behaviour; or perhaps a patient with an existing mental illness might suddenly be destabilised after falling in love. It is very likely that all of these problems would respond to cognitive therapy or one of its variants. In all probability, the commonsense methods of argument, counsel, and persuasion, used by psychotherapists now, are not significantly different from those used by 'doctors' throughout the ages.

Although it might be argued that the fundamentals of psychotherapy haven't changed very much in the last thousand years, the same cannot be said with respect to drug treatments. When Ibn Sina was practising medicine, a number of herbs were thought to dull sexual interest, and were subsequently viewed as helpful in the treatment of love sickness. Modern doctors, however, can prescribe from an extraordinary range of pharmaceuticals, many of which can influence the biological processes that trigger and sustain love.

Certain hormones, antidepressants, and major tranquillisers are known to reduce libido; therefore, theoretically, all might have some role to play in a cure for love. However, sexuality is so central to a person's sense of self, it is doubtful that anyone would endorse 'chemical neutering' as an acceptable treatment, albeit temporary. Moreover, sex hormones and major tranquillisers are associated with very unpleasant side-effects. For example, when female hormones have been administered to male sex offenders to reduce their sex drive, the majority have developed gynaecomastia (breast enlargement). As far as pharmacological interventions are concerned, it is probably wise not to tamper with libido. But libido, of course, is only one aspect of love. Love provides the pharmaceutical industry with many other opportunities for chemical intervention.

Italian psychiatrist Donatella Marazziti's research suggests that falling in love is associated with depletion of the neurotransmitter serotonin. Therefore, drugs that boost serotonin levels – the Selective Serotonin Reuptake Inhibitors or SSRIs – might well reduce the intensity of love. Given what is known about the biochemistry of depression and OCD, a low dose of an SSRI would be expected to relieve melancholy, while a higher dose would be expected to reduce obsessions and compulsions.

American psychiatrist Michael Liebowitz has argued that the emotional 'crash' following a break-up is similar to that experienced by drug addicts during amphetamine withdrawal. When lovers are rejected, amounts of the amphetamine-related substance associated with love's 'rush', PEA, drop dramatically. Liebowitz has suggested that the mood of rejected lovers can be stabilised by Monoamine Oxidase Inhibitors (MAOIs). These are antidepressant drugs that inhibit the breakdown of PEA. In other words, MAOIs will let the unrequited lover down slowly, thus avoiding a precipitous and potentially damaging mood swing. Clearly, a gentle, gliding descent from love's giddy heights would give the unrequited lover more time to make a healthy psychological adjustment.

Although it is extremely unlikely that any doctor would prescribe an MAOI or an SSRI for love sickness, most would be happy to prescribe such medication if a patient met diagnostic criteria for depression. Yet, as we have already established, the symptoms of love sickness and depression overlap considerably. Thus, under the legitimising banner of depression, many doctors routinely prescribe psychoactive drugs as a treatment for love sickness. Interestingly, many patients comply with their medication regimen because the drugs seem to work.

It should also be remembered that medication is frequently prescribed for those features of love sickness that have survived the collapse of the humoral model and are still recognised in contemporary diagnostic systems: namely, erotomania and morbid jealousy. Antipsychotic drugs such as pimozide are said to have a specific and therapeutic effect with respect to these two conditions.

Eventually, as the biochemistry of love becomes better understood, it is inevitable that newer and more refined drugs will be able to correct even the most subtle neurotransmitter imbalance. In effect, we will have developed pills that can reliably tame passion and/or mend a broken heart.

Medicine has always worked on the principle that prevention is better than cure. Thus, ultimately, we are faced with the frightening prospect of drugs that can prevent us from falling in love. Something like an oxytocin-blocker could potentially allow individuals to enjoy sex without risking the formation of a strong emotional attachment. In the Brave New World that awaits us, the contraceptive pill blister-pack might be supplemented with O-blockers, to make doubly sure that recreational sex is just for fun. The legions of women who currently 'love too much' or are tricked by their biology into forming unsuitable, addictive relationships might become a thing of the past.

But do we really want absolute control over our emotions?

There are many great psychologists and psychiatrists, such as Carl Gustav Jung and R.D. Laing, who have argued that mental illness is not an affliction, but a journey. In the annals of psychiatry, we can find many references to the idea of 'creative illness' – a painful but necessary process of self-discovery, which enriches the individual's inner world. This notion seems particularly pertinent to the special form of madness we call love. It is a journey we must all complete to become who we are, and those who never embark on that journey remain curiously unfinished. One is reminded of the numerous lyrics, poems, and adages, that follow Tennyson's famous example:

> 'Tis better to have loved and lost
> Than never to have loved at all.

Love may be a mental illness, but it is an illness for which, in reality, we may never want a cure. Perhaps we would do better to divest ourselves of the notion of curing love – replacing it with a more realistic and acceptable aspiration: making love healthier.

By taking the illness metaphor seriously, we have learned a great deal about love: why it happens, how it works, and what it does to us. Armed with this knowledge, it is now possible to propose some general guidelines for the formation of more satisfying and durable relationships.

How, then, can we turn love sickness into love fitness?

Love has evolved over thousands of years, to ensure that we achieve our evolutionary destiny – the transmission of our genes into subsequent generations. Unfortunately, evolutionary pressures tend to produce parsimonious solutions. We do not need to be in love for ever to reproduce. Therefore, passionate love tends to be relatively short-lived – the time it would have taken our ancestors to mate and raise one or two children.

A relationship that is based solely on passion and sexual attraction is unlikely to last beyond the limits established in the ancestral environment. Thus, most relationships based primarily on sexual attraction will not survive for more than two or three years, the majority breaking down before seven years have elapsed.

Desire must be complemented by amity. In the absence of amity, when passion inevitably diminishes or fails there will be little left to sustain the relationship. Needless to say, amity also insures against diminishing and failing beauty. When beauty (or its hallucination) fades, it is essential that a couple still find each other attractive. Necessarily, this mutual attraction must be based on something deeper than 'good looks'.

An appreciation of 'inner beauty' makes it possible to examine a wrinkled face and see not decrepitude but lines of kindness, compassion and good humour. Most people – when free of love's madness – place an extremely high value on such characteristics. Men and women all over the world endorse kindness as the single most important personality trait a partner can possess. In a recent survey conducted in the USA, when respondents were asked which traits they would most like their children to possess, almost 60 per cent chose kindness. Less than 15 per cent chose good looks.

The idea of romantic love is well established in the Western psyche. Although many romantic conventions have an evolutionary origin, the superstructure of romance is very much a cultural phenomenon: a way of thinking about love that began among the Arab Bedouin and later found favour in the courts of medieval Europe. Unfortunately, the roots of romantic idealism are tangled, such that sexual desire and spiritual aspirations are confusingly knotted together. A consequence of this is that we unwittingly expect love to deliver the kind of happiness that was formerly associated with a direct experience of the numinous. In effect, we look to another human being to give life meaning and purpose. Inevitably, such high expectations are likely to end in disappointment.

Romantic idealism also tends to isolate couples from their social context. In romantic literature, for example, the interests of lovers are traditionally opposed by parents, relatives and the host culture. Couples set themselves against an unsympathetic world, and may even choose to become outcasts. Elopement is viewed as escape from oppression and constraint – but in the social vacuum the couple subsequently occupy, there are few forces that will help to keep them together. Even children will not perform this function (as we know from observations of the notoriously brittle 'nuclear family'). A relationship embedded in a rich network of friends and relatives, however, is much more likely to survive. This is where Oriental and Asian cultures seem to have an advantage over the West. In such cultures, a relationship is not defined by one bond, but countless interconnected bonds. From such a perspective, the 'romantic' relationship begins to look somewhat displaced – even lonely.

Love in the Western world is also complicated by a laissez-faire attitude to sex. It is no longer special – it's just a recreational activity, something that we can sample at leisure and walk away from, something that does not necessarily have consequences. Yet this couldn't be further from the truth. Sex is fundamentally different from playing a game of tennis or listening to the radio. It has profound psychological and emotional consequences. When we have sex, we are playing with evolutionary fire.

Sexual intimacy engenders chemical changes in the brain that make us feel attached. These same chemical changes underlie positive perceptual distortions. Thus, sexual partners appear more attractive than they actually are. Further, if a sexual partner is judged beautiful, they are likely to benefit from the halo effect – positive inferences about character and personality. In other words, sex makes us more likely to hallucinate an ideal. The longer we abstain from sex (within reason), the more likely it is that we will form an accurate impression of the person we are falling in love with.

In the modern world, where consumerism and liberal attitudes have created a culture of instant gratification, the idea of courtship seems old-fashioned and inhibiting. Yet, it is an eminently sensible strategy. Jacob Bronowski writes: 'All that tenderness, the postponement of marriage, the preparations and preliminaries that are found in all cultures, are an expression of the weight that we give to the hidden qualities in a mate.' Love's madness (inflamed by sex) obscures those 'hidden qualities'. Our attachment is predominantly chemical rather than psychological.

Enduring love is necessarily built on a foundation of mutual understanding: the kind of understanding that requires time, conversation, stillness and clarity – an intimacy of being, rather than body. Once this level of intimacy has been achieved, sexual intimacy becomes a logical consummation. We reduce the risk of waking one day to discover we have been sharing our bed with a stranger.

John Bowlby's attachment theory shows that if a child is securely attached to its mother, then it will have sufficient confidence to behave in ways consistent with its natural tendency to be curious. It will explore and acquire experiences essential for its healthy development. In the same way, securely attached adults can explore the highs and lows of love, fearlessly acquiring the essential experiences that make us feel complete.

The idea of loving sanely might, at first sight, seem rather pedestrian. Yet, those who enjoy the benefits of a secure attachment are truly liberated. They can divest themselves of the hopeless, confused, deluded and insecure posturing that characterises 'romance', and replace it with something of far greater value: true love – an elusive but many-splendoured thing.

A Brief Note on Language and Sexual Orientation

The terms madness and mental illness are used knowingly. I use them because they possess many subtle and important resonances. I am not against the use of politically correct language. There is nothing wrong with being sensitive. Unfortunately, politically correct language tends to be cumbersome and curiously sterile. Moreover, I have generally found it to be the case that people who suffer from 'mental illness' are quite comfortable with words such as 'mad', 'crazy' or 'insane'. Even so, if the traditional language I have used in this book has caused offence to anyone, then I apologise unreservedly.

Almost all the literature and scientific research on love concerns heterosexual love. This has necessarily influenced the way certain ideas in this book have been expressed. However, it should be assumed that gay men and women (or bisexual men and women) experience love in exactly the same way as straight men and women. The evolutionary foundations of my thesis – which give considerable emphasis to the dynamics of reproduction – do not invalidate or depreciate love between people of the same sex.

Acknowledgements

I would like to thank Clare Alexander and Mark Booth for recognising an idea with potential, Hannah Black for editorial assistance and Kate Shaw for doing some hand-holding duty in the early stages. I would also like to thank Helen Moyes for some impromptu Classics tuition and Nicola Fox for her elevated IQ and remarkable processing speed. As usual, any errors in the text are necessarily down to me.

Frank Tallis

References

P *lease note that reference dates refer to the book editions*
that I actually used as source material. Therefore, they
do not necessarily show the date a book was first published.
Thus, Darwin's Origin of Species *is dated 1985 rather than*
1859. This does not apply to articles from newspapers or
scientific publications.

Agathon (2002), *The Divine Sappho*, http//classicpersuasion.org/
   pw/sappho
American Psychiatric Association (1994), *Diagnostic and
   Statistical Manual of Mental Disorders* (4th edition), APA:
   Washington DC.
Anderson, C., Keltner, D. and John, O.P. (2003), 'Emotional
   convergence between people over time', *Journal of Personality
   and Social Psychology*, 84, 1054–68.
Andrews, Jonathan and Scull, Andrew (2001), *Undertaker of the
   Mind: John Monro and mad-doctoring in eighteenth-century
   England*, University of California Press: Berkeley.
Austen, Jane (1994), *Sense and Sensibility*, Penguin Popular
   Classics, Penguin: Harmondsworth.
Babb, L. (1951), *The Elizabethan Malady: a study of melancho-
   lia in English literature from 1580 to 1642*, Michigan State
   College Press: East Lansing, Michigan.

Baker, R.R. and Bellis, M.A. (1995), *Human Sperm Competition*, Chapman & Hall: London.

Bancroft, John (1989), *Human Sexuality and its Problems* (2nd edition), Churchill Livingstone: London.

Bartels, A. and Zeki, S. (2000), 'The neural basis of romantic love', *NeuroReport*, 17, 3829–34.

Berlioz, H. (1966), *Memoirs of Hector Berlioz from 1803 to 1865* (annotated, and the translation revised by Ernest Newman), Dover: New York.

Bookshelf – British Reference Collection (1996), CD-ROM, Microsoft.

Boyle, Mary (2002), *Schizophrenia: A Scientific Delusion* (2nd edition), Routledge: London.

Breuer, J. and Freud, S. (1991), *Studies on Hysteria*, in the Penguin Freud Library, volume 3 (trans. James and Alix Strachey, ed. James Strachey, Alix Strachey and Angela Richards), Penguin: Harmondsworth.

Briggs, Helen (2001), *BBC News, Sci/Tech*, 'How pretty faces light up the brain', http:news.bbc.co.uk/1/hi/sci/tech/1590847.stm

Bronowski, J. (1977), *The Ascent of Man*, BBC: London.

Brontë, Emily (1985), *Wuthering Heights*, Penguin: Harmondsworth.

Burton, Robert (2001), *The Anatomy of Melancholy*, New York Review Books: New York.

Buss, David M. (2001), *The Dangerous Passion: Why jealousy is as necessary as love or sex*, Bloomsbury: London.

Buss, D.M., Abbott, M., Angleitner, A., Asherian, A., Biaggio, A. (and 45 other co-authors) (1990), 'International preferences in selecting mates: a study of 37 cultures', *Journal of Cross-cultural Psychology*, 21, 5–47.

Buss, D.M., Larsen, R., Westen, D. and Semmelroth, J. (1992), 'Sex differences in jealousy: evolution, physiology, and psychology', *Psychological Science*, 3, 251–5.

References

Capelanus, Andrew (1990), *The Art of Courtly Love*, Columbia University Press: Columbia.

Carey, John (ed.) (1995), *The Faber Book of Science*, Faber & Faber: London.

Carmichael, M.S., Humbert, R. et al. (1987), 'Plasma oxytocin increases in the human sexual response', *Journal of Clinical Endocrinology and Metabolism*, 64, 27–31.

Carter, Rita (2000), *Mapping the Mind*, Phoenix: London.

Cartwright, John H. (2001), *Evolutionary Explanations of Human Behaviour*, Routledge: Hove.

Chaucer, Geoffrey (1988), *The Canterbury Tales* (trans. Nevill Coghill), Penguin: Harmondsworth.

Cheyne, George (1991), *The English Malady* (ed. Roy Porter), Routledge: London.

Clare, Anthony (1986), *Lovelaw: Love, Sex & Marriage around the World*, BBC Publications: London.

Clay, John (1997), *R.D. Laing: A Divided Self*, Sceptre: London.

Clifford, J. (2001), 'Would you let your baby be branded?', *San Diego Union Tribune*, 11 August.

Dalai Lama and Cutler, Howard C. (1999), *The Art of Happiness: A Handbook for Living*, Coronet: London.

Daly, M. and Wilson, M. (1988), *Homicide*, Aldine de Gruyter: Hawthorne, New York.

Dante (1964), *The New Life* (trans. William Anderson), Penguin: Harmondsworth.

Darwin, Charles (1981), *The Descent of Man and Selection in Relation to Sex* (2 vols), Princeton University Press: Princeton, NJ.

Darwin, Charles (1985), *On the Origin of Species by Means of Natural Selection or The Preservation of Favoured Races in the Struggle for Life* (ed J.W. Burrow), Penguin: Harmondsworth.

Darwin, Charles (1999), *The Expression of the Emotions in Man and Animals* (with introduction, afterword and commentaries by Paul Ekman), HarperCollins: London.

Dawkins, Richard (1988), *The Blind Watchmaker*, Penguin: Harmondsworth.

Dawkins, Richard (1999), *The Selfish Gene* (with updated endnotes and bibliography), Oxford University Press: Oxford.

de Rougemont, Denis (1983), *Love in the Western World*, Princeton University Press: Princeton, NJ.

Dickens, Charles (1997), *David Copperfield*, Penguin: Harmondsworth.

Dion, K.K., Berscheid, E. and Wlaster, E. (1972), 'What is beautiful is good', *Journal of Personality and Social Psychology*, 24, 285–90.

Dols, Michael W. (1992), *Majnun: The Madman in Medieval Islamic Society* (ed. Diana E. Immisch), Clarendon Press: Oxford.

Domb, L.G. and Pagel, M. (2001), 'Sexual swellings advertise female quality in wild baboons', *Nature*, 410, 204–6.

Donne, John (1986), *The Complete English Poems* (ed A.J. Smith), Penguin: Harmondsworth.

Donnelly, E.F., Murphy, D.L., Goodwin, F.K. and Waldman, I.N. (1982), 'Intellectual function in primary affective disorder', *British Journal of Psychiatry*, 140, 633–6.

Donovan, Debbi (2002), 'Oxytocin nasal spray: will it help milk ejection?' *Parents' Place*, http://www.parentsplace.com

Dutton, D.G. and Aron, A.P. (1974), 'Some evidence for heightened sexual attraction under conditions of high anxiety', *Journal of Personality and Social Psychology*, 30, 510–17.

Eisler, Benita (2000), *Byron: Child of Passion, Fool of Fame*, Penguin: Harmondsworth.

Eliot, T.S. (1975), *The Complete Poems and Plays of T.S. Eliot*, Faber & Faber: London.

Ellenberger, Henri F. (1994), *The Discovery of the Unconscious: The History and Evolution of Dynamic Psychiatry*, Fontana: London.

Encyclopaedia Britannica (1999), Standard Edition on CD-ROM.

Enoch, David and Ball, Hadrian (2001), *Uncommon Psychiatric Syndromes* (4th edition), Arnold: London.

References

Enright, D.J. (1989), *The Faber Book of Fevers and Frets*, Faber & Faber: London.

Epstein, Robert (2002), 'Calculating Cupid's recipe for love in our cold climate', *Sunday Times*, News Review, 14 July, p. 5.

Etcoff, Nancy (2000), *Survival of the Prettiest*, Abacus: London.

Faraone, Christopher A. (2001), *Ancient Greek Love Magic*, Harvard University Press: Harvard.

Finck, H.T. (1891), *Romantic Love and Personal Beauty: Their Development, Causal Relations, Historic and National Peculiarities*, Macmillan: London.

Frazer, J.G. (1987), *The Golden Bough: A Study in Magic and Religion*, Papermac: London.

Freud, S. (1990), 'From the history of an infantile Nenurosis (the "Wolf Man")' Penguin Freud Library, volume 9, *Case Histories II* (trans. James Strachey, ed. Angela Richards), Penguin: Harmondsworth.

Friedman, M. and Rosenman, R.H. (1974), *Type A Behavior and Your Heart*, Knopf: New York.

Fromm, Erich (1982), *The Art of Loving*, Unwin: London.

Gagemihl, Bruce (1999), *Biological Exuberance: Animal Homosexuality and Natural Diversity*, Profile: London.

Galton, Francis (1878), 'Composite portraits', *Nature*, 18, 97–100.

Gardner, Helen (1988), *The Metaphysical Poets*, Penguin: Harmondsworth.

Gay, P. (1988), *Freud: A Life for Our Time*, J.M. Dent & Sons: London.

Gibran, Khalil (1972), *The Prophet*, Heinemann: London.

Giddon, D.B., Bernier, D.L., Evans, C.A. and Kinchen, J.A. (1996), 'Comparison of two computer-animated imaging programs for quantifying facial profile preference', *Perceptual and Motor Skills*, 82, 1251–64.

Goethe, Johann Wolfgang von (1989), *The Sorrows of Young Werther* (trans. Michael Hulse), Penguin: Harmondsworth.

Goldstein, A.G. and Papageorge, J. (1980), 'Judgements of facial attractiveness in the absence of eye movements', *Bulletin of the Psychonomic Society*, 15, 269–70.

Gould, Stephen Jay (1985), *The Flamingo's Smile: Reflections in Natural History*, Pelican: Harmondsworth.

Graham-Dixon, Andrew (1999), *Renaissance*, BBC: London.

Graves, Robert (1992), *The Greek Myths. Complete Edition*, Penguin: Harmondsworth.

Gregory, Richard L. (ed.) (1988), *The Oxford Companion to the Mind*, Oxford University Press: Oxford.

Haig Gaisser, Julia (ed.) (2001), *Catullus in English*, Penguin: Harmondsworth.

Halsall, Paul (2000), *Internet Medieval Sourcebook*, Fordham University Center for Medieval Studies, http://www.fordham.edu/jalsall/index.html

Hatfield, Elaine (1988), 'Passionate and companionate love', *The Psychology of Love* (eds Robert J. Sternberg and Michael L. Barnes), Yale University Press: New Haven and London.

Hayman, Ronald, *A Life of Jung* (2002), Bloomsbury: London.

Hazm, Ibn (1953), *The Ring of the Dove* (trans. Arthur John Arberry), Luzac & Co.: London.

Healey, Edna (2002), *Emma Darwin: The Inspirational Wife of a Genius*, Review: London.

Hinsliff, Gaby (2003), '"Crime of passion" is no defence', *Guardian*, 19 January 2003.

Hite, Shere (1987), *Women and Love: A Cultural Revolution in Progress*, Penguin: Harmondsworth.

Holy Bible: Revised Standard Version (1971), Collins: London.

Holmes, J. (1993), *John Bowlby and Attachment Theory*, Routledge: London.

Homer (undated edition), *Iliad* (trans. W.H.D. Rouse), Thomas Nelson and Sons: London.

Howatson, M.C. and Chilvers, Ian (1996), *Oxford Concise Companion to Classical Literature*, Oxford University Press: Oxford.

References

Hsu, F.L.K. (1981), *Americans and Chinese: Passage to Difference* (3rd edition), University Press of Hawaii: Honolulu.

Hubbard, Margaret (1974), *Propertius*, Duckworth: London.

Hughes Fowler, Barbara (1994), *Love Lyrics of Ancient Egypt*, University of North Carolina Press: Chapel Hill, NC, London.

Hume, David (1985), *A Treatise of Human Nature*, Penguin: Harmondsworth.

Johnson, Robert A. (1984), *The Psychology of Romantic Love*, Routledge & Kegan Paul: London.

Jones, B.T., Jones, B.C., Thomas, A.P. and Piper, J. (in press), 'Alcohol consumption increases attractiveness ratings of opposite-sex faces. A possible third route to risky sex', *Addiction*, 98.

Jones, Terry and Ereira, Alan (1996), *Crusades*, Penguin/BBC Books: Harmondsworth.

Julian of Norwich (1966), *Revelations of Divine Love* (trans. Clifton Wolters), Penguin: Harmondsworth.

Kaplan, R.M. (1978), 'Is beauty talent? Sex interaction in the attractiveness halo effect', *Sex Roles*, 4, 195–204.

Kenrick, D.T. and Gutierres, S.E. (1980), 'Contrast effects and judgements of physical attractiveness: when beauty becomes a social problem', *Journal of Personality and Social Psychology*, 38, 131–40.

Kenrick, D.T., Gutierres, S.E. and Goldberg, L.L. (1989), 'Influence of popular erotica on judgements of strangers and mates', *Journal of Experimental Social Psychology*, 25, 159–67.

Kesey, Ken (1983), *One Flew over the Cuckoo's Nest*, Picador: London.

Kraepelin, Emil (1976), *Manic-depressive Insanity and Paranoia* (trans. R.M. Barclay, ed. G.M. Roberts), Arno Press: New York.

Kramer, Heinrich and Sprenger, James (1996), *Malleus Maleficarum* (trans. Montague Summers), Bracken Books: London.

Langlois, J.H., Roggman, R.J., Casey, J., Ritter, M., Rieser-Danner, L.A. and Jenkins, V.Y. (1987), 'Infant preferences for attractive faces: rudiments of a stereotype?', *Developmental Psychology*, 23, 363–9.

Lee, John Alan (1973), *Colors of Love*, New Press: Toronto.

Lee, John Alan (1988), 'Love-styles', *The Psychology of Love* (eds Robert J. Sternberg and Michael L. Barnes), Yale University Press: New Haven and London.

Liebowitz, M.R. (1983), *The Chemistry of Love*, Little Brown: Boston.

Lloyd, G.E.R. (ed.) (1983), *Hippocratic Writings* (trans. J. Chadwick, W.N. Mann, I.M. Lonie, E.T. Withington), Penguin: Harmondsworth.

Maisey, D.S., Vale, E.L.E., Cornelissen, P.L. and Tovee, M.J. (1999), 'Characteristics of male attractiveness for women', *Lancet*, 353, 1500.

Malory, Sir Thomas (1976), *Le Morte d'Arthur*, volume 1, Penguin: Harmondsworth.

Malory, Sir Thomas (1976), *Le Morte d'Arthur*, volume 2, Penguin: Harmondsworth.

Mann, Thomas (1990), *Death in Venice & Other Stories* (trans. David Luke), Vintage Classics: London.

Manning, Aubrey (1981), *An Introduction to Animal Behaviour* (3rd edition), Edward Arnold Publishers Ltd: Whitstable.

Manning, J.T. (1995), 'Fluctuating asymmetry and body weight in men and women: implications for sexual selection', *Ethology and Sociobiology*, 15, 145–53.

Marazziti, D., Akiskal, H.S., Rossi, A. and Cassano, G.B. (1999), 'Alteration of the platelet serotonin transporter in romantic love', *Psychological Medicine*, 29, 741–5.

Marie de France (1986), *The Lais of Marie de France* (trans. Glyn S. Burgess and Keith Busby), Penguin: Harmondsworth.

Márquez, Gabriel García (1988), *Love in the Time of Cholera* (trans. Edith Grossman), Penguin: Harmondsworth.

Massie, Robert K. (2000), *Nicholas & Alexandra*, Indigo: London.

McEwan, Ian (1997), *Enduring Love*, Jonathan Cape: London.

References

McNeilly, A.S., Robinson, I.C. et al. (1983), 'Release of oxytocin and prolactin response to suckling', *British Medical Journal*, 257–9.

Meichenbaum, Donald (1994), *A Clinical Handbook/Practical Therapist Manual for Assessing and Treating Adults with Post-Traumatic Stress Disorder (PTSD)*, Institute Press: Ontario.

Miller, Geoffrey (2001), *The Mating Mind: How Sexual Choice Shaped the Evolution of Human Nature*, Vintage: London.

Montaigne, Michel de (1991), *The Complete Essays* (trans. M.A. Screech), Penguin: Harmondsworth.

Morris, Desmond (1967), *The Naked Ape: A Zoologist's Study of the Human Animal*, McGraw-Hill: New York.

Mullen, P.E., Pathe, M. and Purcell, R. (2000), *Stalkers and their Victims*, Cambridge University Press: Cambridge.

Murdoch, Iris (2001), *A Severed Head*, Vintage: London.

Naumann, Earl (2001), *Love at First Sight: The Stories and Science behind Instant Attraction*, Casablanca Press.

Nizami (1997), *Layla and Majnun: The Classic Story of Persian Literature* (trans. Colin Turner), Blake: London.

Obholzer, Karin (1982), *The Wolf-Man: Sixty Years Later. Conversations with Freud's Controversial Patient* (trans. Michael Shaw), Routledge & Kegan Paul: London, Melbourne and Henley.

Odent, Michel (1999), *The Scientification of Love*, Free Association Books: London.

Ovid (1993), *The Art of Love* (trans. James Michie), The Folio Society: London.

Paz, Octavio (1996), *The Double Flame: Essays on Love & Eroticism*, Harvill: London.

Pearson, Helen (2002), 'Eau de dad woos women', *Nature Science Update*. Report on S. Jacob, M.K. McClintock, B. Zelano and C. Ober, 'Paternally inherited HLA alleles are associated with women's choice of male odor', *Nature Genetics*, http://www.nature.com

Pedersen, C.A. and Prange, J.R. (1979), 'Induction of maternal behaviour in virgin rats after intracerebroventricular administration of oxytocin', *Proceedings of the National Academy of Science*, 76, 6661–5.

Peele, Stanton (1988), 'Fools for love: the romantic ideal, psychological theory, and addictive love', *The Psychology of Love* (eds Robert J. Sternberg and Michael L. Barnes), Yale University Press: New Haven and London.

Plato (1973), *Phaedrus* (trans. Walter Hamilton), Penguin: Harmondsworth.

Plato (1986), *The Symposium* (trans. Walter Hamilton), Penguin: Harmondsworth.

Pons, L., Nurnburger, J.L. and Murphy, D.L. (1985), 'Mood-independent aberrancies in associative processes in bipolar affective disorder: an apparent stabilizing effect of Lithium', *Psychiatry Research*, 14, 315–22.

Porter, R. (1997), *The Greatest Benefit to Mankind: A Medical History of Humanity from Antiquity to the Present*, Harper-Collins: London.

Porter, R. (2002), *Madness: A Brief History*, Oxford University Press: Oxford.

Preti, G. et al. (2003), 'Male axillary extracts contain pheromones that affect pubatile secretion of lutenizing hormone and mood in women recipients', *Biology of Reproduction*, 68, 2107–2103.

Propertius, Sextus (1985), *The Poems* (trans. W. G. Shepherd), Penguin: Harmondsworth.

Redfield Jamison, Kay (1994), *Touched with Fire: Manic-depressive Illness and the Artistic Temperament*, Free Press: New York.

Reed, R. (1952), *Bedlam on the Jacobean Stage*, Cambridge University Press: Cambridge.

Rettersol, N. (1967), 'Jealousy-paranoiac psychoses', *Acta Psychiatrica Scandinavica*, 43, 75–107.

References

Richards, Graham (2002), *Putting Psychology in its Place: A Critical Historical Overview* (2nd edition), Routledge: Padstow.

Ridley, Matt (1993), *The Red Queen: Sex and the Evolution of Human Nature*, Penguin: Harmondsworth.

Rollins, B.C. and Feldman, H. (1970), 'Marital satisfaction over the family life cycle', *Journal of Marriage and the Family*, 32, 20–8.

Rostand, Edmond (1991), *Cyrano de Bergerac* (trans. Lowell Blair), Penguin: Harmondsworth.

Roth, Philip (2002), *The Dying Animal*, Vintage: London.

Rubin, Zick (1988), preface to *The Psychology of Love* (eds Robert J. Sternberg and Michael L. Barnes), Yale University Press: New Haven and London.

Rudgley, Richard (1993), *The Alchemy of Culture*, British Museum Press: London.

Russell, Bertrand (1975), *The Conquest of Happiness*, Routledge: London.

Sappho (1958), *Sappho: A New Translation* (trans. M. Barnard), University of Chicago Press: Chicago.

Shakespeare, W. (1988), *As You Like It*, The New Penguin Shakespeare (ed. H.J. Oliver), Penguin: Harmondsworth.

Shakespeare, W. (1987), *King Lear*, The New Penguin Shakespeare (ed. G.K. Hunter), Penguin: Harmondsworth.

Shakespeare W. (1988), *The Merry Wives of Windsor*, The New Penguin Shakespeare (ed. G.R. Hibbard), Penguin: Harmondsworth.

Shakespeare, W. (1988), *A Midsummer Night's Dream*, The New Penguin Shakespeare (ed. Stanley Wells), Penguin: Harmondsworth.

Shakespeare, W. (1988), *Much Ado Bbout Nothing*, The New Penguin Shakespeare (ed. R.A. Foakes), Penguin: Harmondsworth.

Shakespeare, W. (1981), *Othello*, The New Penguin Shakespeare (ed. Kenneth Muir), Penguin: Harmondsworth.

Shakespeare, W. (1988), *Romeo and Juliet*, The New Penguin Shakespeare. (ed. Stanley Wells), Penguin: Harmondsworth.

Shaver, Philip, Hazan, Cindy and Bradshaw, Donna (1988), 'Love as attachment: the integration of three behavioural systems', *The Psychology of Love* (eds Robert J. Sternberg and Michael L. Barnes), Yale University Press: New Haven and London.

Shaver, P.R., Wu, S. and Schwartz, J.C. (1991), 'Cross-cultural similarities and differences in emotion and its representation: a prototype approach', *Review of Personality and Social Psychology*, volume 13 (ed. M.S. Clark), Sage: Newbury Park, CA.

Singh, D. (1993), 'Adaptive significance of female sexual attractiveness', *Journal of Personality and Social Psychology*, 65, 293–307.

Soler, C., Nunez, M., Gutierez, R., Nunez, J., Medina, P., Sancho, M., Alvarez, J. and Nunez, E. (2003), 'Facial attractiveness in men provides clues to semen quality', *Evolution and Human Behaviour*, 24, 199–207.

Sommers, Peter van (1988), *Jealousy: What is it and who feels it?*, Pelican: Harmondsworth.

Stendhal (1975), *Love* (aka *On Love*) (trans. Gilbert and Suzanne Sale, introduction by Jean Stewart and B.C.J.G. Knight), Penguin: Harmondsworth.

Sternberg, Robert (1986), 'A triangular theory of love', *Psychological Review*, 93, 119–35.

Sternberg, Robert (1988), 'Triangulating love', *The Psychology of Love* (eds Robert J. Sternberg and Michael L. Barnes), Yale University Press: New Haven and London.

Stevens, A. and Price, J. (1996), *Evolutionary Psychiatry*, Routledge: London.

Storr, Anthony (1976), *The Dynamics of Creation*, Pelican: Harmondsworth.

Strassburg, Gottfried von (1967), *Tristan – with the 'Tristan' of*

Thomas (trans. Arthur Thomas Hatto), Penguin: Harmondsworth.

Sullivan, Sheila (1999), *Falling in Love*, Macmillan: London.

Sutherland, Stuart (1994), *Irrationality*, Penguin: Harmondsworth.

Szasz, T. (1962), *The Myth of Mental Illness*, Secker & Warburg: London.

Tallis, Frank (1995), *Obsessive Compulsive Disorder: A Cognitive and Neuropsychological Perspective*, John Wiley & Sons: Chichester.

Tallis, Frank (1998), *Changing Minds: The History of Psychotherapy as an Answer to Human Suffering*, Cassell: London.

Tallis, Frank (1999), 'Unintended thoughts and images', *Handbook of Cognition and Emotion* (ed. Tim Dalgleish and Mick Power), John Wiley & Sons: Chichester.

Tennov, Dorothy (1979), *Love and Limerence: The experience of being in love*, Stein & Day: New York.

Tennyson, Alfred Lord (1991), *Selected Poems*, Penguin: Harmondsworth.

Teresa of Avila (1946), *The Complete Works of St. Teresa of Jesus* (trans. E.A. Peers), Sheed & Ward: London.

Thornhill, R. and Gangestad, S.W. (1993), 'Human facial beauty: averageness, symmetry, and parasite resistance', *Human Nature*, 4, 237–69.

Thornhill, R. and Gangestad, S.W. (1994), 'Human fluctuating asymmetry and sexual behaviour', *Psychological Science*, 5, 297–302.

Thornhill, R., Gangestad, S.W. and Comer, R. (1995), 'Human female orgasm and male fluctuating asymmetry', *Animal Behaviour*, 50, 1601–15.

Tilyard, E.M.W. (1988), *The Elizabethan World Picture*, Pelican: Harmondsworth.

Toates, Frederick and Coschug-Toates, Olga (2002), *Obsessive Compulsive Disorder* (2nd edition), Class Publishing: London.

Tolstoy, Leo (1985), *The Kreutzer Sonata and Other Stories* (trans. David McDuff), Penguin: Harmondsworth.

Tovee, M.J., Reinhardt, S., Emery, J.L. and Cornelissen, P.L. (1999), 'Optimal BMI = maximum sexual attractiveness', *Lancet*, 1998, 352, 548.

Turgenev, Ivan Sergeyevich (1980), *First Love* (trans. Sir Isaiah Berlin), Penguin: Harmondsworth.

Valins, S. (1971), 'Cognitive effects of false heart rate feedback', *Journal of Personality and Social Psychology*, 4, 400–8.

Veale, D., Ennis, M. and Lambrou, C. (2002), 'Possible association of Body Dysmorphic Disorder with an occupation or education in art and design', *American Journal of Psychiatry*, 159, 1788–90.

Verbalis, J.G., McCann, M., McHale, C.M. and Stricker, E.M. (1986), 'Oxytocin secretion in response to cholecystokinin and food: differentiation of nausea from satiety', *Science*, 232, 1417–19.

Whitfield, John (2002), 'We like the look of lookalikes', *Nature Science Update*, http://www.nature.com

Wilson, Glenn D. and McLaughlin, Chris, *The Science of Love* (2001), Fusion Press: London.

World Health Organisation (1992), *The ICD-10 Classification of Mental and Behavioural Disorders: Clinical Descriptions and Diagnostic Guidelines*, WHO: Geneva.

Wright, Robert, (1996), *The Moral Animal: Why We Are the Way We Are – The New Science of Evolutionary Psychology*, Abacus: London.

Yalom, Irvin D. (1991), *Love's Executioner (and Other Tales of Psychotherapy)*, Penguin: Harmondsworth.

Yelsma, P. and Athappilly, K. (1988), 'Marital satisfaction and communication practices: comparisons among Indian and American couples', *Journal of Comparative Family Studies*, 19, 37–54.

Zeldin, Theodore (1995), *An Intimate History of Humanity*, Mandarin: Reed Books: London.

Index

Index